AF651152

INDIA BOOKVARSITY

LOTUS CHOICES

Editor: Mahendra Kulasrestha

Classics Revived for an Ultra-modern World

PHILOSOPHY INDIA

The Six Systems of Indian Philosophy

F. MAX MULLER

One of the best
as also the earliest
work on the subject

VEDANTA
PURYA MIMAMSA
SAMKHYA, YOGA
NYAYA, VAISESHIKA

Lotus PRESS

4735/22, Prakash Deep Building
Ansari Road, Darya Ganj,
New Delhi-110002

Philosophy
INDIA
The Six Systems of Indian Philosophy

By the Celebrated Orientalist
F. MAX MULLER

A scholarly yet
easy-to-follow
presentation of the
six systems of
Indian Philosophy

Source: ***The Six Systems of Indian Philosophy,***
By F. Max Muller,
Published by Longman's, U.K., 1899.

Text out of copyright;
form, structure, notes, design, etc.,
© Editor 2026

Philosophy India,
by F. Max Muller

Edition—2026
ISBN: 978-81-8382-273-2 (HB)

Lotus Press : Publishers & Distributors
Unit No. 220, 2nd Floor, 4735/22, Prakash Deep Building,
Ansari Road, Darya Ganj, New Delhi- 110002
Ph.: 41325510, 98118-38000
• E-mail : lotuspress1984@gmail.com
www.lotuspress.co.in

Printed & Published by : **Lotus Press Publisher & Distributors,** New Delhi-02

Editorspeak

'A Land of Philosophers'

Religion and Philosophy, or both, separately or together, have been the concern of all times for the most evolved species, humans, of living beings on our dear dear planet, the Earth, also known by the beautiful word, Gaia. We have lived a life of what we call Culture, for a few thousand years; and it would seem, on the testimony of Buddha who examined life more than 2500 years ago, that life is basically very great Suffering, which should be discontinued at whatever cost and everyone should try to attain salvation from it. The great Lord's influence persists till date, and is expected to contribute something significant to solve humanity's present-day problems of mindless terroristic horrors.

The creation of mind in the human body structure has given an unusual dimension of Thinking, which has gifted us the power of holding life in our own hands and plan it according to our own lights, aimed chiefly at better living. We can analyse, criticise, reject, speculate, plan and devise new ways—and we are fast moving towards unexpected, even mind-boggling, directions, achieving, as well as sometimes losing worthwhile materials and facilities. The 21st century of the third millennium, the point of time at which we are living, is especially imbued with such possibilities.

Life has been a puzzle, a problem, since it flowered in its present form, and we humans are trying to examine as well as control it to as much extent as possible, with the help of religion and philosophy. These have been our major instruments of understanding and controlling of our well-being. Our invention of the concept of God has been a remarkable achievement, despite philosophical criticisms.

This game has been very interesting in various communities. While the China-centered eastern countries did never develop any religion or philosophy, for which reason they cheerfully accepted whatever religion came their way; the three religions of Abraham stuck to the single easy idea of God alone with one single scripture, that, on the one hand, effectively prevented the growth of any worthwhile philosophical ideas, on the other, their fanatic fundamentalism-generated intractable violence wherever they went, and among themselves—Karen Armstrong's tome entitled 'Jerusalem' is an eye-opening work in this regard—which does not seem to subside even after the passage of three thousand years.

The Indian group of religions undertook a different path. It developed the essentially philosophical ideas of Atman and Brahman—both abstract—to understand the human reality and situation, supported by the justice-oriented sub-ideas of Karma and Rebirth, allowing the second place to the concept of God, chiefly in the interests of the common man. They worked enthusiastically on these lines, generating a number of philosophies, religions and sects of various hues and smells, an immense corpus of literature, thousands of gods and goddesses—that women were not discarded remains a special plus point—with a spirit of harmony—a higher stage of tolerance—and inter-relationship among everybody. Here was an essentially continuous picture where philosophy and religion had joined hands to further human welfare. The scenario was—and is—totally different from Abraham's religions, two of which remain prominent in modern times.

If the God-centred concepts are graded as the L.C.M. (Lowest Common Multiple) of people's level, the Atman-Brahman duo would easily be the higtest (H.C.M.), empowering it to frog-jump into the pure arena of philosophy. No wonder, when two or so centuries ago, the West came in contact for the first time with Hindu philosophy and religion, they were flabbergasted, and, starting with the famous French philosopher Schopenhauer, the trend to explore, understand and write tomes after tomes on these subjects started in a rather big way.

F. Max Muller's contribution in this area is the most significant. He not only translated the ancient Indian texts but published an immense volume of material in the 50 volumes of the Sacred Books of the East series, the first major project of its kind, which holds its position till date.

His last work was a 450-page volume entitled 'The Six Systems of Indian Philosophy', the first work on the subject in English. It had a second edition within four years, but by that time he had passed away. I have a feeling that, despite its great value and excellence, it has been overshadowed by his work in other areas.

The systems of Indian, or Hindu, to be exact, are a major achievement of Indian mind and culture. As Indians it is our duty to know as much as we can about its various aspects and interesting arguments. With this view, we have included the work in the present India Bookvarsity Series. But philosophy being a difficult subject, I've condensed the original to a substantial extent to make it accessible to the general educated reader and reset the material. Those interested in the whole work, could have it in the complete volume available in other imprints. The one I've used is Chowkhamba Sanskrit Series publication.

Of late, after the survey of book-reading habits held a few years ago—which concluded that even those who buy books, do not read them in full (which is my own experience also)—I've come to believe that books in condensed form, and suitably edited, are more accessible to human mind and more retainable. Anyway, here is a most wonderful book on the subject of Six Systems of Indian Philosophy:the two Mimansas, Purva and Uttara (known as Vedanta); Samkhya and Yoga; and Nyaya and Vaiseshika. The reader will note that **the author is highly appreciative of the Indian approach and treatment of the otherwise hoary subject and regards**

it as superior to all existing ones till his times. He doesn't hesitate to opine that those who do not know the theories of Vedanta and Samkhya, have no right to call themselves philosophers. It is also well-known that the venerable Swami Vivekananda was keen to develop Vedanta as the religion of the whole world, and had devised a plan to work for it. He deeply influenced the West in this regard, but destiny, or his gods—the goddess, to be exact—did not support him; — and why?, I would question. His own followers in the Ramakrishna Mission also failed him.

And, attainment of the Brahman by the Atman, is now being questioned: the veteran Maharshi (not Maharishi, as they spell the word) Mahesh (of whose this writer has a few interesting memories) who passed away recently in Europe at a hoary old age, is said to have declared that—such a thing is not possible. Bad news indeed, but this is not the point; the point is that we have explored one area, and are now free to think and experiment in other directions. That is the spirit and the meaning of Indian philosophy. Let our thinkers break new ground for the new times. Amen!

Authorspeak

Superior to Western Thought

It was as early as 1852 that I published my first contributions to the study of Indian philosophy in the *Zeitschrift der Deutshen Morgenliandischem Gesellcraft.* This interest was kindled afresh when I had to finish for the Sacred Books of the East (Vols. I and XV) my translation of the Upanishads, the remote sources of Indian philosophy, and especially of the Vedanta philosophy, a system in which human speculation seems to me to have reached its very acme.

It was only in a country like India, with all its physical advantages and disadvantages, that such a rich development of philosophical thought as we can watch in the six systems of philosophy, could have taken place. In ancient India there could hardly have been a very severe struggle for life. The necessaries of life were abundantly provided by nature, and people with few tastes could live there like the birds in a forest, and soar like birds towards the fresh air of heaven and the eternal sources of light and truth. There was hardly any political life in ancient India, such as we know it from the Vedas, and in consequence neither political strife nor municipal ambition. Neither art nor science existed as yet, to call forth the energies of this highly gifted race. Life in a forest was in the warm climate of India and in the absence of the most ordinary means of communication, what was there to do for the members of the small settlements dotted over the country, but to give expression to that wonder at the world which is the beginning of all philosophy? Literary ambition could hardly exist during a period when even the art of writing was not yet known, and when there was no literature except what could be spread and handed down by memory, developed to an extraordinary and almost incredible extent, are under a carefully elaborated discipline. But at a time when people could not yet think of public applause or private gain, they thought all the more of truth; and hence the perfectly independent and honest character of most of their philosophers.

Everyone of the opinions at which the originators of the six principal schools of Indian philosophy arrived, has been handed down to us in the form of short aphorisms or Sutra, so as to leave but little room for uncertainty as to the exact position which each of these philosophers occupied on the great battlefield of thought.

Hindu philosophers seldom leave us in doubt on important points and they certainly never shrink from the consequences of their theories. They never equivocate or try to hide their opinions where they are likely to be unpopular. Kapila, for instance, the author or hero eponymous of the

Samkhya philosophy, confesses openly that his system was atheistic, *an-isvara*, without an active Lord or God, but in spite of that, his system was treated as legitimate by his contemporaries, because it was reasoned out consistently, and admitted, nay, required some transcendent and invisible power, the so-called Purushas. Without them there would be no evolution of Prakriti, original matter, no objective world, nor any reality in the lookers-on themselves, the Purushas or spirits. From a philosophical point of view, no theory of evolution, whether ancient or modern (in Sanskrit, Parinama), can provide any room for a creator or governor of the world, and hence the Samkhya philosophy declares itself fearlessly as *an-isvara*, Lord-less, leaving it to another philosophy, the Yoga, to find in the old Samkhya system some place for an Isvara or personal God. What is most curious is that a philosopher, such as Samkara, the most decided monist and the upholder of Brahman, as a neuter, as the cause of all things, is reported to have been a worshipper of idols and to have seen in them, despite all their hideousness, symbols of the Deity, useful, as he thought, for the ignorant, even though they have no eyes as yet to see what is hidden behind the idols, and was the true meaning of them.

It has sometimes been said that Hindu philosophy asserts but does not prove, that it is positive throughout, but not argumentative. This may be true to a certain extent and particularly with regard to the Vedanta philosophy, but we must remember that almost the first question which everyone of the Hindu systems of philosophy tries to settle is: How do we know? In thus giving the Noetics the first place, **the thinkers of the East seem to me again superior to most of the philosophers of the West.**

This work professes to be no more than a description of some of the salient points of each of the six recognised systems of Indian philosophy. Even thus it could not well be avoided that in giving an account of each of the six systems, there should be much repetition, for they all share so much in common, with but slight modifications, and the longer I have studied the various systems, the more have I become impressed with the truth of the view taken by Vijnana-Bhikshu and others that there is behind the variety of the six systems a common fund of what may be called national or popular philosophy, a large Manasa lake of philosophical thought and language, I have done my best, little as it may be, and my best reward will be if a new interest shall spring up for a **long neglected mine of philosophical thought**, and if my own book was soon to be superseded by a more complete and more comprehensive examination of Indian philosophy.

Oxford, May 1899

Contents

1

Seeking the Truth

Some of the systems of Indian philosophy have from time to time roused the curiosity of scholars and philosophers in Europe and America, and in India itself a revival of philosophic and theosophic studies has taken place, which, if it leads to a more active co-operation between European and Indian thinkers, may be productive in the future of most important results.

It has long been my wish to bring the results of this national Indian philosophy nearer to us, and, if possible, to rouse our sympathies for their honest efforts to throw some rays of light on the dark problems of existence, whether of the objective world at large, or of the subjective spirits, whose knowledge of the world constitutes, after all, the only proof of the existence of an objective world. The mere tenets of each of the six systems of Indian philosophy are by this time well known, or easily accessible, more accessible, I should say, than even those of the leading philosophers of Greece or of modern Europe. We know what an enormous amount of labour had to be spent and is still being spent in order to ascertain the exact views of Plato and Aristotle, nay, even of Kant and Hegel, on some of the most important questions of their systems of philosophy.

There are even living philosophers whose words often leave us in doubt as to what they mean, whether they are materialists or idealists, monists or dualists, theists or atheists. Mere names have acquired with us such a power that the authors of systems in which there is clearly no room for an active God, never-the-less shrink from calling themselves atheists, nay, try even by any means to foist an active God into their philosophies, in order to escape the damaging charge of atheism. This leads to philosophical ambiguity, if not dishonesty, and has often delayed the recognition of a Godhead, free from all the trammels of human activity and personality but yet endowed with wisdom, power, and will.

What I admire in Indian philosophers is that they never try to deceive us as to their principles and the consequences of their theories. If they are idealists, even to the verge of nihilism, they say so, and if they hold that the objective world requires a real, though not necessarily a visible or tangible substratum, they are never afraid to speak out. They are bona fide idealists or materialists, monists or dualists, theists or atheists, because their reverence for truth is stronger than their reverence for anything else. The Vedantist, for instance, is a fearless idealist, and, as a monist, denies the reality of anything but the One Brahman, the Universal Spirit, which is to account for the whole of the phenomenal world. The followers of the Samkhya, on the contrary, though likewise idealists and believers in an unseen Purusha (subject), and an unseen Prakriti (objective substance), leave us in no doubt that they are and mean to be atheists, so far as the existence of an active God, a maker and ruler of the world, is concerned. They do not allow themselves to be driven one inch beyond their self-chosen position. They first examine the instruments of knowledge which man possesses. These are sensuous perception, inference, and verbal authority and as none of these can supply us with the knowledge of a Supreme Being, as a personal creator and ruler of the world, Kapila never refers to Him in his Sutras.

As a careful reasoner, however, he does not go so far as to say that he can prove the non-existence of such a Being, but he is satisfied with stating, like Kant, that he cannot establish His existence by the ordinary channels of evidential knowledge. In neither of these statements can I discover, as others have done, any trace of intellectual cowardice, but simply a desire to abide within the strict limits of knowledge, such as is granted to human beings. He does not argue against the possibility even of the gods of the people, such as Siva, Vishnu, and all the rest, he simply treats them as Janesvaras or Karyesvaras, produced and temporal gods, and he does not allow, even to the Supreme lsvara, the Lord, the creator and ruler of the world, as postulated by other systems of philosophy or religion, more than a phenomenal existence, though we should always remember that with him there is nothing phenomenal, nothing confined in space and time, that does not in the end rest on something real and eternal.

We must distinguish however. Kapila, though he boldly confessed himself an atheist, was by no means a nihilist or Nastika. He recognised in every man a soul which he called Purusha. literally man, or spirit, or subject, because without such a power. without such endless Purushas, he held that Prakriti, or primordial matter with its infinite potentialities, would for ever have remained dead, motionless and thoughtless. Only through the presence of this Purusha and through his temporary interest in Prakriti could her movements-her evolution, her changes and variety be accounted for, just as the movements of iron have to be accounted for by the presence of a magnet. All this movement, however, is temporary only, and the highest object of Kapila's philosophy is to make Purusha turn his eyes away from Prakriti, so as to stop her acting and to regain for himself his oneness, his aloneness, his independence, and his perfect bliss.

Whatever we may think of such views of the world as are put forward by the Samkhya, the Vedanta, and other systems of Indian philosophy, **there is one thing which we cannot help admiring, and that is the straightforwardness and perfect freedom with which they are elaborated.** However imperfect the style in which their theories have been clothed may appear from a literary point of view, it seems to me the very perfection for the treatment of philosophy. It never leaves us in any doubt as to the exact opinions held by each philosopher. We may miss the development and the dialectic eloquence with which Plato and Hegel propound their thoughts, but we can always appreciate the perfect freedom, freshness. and downrightness with which each searcher after truth follows his track without ever looking right or left.

It is in the nature of philosophy that every philosopher must be a heretic, in the etymological sense of the word, that is, a free chooser, even if, like the Vedantists, he, for some reasan or other, bows before his self-chosen Veda as the seat of a revealed authority.

Generally speaking, they admitted three legitimate channels by which knowledge can reach us, perception, inference, and authority, but authority freely chosen or freely rejected. In some systems that authority is revelation, Sruti, Sabda, or the Veda, in others it is the word of any recognised authority ,Apta-vakya. Thus it happens that the Samkhya philosophers, who profess themselves entirely dependent on reasoning (Manana), may nevertheless accept some af the utterances of the Veda as they would accept the opinions af eminent men or Sishtas, though always with the proviso that even the Veda could never make a false opinion true. The same relative authority is granted to Smriti ar tradition, but there with the proviso that it must not be in contradiction with Śruti or revelation.

Such an examinatian of the authorities of human knowledge (Pramanas) aught, of course, to form the introductian to every system of philosophy, and to have clearly seen this is, as it seems to me, a very high distinction of Indian philosophy. ***How much useless controversy would have been avoided. particularly among Jewish, Mohammedan, and Christian philosophers, if a proper place had been assigned in limine to the question of what constitutes our legitimate or our only possible channels of knowledge, whether perception, inference, revelation, or anything else!***

Supported by these inquiries into the evidences of truth, Hindu philosophers have built up their various systems of philosophy, or their various conceptions of the world, telling us clearly what they take for granted, and then advancing step by step from the foundations to the highest pinnacles of their systems. The Vedantist, after giving us his reasons why revelation or the Veda stands higher with him than sensuous perception and inference, at least for the discovery of the highest truth (Paramartha), actually puts Sruti in the place of sensuous perception, and allows to perception and inference no more than an authority restricted to the phenomenal (Vyavaharika) world.

The conception of the world as deduced from the Veda, and chiefly from the Upanishads, is indeed astounding. It could hardly have been arrived at by a sudden intuition or inspiration, but presupposes a long preparation of metaphysical thought, undisturbed by any foreign influences. All that exists is taken as One, because if the existence of anything besides the absolute One or the Supreme Being were admitted, whatever the Second by the side of the One might be, it would constitute a limit to what was postulated as limitless, and would have made the concept of the One self-contradictory. But then came the question fot Indian philosophers to solve, how it was possible, if there was but the One, that there should be multiplicity in the world, and that there should be constant change in our experience. They knew that the one absolute and undermined essence, what they called Brahman, could have received no impulse to change, either from itself, for it was perfect, nor from others, for it was Second-less.

Then what is the philosopher to say to this manifold and ever-changing world? There is one thing only that he can say, namely, that it is not and cannot be real, but must be accepted as the result of nescience or Avidya, not only of individual ignorance, but of ignorance as inseparable from human nature. That ignorance, though unreal in the highest sense, exists, but it can be destroyed by Vidya, knowledge, i.e., the knowledge conveyed by the Vedanta, and as nothing that can at any time be annihilated has a right to be considered as real, it follows that this cosmic ignorance also must be looked upon as not real, but temporary only. It cannot be said to exist, nor can it be said not to exist, just as our own ordinary ignorance, though we suffer from it for a time, can never claim absolute reality and perpetuity.

It is impossible to define Avidya, as little as it is possible to define Brahman, with this difference, however, that the former can be annihilated, the latter never. The phenomenal world which, according to Vedanta, is called forth, like the mirage in a desert, has its reality in Brahman alone. Only it must be remembered that what we perceive can never be the absolute

Brahman, but a perverted picture only, just as the moon which we see manifold and tremulous in its ever changing reflections on the waving surface of the ocean, is not the real moon, though deriving its phenomenal character from the real moon which remains unaffected in its unapproachable remoteness. Whatever we may think of such a view of the cosmos, a cosmos which, it should be remembered, includes ourselves quite as much as what we call the objective world, it is clear that our names of nihilism would be by no means applicable to it.

The One Real Being is there, the Brahman, only it is not visible, nor perceptible in its true character by any of the senses; but without it, nothing that exists in our knowledge could exist, neither our Self nor what in our knowledge is not our Self.

This is one view of the world, the Vedanta view; another is that of the Samkhya, which looks upon our perceptions as perceptions of a substantial something, of Prakrlti, the potentiality of all things, and treats the individual perceiver as eternally individual, admitting nothing besides these two powers, which by their union or identification cause what we call, the world, and by their discrimination or seperation produce final bliss or absoluteness.

These two, with some other less important views of the world, as put forward by the other systems of Indian philosophy, constitute the real object of what was originally meant by philosophy, that is, an explanation of the world. This determining idea has secured even to the guesses of Thales and Heraclitus their permanent place among the historical representatives of the development of philosophical thought by the side of Plato and Aristotle, of Descartes and Spinoza. **It is in that Walhalla of real philosophers that I claim a place of honour for the representatives of the Vedanta and**

Samkhya. Of course, it is possible so to define the meaning of philosophy as to exclude men such as even Plato and Spinoza altogether, and to include, on the contrary, every botanist, entomologist, or bacteriologist. The name itself is of no consequcnce, but its definition is. And if hitherto no one would have called himself a philosopher who had not read and studied the works of Plato and Aristotle, of DesCartes and Spinoza, of Locke, Hume, and Kant in the original. **I hope that the time will come when no one will claim that name who is not acquainted at least with the two prominent systems of ancient Indian philosophy, the Vedanta and the Samkhya.** A President, however powerful, does not call himself His Majesty, why should an observer, a collector and analyser, however full of information, claim the name of philosopher?

A friend of mine, a native of India, whom I consulted about the various degrees of popularity enjoyed at the present day by different systems of philosophy in his own country, informs me that the only system that can now be said to be living in India is the Vedanta with its branches, the Advaitis, the Madhvas, the Ramanujas, and the Vallabhas. The Vedanta, being mixed with religion, he writes, has become a living faith, and numerous Pandits can be found to-day in all these sects who have learnt at least the principal works by heart and can expound them, such as the Upanishads, the Brahma-Sutras, tlie great commentaries of the Acharyas and the Bhagavad-gita. Some of the less important treatises also are studied, such as tlie Panchadasi and Yoga-Vasishtha. The Purva-Mimamsa is still studied in Southern India, but not much in other parts, although expensive sacrifices are, occasionally performed. The Agnishtoma was performed last year at Benares.

Of the other systems, the Nyaya only finds devotees, especially in Bengal, but the works studied are generally the later controversial treatises, not the earlier ones.

The Vaiseshika is neglected and so is the Yoga, except in its purely practical and degenerate form.

It is feared, however, that even this small remnant of philosophical learning will vanish in one or two generations, as the youth of the present day, even if belonging to orthodox Brahmanic families, do not take to these studies, as there is no encouragement.

SEARCH FOR A SUPREME DEITY

The human yearning for one supreme deity led the Vedic priests to address their hymns to the Visve Devas or to Visvakarman as the maker of all things, induced them likewise to give a more personal character to Prajapati. This name, meaning lord of creatures, is used in the Rig-veda as a predicate of several gods, such as Soma, Savitri, and others. His later origin has been inferred from the fact that his name occurs but three times in the Rig-veda. These arithmetical statistics should, however, be used with great caution. First of all, the index verborum is by no means infallible, and secondly, our Samhita of the Rig-veda is but a segment, probably a very small segment, of the mass of religious poetry that once existed. In the case of Prajapati I had left out in my Index one passage, X, 121, 10, and though, for very good reasons, I considered and still consider this verse as a later addition, this was probably no excuse for omitting it, like all that is omitted in the Pada-text of the Rig-veda. The whole hymn must have been, as I thought, the expression of a yearning after one supreme deity, who had made heaven and earth, the sea and all that in them is. But many scholars take it as intended from the very first verse for the individualised god, Prajapati. I doubt this still, and I give therefore the translation of the hymn as I gave it in 1860, in my 'History of Ancient Sanskrit Literature'. It has been translated many times since, but it will be seen that I have had but little to alter.

HYMN TO THE UNKNOWN GOD

1. In the beginning there arose the germ of golden light, Hiranya-garbha; he was the one born lord of all that is. He established the earth and this sky—Who is the god to whom we should offer our sacrifice?
2. He who gives life, he who gives strength; whose command all the bright gods revere; whose shadow is immortality and mortality (gods and men)—Who is the god to whom we should offer our sacrifice?
3. He who through his power became the sole king of this breathing and slumbering world—he who governs all, man and beast—Who is the god to whom we should offer our sacrifice?
4. He through whose greatness these snowy mountains are, and the sea, they say, with the Rasa, the distant river, he whose two arms these regions are—Who is the god to whom we should offer our sacrifice?
5. He through whom the sky is strong, and the earth firm, he through whom the heaven was established, nay, the highest heaven, he who measured the light in the air—Who is the god to whom we should offer our sacrifice?
6. He to whom heaven and earth (or, the two armies) standing firm by his help, look up, trembling in their minds, he over whom the rising sun shines forth—Who is the god to whom we should offer our sacrifice?

7. When the great waters went everywhere, holding the germ and generating fire, thence he arose who is the sole life of the bright gods–Who is the god to whom we should offer our sacrifice?
8. He who by his might looked even over the waters, which gave strength and produced the sacrifice, he who alone is god above all gods–Who is the god to whom we should offer our sacrifice?
9. May he not destroy us, he, the creator of the earth, or he, the righteous, who created the heaven, he who also created the bright and mighty waters–Who is the god to whom we should offer our sacrifice?

Then follows the verse which I treated as a later addition, because it seemed to me that, if Prajapati had been known by the poet as the god who did all this, he would not have asked, at the end of every verse, who the god was to whom sacrifice should be offered. However, poets have their own ways. But the strongest argument against the final verse, which my critics have evidently overlooked, is the fact that this verse has not been divided by the Padakara. I still hold, therefore, that it was a later addition, that it is lame and weak, and spoils the character of the hymn. It runs as follows:

10. O Prajapati, no other but thou has held together all these things; whatever we desire in sacrificing to thee, may that be ours, may we be the lords of wealth.

With this conception of Prajapati as the lord of all created things and as the supreme deity, the monotheistic yearning was satisfied, even though the existence of other gods was not denied. And what is curious is that we see the same attempt repeated again and again. Like Visvakarman and Prajapati we find such names as Purusha, man; Hiranyagarbha, golden germ; Prana, breath, spirit; Skambha, support; Dhatri, maker; Vidhatri, arranger; Namadha, name-giver of the gods, all names for the Eka Deva, the one god, though not, like Prajapati, developed into full-grown divine personalities. These names have had different fates in later times. Some meet us again during the Brahmana period and in the Atharvana hymns, or rise to the surface in the more modern pantheon of India; others have disappeared altogether after a short existence, or have resumed their purely predicative character.

But the deep groove which they made in the Indian mind has remained, and to the present day the religious wants of the great mass of the people in India seem satisfied through the idea of the one supreme god, exalted above all other gods, whatever names may have been given to him. Even the gods of modern times such as Siva and Vishnu, nay, goddesses even, such as Kali, Parvati, Durga, are but new names for what was originally embodied in the lord of created things (Prajapati) and the maker of all things (Visvakarman). In spite of their mythological disguises, these modern gods have always retained in the eyes of the more enlightened of their worshippers traces of the character of omnipotence that was assigned even in Vedic times to the one supreme god, the god above all gods.

The same postulated Being is most fully described in hymn X, 129, I, of which I likewise gave a translation in my 'History iof Ancient Sanskrit Literature'. It has been frequently translated since, but the meaning has on the whole remained much the same.

THE NASADIYA HYMN

1. There was then neither what is nor what is not, there was no sky, nor the heaven which is beyond. What

covered? Where was it, and in whose shelter? Was the water the deep abyss (in which it lay)?

2. There was no death, hence was there nothing immortal. There was no light (distinction) between night and day. That One breathen nothing.
3. Darkness there was, in the beginning all this was a sea without light; the germ that lay covered by the husk, that One was born by the power of heat (Tapas).
4. Love overcame it in the beginning, which was the seed springing from mind; poets having searched in their heart found by wisdom the bond of what is in what is not.
5. Their ray which was stretched across, was it below or was it above? There were seed-bearers, there were powers, self-power below, and will above.
6. Who then knows, who has declared it here, from whence was born this creation? The gods came later than this creation, who then knows whence it arose?
7. He from whom this creation arose, whether he made it or did not make it, the Highest Seer in the highest heaven, he forsooth knows; or does even he not know?

It is strange to meet with this bold guess in a collection of hymns the greater part of which consists of what must seem to us childish petitions addressed to the numerous Devas or gods of nature. Even the question which in Europe was asked at a much later date, where the Creator could have found something for creating the world out of matter or out of nothing, had evidently passed through the minds of the Vedic seers when they asked: 'What was the stand, what was the support, what and how was it, from whence the all-seeing Visvakarman produced by his might the earth and stretched out the sky?

We must not measure every nation with the same measure. It is not necessary that the historical progress of thought, whether religious or philosophical, should have been exactly the same in every country, nor must we forget that there always have been privileged individuals whose mind was untrammelled by the thoughts of the great mass of the people, and who saw and proclaimed, as if inspired by a power not themselves, truths far beyond the reach of their fellow men. The poets who utter these higher truths seem fully conscious of their own weakness in grasping them. Thus, in I, 167, 5 and 6, the poet says:

'As a fool, ignorant in my own mind, I ask for the hidden places of the gods; the sages, in order to weave, stretched the seven strings over the newborn calf.'

'Not having discovered I ask the sages who may have discovered, not knowing, in order to kuow: he who supported the six skies in the form of the unborn—was he perchance that One?'

And again in the same hymn:

'Who has seen the firstborn, when he who had no bones (no form) bears him that has bones (form)? Where is the breath of the earth, the blood, the self? Who went to one who knows, to ask this?'

In all this it is quite clear that the poets themselves who proclaimed the truth of the One, as the substance of all the gods, did not claim any inspiration *ab extra*, but strove to rise by their own exertions out of the clouds of their foolishness towards the perception of a higher truth. The wise, as they said, had perceived in their heart what was the bond between what is and what is not, between the visible and the invisible, between the phenomenal and the real, and hence also between, the individual visual gods worshipped by the multitude. All this represented an enormous progress, and it is certainly difficult to imagine how it could have been achieved at that early period and, as it were, in the midst of prayers and sacrifices addressed to a crowd of such decidedly personal and mythological Devas as Indra and Agni and all the rest. Still it was achieved; and whatever is the age when the collection of our Rig-veda Samhita was finished, it was before that age that the conviction had been formed that there is but One, One Being, neither male nor female, a Being raised high above all the conditions and limitations of personality and of human nature; and nevertheless the Being that was really meant by all such names as Indra, Agni, Matarisvan, nay, even by the name of Prajapati, lord of creatures. In fact the Vedic poets had arrived at a conception of the Godhead which was reached once more by some of the Christian philosophers of Alexandria, but which even at present is beyond the reach of many who call themselves Christians.

Before that highest point of religious speculation was reached, or, it may be, even at the same time, for chronology is very difficult to apply to the spontaneous intuitions of philosophical truths, many efforts had been made in the same direction. **Such names as Brahman and Atman, do not spring into life without a long previous incubation.**

BRAHMAN, ITS VARIOUS MEANINGS

We naturally ask, first of all, whence came these names? What did Brahman mean so as to become fit to signify the truths? It is curious to observe how lightly this question has been answered. Brahman, it was said by Dr. Haug, means prayer, and was derived from the root Barh or Brih, to swell or to grow, so that originally it would have meant what swells or grows. He then assigned to Brahman the more abstract meaning of growth and welfare, and what causes growth and welfare, namely, sacred songs. Lastly, he assigned to Brahman the meaning of force as manifested in nature, and that of universal force as the Supreme Being. I confess I can see no continuity in this string of thought. Other scholars, however, have mostly repeated the same view. Dr. Muir starts from Brahman in the sense of prayer, while with the ordinary change of accent Brahman means he who prays.

Here the first question seems to be how Brahman could have come to mean prayer. Prof. Roth maintained that Brahman expressed the force of will directed to the gods; and he gave as the first meaning of Brahman, 'Die als Drang und Fulle des Gemuths auftratende und den Gottern zustrebende Andarht,' words difficult to render into intelligible English. The second meaning, according to him, is a sacred or magic formula; then sacred and divine words, opposed to ordinary language; sacred wisdom, holy life; lastly, the absolute or impersonal god. These are mighty strides of thought, but how are they to be derived one from the other?

Prof. Paul Deussen sees in Brahman 'prayer,' the lifting up of the will above one's own individuality of which we become conscious in religious meditation. I must confess that here too there seem to be several missing links in the chain of meanings. Though the idea of prayer as swelling or exalted thought may be true with us, there is little, if any, trace of such thoughts in the Veda. Most of the prayers there are very matter-of-fact petitions, and all that has been said of the swelling of the heart, the elevation of the mind, the fervid impulse of the will, as expressed by the word Brahman, seems to me decidedly modern, and without any analogies in the Veda itself. When it is said that the hymns make the gods grow (Vridh), this is little more than what we mean by saying that they magnify the gods. Even if a more profound intention was supposed to be necessary for the word Brahman in the sense of prayer, there would be nothing to prevent its having originally grown out of Brahman in the sense of word. Of course we cannot expect perfect certainty in a matter like this, when we are trying to discover the almost imperceptible transitions by which a root which expresses the idea of growing forth (Vriddhau), growing strong, bursting forth, increasing, came to supply a name for prayer as well as for deity. This evolution of thought must have taken place long hefore the Vedic period, long before the Aryan separation, long before the final constitution of the Aryan language of India. We can but guess therefore, and we should never forget this in trying to interpret the faint traces which the earliest steps of the human mind have left on the half-petrified sands of our language. That Brahman means prayer is certain, and that the root Brih meant to grow, to break forth, is equally certain, and admitted by all. What is uncertain are the intermediate links connecting the two.

I suppose, and I can say no more, that Vrih or Brih, which I take to be a parallel form of Vridh, to grow, meant to grow, to come forth, to spread. Hence Brihat means simply great (like great from growing), broad, strong, Brahishtha, strongest. We should note, however, though we cannot attribute much importance to the fact, that Brimhati and Brimhayati also were quoted by Indian grammarians in the sense of speaking and shining. Here we can see that speaking could originally have had the meaning of uttering, and that 'word' has been conceived as that which breaks forth, or is uttered, an utterance, as we say.

The next step to consider is the name Brihaspati. We must start from the fact that Brihaspati is synonymous with Vachaspati, lord of speech. Unless Brih had once meant speech, it would have been impossible to form such a name as Brihaspati, as little as Brahmanas-pati could have been possihle without Brahman.

From this point once gained I make the next step and suppose that Brah-man was formed to express what was uttered, what broke forth, or shone forth, that is, the word or speech. If we have arrived at this, we can easily understand how the general concept of the word was specialised in the sense both of sacred utterance or formula and of prayer; without any idea of swelling meditation or lifting up of hearts, so alien to Vedic poets, such as they are known to us. But if I am right in seeing in Brahman the original meaning of what breaks forth, of a force that manifests itself in audible speech, it will become easy to understand how Brahman cculd also, from the very beginning though in a different direction, have ueen used as a name of that universal force which manifests itself in the creation of a visible universe. We need not suppose that it had to ascend a scale first from holy word, holy wisdom to the source of that wisdom, the absolute god.

BRIH AND BRAHMAN, WORD

We may suppose therefore—I say no more—that Brahman meant force or even germ, so far as it bursts forth, whether in speech or in nature. But now comes a much more perplexing question. It can hardly be doubted that Vrih or Brih is a parallel form of Vridh; and it is a well-known fact that both the Latin Verbum and the German Wort can be regularly derived from the same root, corresponding to a possible Sanskrit Vrih-a or Vridh-a. In that case Brahman also may be taken as a direct derivation in the sense of the uttered word, and brahman as the speaker, the utterer. So far we are still on safe ground, and in the present state of our knowledge I should not venture to go much beyond. But Colebrooke and other Vedic scholars have often pointed out the fact that in the Veda already we find a goddess Vach, speech, which we met in Vachas-pati and Brihas-pati, the lord of speech. This Vach, as Colebrooke pointed out as early as 1805, was 'the active power of Brahma, proceeding from him.' After reading Colebrooke's remarks on it, few Sanskrit scholars could help being reminded of the Logos or the Word that was in the beginning, that was with God, and by whom all things were made.

The important question, however, which, even after Colebrooke's remarks, remained still undecided, was whether this idea of the creative Word was borrowed by the Greeks from India, or by the Indians from Greece, or whether it was an idea that sprang up independently in both countries. This is a question the answer of which must lead to the most far-reaching consequences. Professor Weber in his 'Indische Studien,' IX, 47.3, published an article with the object of showing that 'the Logos-idea had no antecedents in Greece to account for it.' This was certainly a startling assertion, but in the face of well-known facts he added: 'Without wishing to give a decision on this question, the surmise is obvious, **considering the close relations at that time existing between Alexandria and India, that the growth of this Neoplatonic idea was influenced by the like views of the philosophical systems of India.'** He says again, 'that it may have been simply on account of the invigorating influence which the gods were believed to derive from the hymns, that the goddess of Speech was conceived as furnishing to Prajapati the strength of creation, though at last, particularly in the shape of Om, she obtained the highest position, being identified with the absolute Brahman.'

I hope I have thus given a correct account of Professor Weber's somewhat vague yet startling assertion, that the Alexandrian Logos idea had no antecedents in Greek philosophy, but was influenced by the Vedic Vach. There are, no doubt, similarities, but there are dissimilarities also which ought not to be ignored. To say nothing else, Vach is a feminine, Logos a masculine, and that involves more than a difference of grammatical gender.

I have tried to show in my 'Lectures on Theosophy,' that the facts of the case lead us to a very different, nay, to the very opposite, opinion. If I did not enter on a discussion of the arguments which were intended to prove the absence of antecedents of the Alexandrian Logos idea in Greek philosophy, it was because I thought it better to state the facts as they really are, without entering on any useless controversy, leaving classical and Sanskrit scholars to form their own conclusions. While Professor Weber had asserted that the Logos appears in Alexandria without any preparatory steps, I did my best to point out these very steps leading up to the Logos, which are very well known to every student of the early history of Greek philosophy. If I have succeeded in this, the presumption in favour of any Indian influence having been exercised on the philosophers of Alexandria, would fall to the ground of itselt, and the claims of India and Greece would be equal so far as the original idea of the Word, as a *potentia* of the absolute Being, was concerned. 'Real Indian philosophy,' I had said before, 'even in that embryonic form in which we find it in the Upanishads, stands completely by itself. We cannot claim for it any historical relationship with the earliest Greek philosophy. The two are as independent of each other as the Greek Charis, when she has become the wife of Hephaestos, is of the Haritas, the red horses of the Vedic Dawn'.

Then the question arose, was there at least a distant relationship, such as exists between Charis and the Haritas, between Zeus and Dyaus, between Vach and the Logos also? As there were no linguistic indications whatever in support of such a view, I arrived in the end at the conclusion, that striking as are the coincidences between the Vedic Vach and the Greek Logos, we must here also admit that what was possible in India was possible in Greece likewise, and that we have no evidence to support us in any further conclusions. In all this I thought that facts would speak far better than words. It is quite true that Professor Weber was careful to add the clause 'that he did not intend to give any opinion on this question,' but after such a confession it is hardly becoming to hint that those who have given an opinion on this question, have derived their information from him. It is easy to state the pros and cons, the Purvapaksha and the Uttarapaksha, but both are meant in the end to lead on to the Siddhanta, the conclusion. Even stronger coincidences between Vach and the Sophia of the Old Testament might have been adduced, for as we read of Vach as the companion of Prajapati, Wisdom, is made to say, 'I was by him, as one brought up with him and I was daily his delight, rejoicing always before him.'

While in the Kathaka we read of Vach being impregnated by Prajapati, we read in Provo, viii. 22, 'The Eternal possessed me in the beginning of his way, before his works of old.'

But with all this I cannot admit that there is any evidence of borrowing or of any kind of interaction between Indian and Greek philosophy, and I should have thought that after the historical antecedents of the Logos and the Logoi in Greece had been clearly laid open, the idea of the Greeks having borrowed their Logos from Vedic Vach or from the O.T. Sophia, would not have been revived. The historical consequences of such an admission would carry us very far indeed, and it would require a far stronger lever to lift and to remove the weight of evidence on the other side than the arguments hitherto brought forward. If the Greeks had really borrowed their idea of the Logos from India, why should they not have adopted any of the consequences that followed from it?

EAST AND WEST

This requires some fuller consideration. Every indication of a possible intellectual intercourse between Greeks and Hindus in ancient as well as in more modern times, has been carefully noted and strongly urged of late, but I feel bound to say that, particularly for ancient times, nothing beyond mere possibilities of an exchange of religious or philosophical ideas between Greece and India has as yet been established. It seems not to have been perceived that an exchange of philosophical thought is very different from an adoption of useful arts, such as alphabetic writing, astronomical observations, coined money, or articles of trade whether jewels, wood, or clothing materials. It is only a philosopher that can teach or influence a philosopher, and even in the cases of two such men meeting, the difficulties of an interchange of thought, without a perfect knowledge of the languages, are far greater than we imagine.

We have an instance of a foreign philosopher becoming a proficient in the philosophical language of India in the case of Hiuen-thsang. Has he left any trace of Chinese thought, whether derived from Confucius or Laotze, in India? Modern missionaries, if unsuccessful in conversions, may, no doubt, have left some imprint of Christianity and European philosophy on the native mind, but the position of the Christian missionary in India, accredited by membership in the ruling race, is very different from what the position of a few Buddhist monks could possibly have been in ancient times, even if they had reached Alexandria, and learnt to speak and converse on certain subjects in Greek or Egyptian. A courier may be very conversant with French or Italian, but let him try to discuss metaphysical questions, or even to translate a book of Vico's into English, and it will be perceived what difference there is between an interpreter and a philosopher capable of discussing religious and metaphysical problems.

That there was a time when the ancestors of the Aryan speakers had the same language and held many of their mythological and religious names and ideas in common, is no longer doubted, though, even here, we must be satisfied with names, and could not expect common mythological speculations. Later contact between Indians and Greeks, whether in Persia, Asia Minor, or Greece, assumed no importance till we come to the invasion of Asia Minor, Persia, and India by Alexander the Great. But long before that time both Greeks and Hindus had invented many things, such as kings, priests, numbers, and seasons, marriages and funerals, without our having to imagine that there was at that time any exchange of ideas between the two countries on such points. If then we meet in India as well as in Greece with similar philosophic ideas, as, for instance, with a name meaning atom and with the atomic theory, should we suggest at once that Epicurus must have borrowed his atoms from Kanada, or Kanada his Anus from Epicurus?

It is interesting, no doubt, to point out coincidences between Kapila and Zenon, Pythagoras, Plato and Aristotle, but it is even more interesting to point out the shades of difference in cases where they seem most to agree. If the Vedanta could elaborate an ideal Monism, why not the Eleatics as well? And yet where is there a trace of such a philosophical theory as the absolute identity of Atman (the Self), and Brahman (the absolute being), to be found in Greek philosophy? Who would see more than a very natural coincidence between the Sanskrit triad of Dharma, virtue, Artha, wealth, Kama, love, and the

Platonic τα καλα, what is good, τα ωφελτυα, what is useful, and ταηδεα, what is pleasant. How widely the triad of thought, word, and deed is spread has been shown very clearly by my old friend Professor Cowell and others, but no one would venture to accuse either Greeks or Indians of borrowing or of theft on such evidence.

The real character of most of these coincidences between Greek and Hindu philosophy, is best exhibited by the often attempted identification of the names of Pythagoras and Buddha-guru. At first sight it is certainly startling, but if traced back to its origin, it evaporates completely. First of all, Buddha-guru does not occur, least of all as a name of the teacher Buddha, and whether as a common Aryan name or as borrowed, Pytha could never be the same as Buddha, or Goras as Guru. The belief in transmigration among the Buddhists, besides being borrowed from the Veda, is very different from that of Pythagoras and other philosophers, both civilised and uncivilised, while ascetic practices were certainly not confined to either India or Greece.

It is quite true that after Alexander's conquests, and after the establishment of a Bactrian kingdom, in the North of India, there was a more real intercourse even between philosophers of Greek and Indian origin, and many of the facts bearing on this subject have been very carefully put together by Count Goblet d'Alviella in his 'Ce que Inde doit a la Grece,' 1897. But even he brings forward coincidences, which require more convincing proofs. With regard to Indian coinage, it should be observed that the three gods mentioned by Patanjali as used for commerce, i.e., on coins, are the very gods found on the earliest Mauryan coins, Siva, Skanda, and Visakha, provided that Visakha can refer to Kama shooting his arrows?

It cannot be doubted that the art of coining money was introduced into India by the Greeks, and if the images of Indian gods and even of Buddha on ancient coins, may be supposed to have favoured idolatry in India, that too may be admitted. Indian gods, however, were anthropomorphic, had legs and arms, heads, noses and eyes, as early as the Veda, and the absence of workable stone in many parts of India would naturally have been unfavourable to a development of sculptured idols. The Hindus had a god of love in the Veda, but he was very different from the Kama, imaged on more modern coins as an archer sitting on the back of a parrot.

We are now in possession of specimens of much earlier Greek workmanship in India, than this Kama on the back of a parrot, nor is there any reason to doubt that the idea of temples or monasteries or monument, built and carved in stone, came from Greece, while some of the Indian architecture, even when in stone, shows as clear surviving traces of a native wood-architecture as, for instance, the Lycian tombs.

The later influence which Christianity is supposed to have exercised in originating or in powerfully influencing the sectarian worship of Krishna does not concern us here, for, if it should he admitted at all, it would have to be referred to a much later period than that which gave rise to the six systems of philosophy. Ever since the beginning of Sanskrit studies, nay, even before, these startling similarities between Krishna and Christos have been pointed out again and again. But iteration yields no strength to argument, and we are as far as ever from being able to point to any historical channel through which the legends of Christ or Krishna could have travelled. No one can deny the similarities, such as they are, but no one, I believe, can account for them. Some of those who have been most anxious to gather coincidences between the Bhagavad-gita and the New Testament, have been rightly warned by native scholars themselves, that they should learn to translate both Sanskrit and Greek before they venture to compare. It should not be forgotten that as the Bhagavad-gita bears the title of Upanishad, it may belong to the end of the Upanishad-period, and may, as the late Professor Telang maintained, be older even than the New Testament. If Damascius tells us that there were Brahmans living at Alexandria, we must not forget that this refers to the end of the fifth century A. D., and does not help us much even as indicating the way by which the idea of the Creative Word could have reached Clement of Alexandria or Origen. That Clement of Alexandria knew the name of Butta is well known, he even knew that he had been taken for a god. Nor should it be forgotten, that Pantaenus who, according to Eusebius, had preached the Gospel in India, was one of the teachers of Clement. But all this is far from proving that Clement or Origen was able to study the Vedanta-Sutras or the Buddhist Abhidharmas, or that their opinions were influenced by a few Indian travellers staying at Alexandria who cared for none of these things.

Some of the coincidences between Buddhism and Christianity are certainly startling, particularly by their number, but in several cases they exist on the surface only and are not calculated to carry conviction on one side or the other. I have treated of them on several occasions, for the last time in my paper on 'Coincidences,' but the same coincidences, which have been proved to be anything but real coincidences, are repeated again and again. The story of Buddha sitting under an Indian fig-tree (ficus religiosa) has nothing whatever in common with Nathaniel sitting under a Palestinian fig-tree, and the parable of the Prodigal Son in the Buddhist scriptures is surely very different in spirit from that in the New Testament. There remain quite sufficient similarities to startle and perplex us, without our dragging in what has no power of proving anything. No critical historian would listen for one moment to such arguments as have been used to establish a real exchange of thought between India and Europe in ancient times.

On this point we owe a great deal to students of ethnology, who have pointed out coincidences quite as startling between the religious and philosophical folklore of uncivilised and civilised races, without venturing to suggest any borrowing or any historical community of origin. The Chinvat bridge, for instance, which seems so peculiar to the Persians, had its antecedents as far back as the Veda, and is matched by a similar bridge among the North American Indians. I say, a similar bridge, for it differs also, as I pointed out, very characteristically from the Persian bridge. Again, it is well known that the creation of the world by the Word has been discovered among Iowa race as the Klamaths, but no one has ventured to say that the two accounts had a common origin or were borrowed one from the other. This should serve as a useful warning to those who are so fond of suggesting channels through which Indian thought might have influenced Palestine or Greece, and vice versa.

No doubt, such channels were there; neither mountains nor seas would have formed impassable barriers. Besides, Buddhism, as early as the third century B. C., was certainly a missionary religion quite as much as Christianity was at a later time. Alexandria was known by name, as Alasando, to the author of the Mahavamsa. On the other hand, the name of King Gondaphoros, who is mentioned in the legend of St. Thomas' travels to India, has been authenticated on Indo-Parthian coins as Gondophares, likewise the name of his nephew Abdayases, and possibly, according to M. S. Levi, that of Vasu Deva as Misdeos. All this is true, and shows that the way between Alexandria and Benares was wide open in the first century A.D. Nor should it have been forgotten that in the Dialogues between Milinda and Nagasena we have a well-authenticated case of a Greek king (Menandros), and of a Buddhist philosopher, discussing together some of the highest problems of philosophy and religion.

All this is true, and yet we are as far as ever from having discovered a Greek or Indian go-between in *flagrante delicto.* We have before us ever so many possibilities, nay, even probabilities, but we could not expect any bona fide historian to accept anyone of them as a proof of a real influence having been exercised by Greece on India or by India on Greece, at a time when Greek philosophy and religion might still have been amenable to Eastern guides, or Indian schools of thought might have gratefully received fresh impulses from the West. Though the literature of India has no trustworthy chronology, still, unless the whole structure of the literary development of India is once more to be revolutionised, we can hardly imagine that the occurrence of such names as Bodda and Zarades (Zoroaster) among the followers of Mani, or that of Terebinthos, the pupil of Scythianos, the very founder of the Manichaean sect in Babylon, would help us to discover the secret springs of the wisdom of Kapila or Buddha Sakya Muni.

They may point out whence these hereiarchs derived their wisdom, but they leave the question which concerns us here totally untouched. Gorres, in spite of all his mysticism, was right when he looked for a similarity in technical terms in order to establish an Indian influence on Greek or a Greek influence on Indian philosophy. His principle was right, though he applied it wrongly. It is the same as in Comparative Mythology. There may be ever so many similarities between two mythologies, such as changes of men and women into animals or plants, worship of trees and ancestors, belief in spirits and visions in sleep or dreams, but, one such equation as Dyaus=Zeus, is more convincing than all of them taken together. If people ask why, they might as well ask why the discovery of one coin with the name of Augustus on it is a more convincing proof of Roman influence in India than the discovery of ever so many pieces of uncoined gold.

To return to the origin of the word Brahman. Tempting as the distant relationship between Brahman and Brih, in the sense of speech, with Verbum and Word may be, we could not admit it without admitting at the same time a community of thought, and of deep philosophical thought, at a period previous to the Aryan separation; and we certainly have no evidence sufficiently strong to support so bold a hypothesis. What we may carry away from a consideration of the facts hitherto examined is that in India itself, Brahman need not have passed through a stage when Brahman meant prayer only, and that Brahman, prayer, could not have assumed the meaning of the object of prayers, that is, the Universal Spirit, who never required any prayers at all.

In order to show what direction the thoughts connected with Vach took in the Veda, I shall first of all subjoin here a few passages from the hymns, the Brahmanas and Upanishads:

Vach, speech, speaking in her own name, is introduced in hymn X, 125, also in Atharva-veda IV, 30, as saying:

1. I wander with the Vasus and the Rudras, I wander with the Adityas and the Visve Devas, I support Mitra and Varuna both, I support Agni and the two Asvins;

2. I support the swelling Soma, I support Tvashtri and Pushan and Bhaga. I bestow wealth on the zealous offerer, on the sacrificer who presses Soma.
3. I am the queen, the gatherer of riches, the knowing, first of those who merit worship; the gods have thus established me in many places, staying with many, entering into many.
4. By me it is that he who sees, he who breathes, he who hears what is spoken, eats food; without knowing it, they rest on me. Hear, one and all! I tell thee what I believe:
5. I, even I myself, say this, what is good for gods, and also for men; whomsoever I love, him I make formidable, him I make a Brahman, him a Rishi, him a sage.
6. I bend the bow for Rudra (the storm-god) that his arrow may strike the hater of Brahman; I make war for the people, I have entered both heaven and earth.
7. I bring forth the (my ?) father (Dyaus) on the summit of this world, my origin is in the waters, in the sea; from thence I spread over all beings, and touch yonder heaven with my height.
8. I indeed spread forth like the wind, to lay hold on all things, beyond the sky, beyond the earth; such have I become through my greatness.

I ask, is there any trace in these utterances of the thoughts that led in the end to the conception of the Greek Logos? There is another hymn (X, 71) which is very obscure and has for the first time been rendered more intelligible by Professor Deussen where we meet with some important remarks showing that language formed an object of thought even at that early time.

But here also there is nothing, as yet, approaching to the conception of the Word as a creative power. We meet with such observations as that words were made in the beginning in order to reveal what before had been hidden. This is, no doubt, an important thought, showing that those who uttered it had not yet ceased, like ourselves, to wonder at the existence of such a thing as language. The struggle for life that is going on among words is alluded to by saying that the wise made speech by mind (Manas), sifting as by a sieve the coarsely ground flour. The power of speech is greatly extolled, and eloquence is celebrated as a precious gift. All men shout when the eloquent man appears, holding the assembly subdued or spellbound by his words (Sabhasaha), nay, he is supposed to remove all sin and to procure sustenance for his friends. The knowledge of all things or, as Deussen says, the knowledge of the origin of things, is taught by the Brahman.

We meet with passages of a very similar character, in various parts of the Brahmanas. One of the most startling is found in a verse inserted in the Purusha-hymn, as given in the Taittiriya-aranyaka (III, 12,17), 'I know that great sun-coloured Purusha, when on the verge of darkness, he, the wise, rests, addressing them, after having thought all forms, and having made their names.'

But although we can discover in this hymn an appreciation of the mysterious nature of speech, we look in vain for the clear and definite idea that language and thought are one, which can be so clearly read in the Greek word Logos, both word and thought, nor do we find more than slight anticipations of the Neo-platonist dogma that the creation of the universe was in reality an utterance of the hidden thoughts and words of the Deity.

MIND AND SPEECH

The following passages will give some idea of what was thought in India about mind and language and their mutual relation. They may be vague and mystical, but they show at all events that a good deal of thought must have been expended by the early thinkers of India on this problem, the nature of speech and the relation between speech and thought.

Satap. Brahmana VI, I, I: 'Prajapati, after having created the Veda (Brahman, neut.), created the waters out of Vach (speech), for Vach was his. That was created (sent forth). He then entered the waters with Brahman, i.e., the threefold Veda, and there arose from the water an egg which he touched and commanded to multiply. Then from the egg there arose first Brahman, neut., that is, the threeold Veda.'

Panchavimsa Brahmana XX, 14, 2: 'Prajapati alone was his, and Vach was his own, Vach as the second. He thought, let me create (send forth) this Vach, for she will go and become all this.'

Satap. Brahm. VII, 5, 2, 21: 'The unborn is Vach, and from Vach Visvakarman (the all-maker) begat living beings.'

Brih. Ar. Up. I, 5, 3: 'The Atman consists of speech, mind, and breath. There are also the three worlds; speech is this world, mind the air, breath the sky. The same are the three Vedas, speech the Rig-veda, mind the Yajur-veda, breath the Sama-veda. The same are gods, ancestors, and men, speech the gods, mind the ancestors, breath men, etc.'

Brih. Ar. Up. I, 4, 24: 'He desired, let a second body be born of me, and he (death or hunger) embraced speech with his mind.'

And ibid. I, 4, 17: 'This world in the beginning was Atman (Self), alone and lonely. He desired, May I have a wife.... Manas (mind) is the Self, speech the wife, breath the child.'

The same or very similar and often contradictory ideas occur in later works also. Thus we read in Manu I, 21: 'In the beginning he (Brahma) fashioned from the words of the Veda, the several names, works, and conditions of all things.'

And to quote but one passage from the Mahabharata, Santi-parva, 8533: 'In the beginning Vidya (knowledge, Sophia) without beginning or end, the divine Vach (speech) of the Vedas, was sent forth by Svayambhtu, the self-existent.'

Samkara, when treating of Sphota (word), of which we shall have to treat further on, quotes from the Brih. Ar. Up. I, 2,4: 'He with his mind united himself with speech,' and he adds an important verse from some Smriti: 'In the beginning divine Vach, Speech, eternal, without beginning or end, consisting of Veda, was uttered by Svayambhu from which all activities proceeded';

And again: 'In the beginning Mahesvara shaped from the words of the Veda the names and forms of all beings and the procedure of all activities.'

The Laws of Manu, or, more correctly, of the Manavas, the clan of Manu, are no doubt later than the Brahmanas but they often contain old thoughts.

These utterances, to which many more might be added, are certainly vague, and chaotic, and often contradictory, because they sprang from different minds without any prearranged system; but they seem to me to show at all events that **thought and language must have occupied the philosophers of India far more than they did the philosophers of Greece, and even in later times those of modern Europe.** And if some of them assigned the first place to thought and others to speech, this also serves to show that at all events these early guessers did not accept language simply as a matter of conrse, as most of our modern philosophers are so apt to do, but tried hard to discover whence it came and what was its true relation to thought. Thus we read in the Satap. Br. I, 4, 5, 8: 'A dispute once took place between Mind and Speech as to which was the better of the two. Both said, "I am excellent." Mind said: "Surely I am better than thou, for thou dost not speak anything that is not understood by me, and since thou art only an imitator of what is done by me and a follower in my wake, I am surely better than thou." Speech said: "Surely I am better than thou, for what thou knowest I make known, I communicate."

They went to appeal to Prajapati for his decision, and Prajapati decided in favour of Mind, etc.

In the Anuglta we read on the contrary: 'Then the lord of speech was produced, that lord of speech looks up to the mind. First, verily, are words produced, and the mind runs after them.'

Some of the Brahmanic thinkers say in so many words that Speech is Brahman (Satap. Br. II, I, 4, 10, Vag vai Brahma), and the co-existence of Brihas-pati and Brahmanas-pati could hardly have failed to suggest to them the identity of Brahman and Brih in the sense of speech, just as every thoughtful Greek must have known that there was a reason why Logos meant both word and thought. But that ancient chapter of thought which lies beyond the childhood of all philosophy is for ever lost to us and can be reconstructed by conjectures only, which, though they produce conviction in some minds, cannot be expected to produce the same in all.

Taking into account all these scattered indications, I cannot bring myself to accept the evolution of the various meanings of the word Brahman as elaborated by former scholars. I am particularly reluctant to differ on such a point from Professor Deussen. Professor Deussen holds that Brahman had a ritualistic origin, and from prayer came to mean he who is prayed to, the *Urgrund der Welt.* He calls *it der zum Heiligen, Gottlichen empor-strebende Wille des Menschen*, which is much the same idea to which Roth and others have given currency, but which certainly requires a fuller justification. Instead of beginning with the specialised meaning of prayer, whether ritualistic or unpremeditated, and then rising to the object of prayer, I prefer to begin with Brahman as a synonym of Brih in Brihaspati, meaning word or speech, and to admit by the side of it another Brahman, meaning that which utters or drives forth or manifests or creates, that which is the universal support (Skambha) or force (Daksha), in fact the Brahman, such as we find it afterwards, whether as a neuter, Brahman, or, for more popular purposes, as a masculine, Brahma. No doubt in those dark passages through which words passed silently before they emerged into the full light of literature, we may often fail to discover the right footsteps of their progress, and we must be prepared for differences of opinion. But the really important point is that on which all scholars agree, by assigning to Brahman the final meaning of those terms, Though as we shall see, not one corresponds fully and exactly to the character of Brahman as developed in the history of the Indian mind.

PRASTHANA BHEDA

What the Brahmans themselves thought of their philosophical literature we may learn even from such modern treatises as the Prasthana-bheda, from which I gave some extracts by way of introduction to some papers of mine on one of the systems of Indian philosophy, published as long ago as

1852 in the Journal of the German Oriental Society. It is but fair to state that the credit of having discovered that tract of Madhusudana Sarasvati, and perceived its importance, belonged really to Colebrooke. I myself came to be acquainted with it through my old friend, Dr. Trithen, who had prepared a critical edition of it, but was prevented by illness and death from publishing it. It was published in the meantime by Professor Weber in his 'Indische Studien,' 1849, and I think it may be useful to give once more some extracts from it.

'Nyaya,' he writes,' is logic, as promulgated by Gotama in five Adhyayas (lessons). Its object is knowledge of the nature of the sixteen Padarthas by means of name, definition, and examination.' These Padarthas are the important or essential topics of the Nyaya philosophy; but it has proved very misleading to see Padartha here translated by categories. No one could understand why such things as doubt, example, wrangling, etc., could possibly be called categories or *praedicabilia*, and it is no wonder that Ritter and others should have spoken of the Nyaya with open contempt, as they have done, if such things were represented to them as the categories of Indian logic.

'There is also the Vaiseshika philosophy in ten lessons, promulgated by Kanada. Its object is to establish by their similarities and dissimilarities the six Padarthas,

1. Dravya, substance.
2. Guna, quality.
3. Karman, activity.
4. Samanya, what is general and found in more than one object. The highest Samanya is Satta or being.

5. Visesha, the differentia or what is special, residing in eternal atoms, etc.
6. Samavaya, inseparable inherence, as between cause and effect, parts and the whole, etc.

To which may be added

7. Abhava, negation.

This philosophy also is called Nyaya.'

These Padarthas of the Vaiseshikas, at least 1-5, may indeed be called categories, for they represent what can be predicated, in general, of the objects of our experience, or, from an Indian point of view, what is predicated by, or what is the highest sense (Artha) of words (Pada). Thus it has come to pass that Padartha, literally the meaning of a word, was used in Sanskrit in the sense of things in general, or objects. It is rightly translated by category when applied to the five Padarthas of Kanada, but such a translation, doubtful even in the case of the sixth or seventh Padartha of the Vaiseshikas, would of course be quite misleading when applied to the Padarthas of Gotama. The real categories would, in Gotama's system, find their place mostly under Prameya, meaning not so much what has to be proved or established, as what forms the object of our. knowledge.

Madhusudana continues: 'The Mimarnsa. also is twofold, the Karma-Mimamsa (work-philosophy) and the Sariraka-Mimamsa (philosophy of the embodied spirit). The Karma-Mimamsa has been brought out by the venerable Jaimini in twelve chapters.'

The objects of these twelve chapters are then indicated very shortly, and so as to be hardly intelligible without a reference to the original Sutras. Dharma, the object of this philosophy, is explained as consisting of acts of duty, chiefly sacrificial. The second, third, and fourth chapters treat of the differences and varieties of Dharma, its parts (or appendent members, contrasted with the main act), and the principal purpose of each sacrificial performance. The fifth chapter tries to settle the order of all sacrificial performances, and the sixth the qualifications of its performers. The subject of indirect precepts is opened in the seventh chapter and carried on more fully in the eighth. Inferrible changes, adapting to any variation or copy of certain sacrificial acts, what was designed for the types or models of them, are discussed in the ninth, and bars or exceptions in the tenth. Concurrent efficacy is considered in the eleventh chapter, and co-ordinate effect in the twelfth; that is, the co-operation of several acts for a single result is the subject of the one, and the incidental effect of an act, of which the chief purpose is different, is discussed in the other.

'There is also the Samkarshana-kanda, consisting of four chapters, composed by Jaimini, and this, which is known by the name of Devata-kanda, belongs to the Karma-Mimamsa, because it teaches the act called Upasana or worship.

'Next follows the Sariraka-Mimamsa, consisting of four chapters. Its object is to make clear the oneness of Brahman and Atman (Self), and to exhibit the rules which teach the investigation of it by means of Vedic study, etc. It is in fact much more what we call a system of philosophy than the Purva-Mimamsa, and it is quoted by different names, such as Uttara-Mimamsa, Brahma-Mimamsa, Vedanta, etc.

'In the first lecture is shown the agreement with which all Vedanta passages refer, directly or indirectly, to the inward, undivided, second-less Brahman. In the first section are considered Vedic passages which have clear indications of

Brahman; in the second, passages which have obscure indications of Brahman, and refer to Brahman so far as he is an object of worship; in the third, passages which have obscure indications of Brahman, and mostly refer to Brahman so far as he or it is an object of knowledge. Thus the consideration of the Vedanta texts has been finished, and in the fourth section such words as Avyakta, Aga, etc., are considered, of which it can be doubtful whether they may not refer to ideas, adapted and formulated by the Samkhya philosophers, such as Pradhana, Prakriti, which is generally, though quite wrongly, translated by nature, as independent of Brahman or Purusha.

'The convergence of all Vedanta texts on the second-less Brahman having thus been established, Vyasa or Badarayana, fearing an opposition by means of arguments such as have been produced by acknowledged Smritis and various other systems, undertakes their refutation, and tries to establish the incontrovertible validity of his own arguments in the second lecture. Here, in the first section, the objections to the convergence of the Vedanta passages on Brahman, as stated by the Smritis of the Samkhya-yoga, the Kanadas, and by the arguments employed by the Samkhyas, are disposed of. In the second section is shown the faultiness of the views of the followers of the Samkhya, because every examination should consist of two parts, the establishment of our own doctrine and the refutation of the doctrine of our opponents. In the third section the contradictions between the passages of the Veda, referring to the creation of the elements and other subjects, are removed in the first part, and in the second those referring to individual souls. In the fourth section are considered all apparent contradictions between Vedic passages referring to the senses and their objects.

'In the third chapter follows the examination of the means of salvation. Here in the first section, while considering the going to and returning from another world (transmigration), dispassionateness has to be examined. In the second section the meaning of the word Thou is made clear, and afterwards the meaning of the word That. In the third section there is a collection of words, if not purely tautological, all referring to the unqualified Brahman, as recorded in different Sakhas or branches of the Veda; and at the same time the question is discussed whether certain attributes recorded by other Sakhas in teaching a qualified or unqualified Brahman, may be taken together or not. In the fourth section the means of obtaining a knowledge of the unqualified Brahman, both the external, such as sacrifices and observing the four stations in life, and the internal, such as quietness, control, and meditation, are investigated.

'In the fourth chapter follows an inquiry into the special rewards or fruits of a knowledge ot the qualified and unqualified Brahman. In the first section is described salvation of a man even in this life, when free from the influence of good or bad acts, after he has realised the unqualified Brahman by means of repeated study of the Veda, etc. In the second section the mode of departure of a dying man is considered. In the third, the further (northern) road of a man who dies with a full knowledge of the unqualified Brahman is explained. In the fourth section the obtainment of disembodied aloneness by a man who knows the unqualified Brahman is first described, and afterwards the abode in the world of Brahman, promised to all who know the qualified (or lower) Brahman.

'This, the Vedanta, is indeed the principal of all doctrines, any other doctrine is but a complement of it, and therefore it alone is to be reverenced by all who wish for liberation, and this according to the interpretation of the venerable Samkara—this is the secret!'

Here we see clearly that Madhusudana considered the Vedanta-philosophy as interpreted by Samkara, if not as the only true one, still as the best of all philosophies. He made an important distinction also between the four, the Nyaya, Vaiseshika, Purva, and Uttara-Mimamsa on one side, and the remaining two, the Samkhya and Yoga-philosophies on the other. It is curious indeed that this distinction has been hitherto so little remarked: According to Madhusudana, the philosophies of Gotama and Kanada are treated simply as Smritis or Dharmasastras, like the Laws of Manu, nay, like the Mahabharata of Vyasa, and the Ramayana of Valmiki. Of course, these systems of philosophy cannot be called Smriti in the ordinary sense of Dharmasastra; but, as they are Smriti or tradition, and not Sruti or revelation, they may be said to teach Dharma, if not in legal, at least in the moral sense of that word. Anyhow, it is clear that Samkhya and Yoga were looked upon as belonging to a class different from that to which the two Mimamsas, nay, even Nyaya and Vaiseshika, and the other recognised branches of knowledge belonged, which together are represented as the eighteen branches of the Trayi (the Veda). Though it may be difficult to understand the exact reason of this distinction, the distinction itself should not be passed over.

'The Samkhya,' Madhusudana continues, 'was brought out by the venerable Kapila in six Adhyayas. In the first Adhyaya the objects for discussion are considered; in the second the effects or products of Pradhana, or original matter; in the third aloofness from sensuous objects; in the fourth stories about dispassionate persons, such as Pingala, the fletcher, etc.; in the fifth there is refutation of opposite opinions; in the sixth a resume of the whole. The, chief object of the Samkhya-philosophy is to teach the difference between Prakriti and the Purushas.

'Then follows the Yoga-philosophy as taught by the venerable Patanjali, consisting of four parts. Here in the first part meditation, which stops the activity and distraction of the mind, and, as a means towards it, repeated practice and dispassionateness, are discussed; in the second the eight accessories which serve to produce deep meditation even in one whose thoughts are distracted, such as restraint, observances, posture, regulation of breath, devotion, contemplation, and meditation; in the third, the supernatural powers; in the fourth aloneness. The chief object of this philosophy is to achieve concentration by means of stopping all wandering thoughts.'

After this follows a short account of the Pasupata and Pancharatra-systems, and then a recapitulation which is of interest. Here Madhusudana says, that 'after the various systems have been explained, it should be clear that there are after all but three roads:

1. The Arambha-vada, the theory of atomic agglomeration.
2. The Parinama-vada, the theory of evolution.
3. The Vivarta-vada, the theory of illusion.

'The first theory holds that the four kinds of atoms (Anu), those of earth, water, fire, and air, by becoming successively double atoms, etc., begin the world which culminates in the egg of Brahman.

'This first theory, that of the Tarkikas (Nyaya and Vaiseshika) and the Mimamsakas, teaches that an effect which was not (the world), is produced through the activity of causes which are.

'The second theory, that of the Samkhyas, Yoga-patanjalas, and Pasupatas, says that Pradhana alone, sometimes called Prakriti or original matter, composed, as it is, of the Gunas of Sattva (good), Rajas (moderate), and Tamas (bad), is evolved through the stages of Mahat (perceiving) and Ahamkara (subjectivity) into the shape of the (subjective and objective) world. From this point of view the effected world existed before as real, though in a subtile (invisible) form, and was rendered manifest through the activity of a cause.

'The third theory, that of the Brahmavadins (Vedanta), says that the self-luminous and perfectly blissful Brahman which has no second, appears by mistake, through its own power of Maya, as the world, while the Vaishnavas (Ramanuja etc.) hold that the world is an actual and true evolution of Brahman.

But in reality all the Munis who have put forward these theories agree in wishing to prove the existence of the one Supreme Lord without a second, ending in the theory of illusion (Vivarta). These Munis cannot be in error, considering that they are omniscient; and these different views have only been propounded by them, in order to keep off all nihilistic theories, and because they were afraid that human beings, with their inclinations towards the objects of the world, could not be expected at once to know the true goal of man. But all comes right when we understand that men, from not understanding their true object, imagined that these Munis would have propounded what is contrary to the Veda, and thus, accepting their opinions, have become followers of various paths.'

Much of what has here been translated from Madhusudana's Prasthana-bheda, though it gives a general survey, is obscure, but will become more intelligible hereafter when we come to examine each of the six philosophies by itself; nor is it at all certain that his view of the development of Indian philosophy is historically tenable. But it shows at all events a certain freedom of thought, which we see now and then in other writers also, such as Vijnana-bhikshu, who are bent on showing that there is behind the diversity of Vedanta, Samkhya, and Nyaya one and the same truth, though differently expressed; that philosophies, in fact, may be many, but truth is one.

THE SIX SYSTEMS OF PHILOSOPHY

No one can suppose that those whose names are mentioned as the authors of these six philosophical systems, were more than the final editors or redactors of the Sutras as we now possess them. If the third century B.C. should seem too late a date for the introduction of writing for literary purposes in India, we should remember that even inscriptions have not yet been found more ancient than those of Asoka, and there is a wide difference between inscriptions and literary compositions. The Southern Buddhists do not claim to have reduced their Sacred Canon to writing before the first century B. C., though it is well known that they kept up close relations with their Northern co-religionists who were acquainted with writing. During all that time, therefore, between 477 and 77 B.C., ever so many theories of the world, partaking of a Vedanta, Samkhya or Yoga, nay, even of a Buddhist character, could have sprung up and have been reduced to a mnemonic form in various Asramas. We need not wonder that much of that literature, considering that it could be mnemonic only, should have been irretrievably lost, and we must take care also not to look upon what has been left to us in the old Darsanas, as representing the whole outcome of the philosophical activity of the whole of India through so many generations.

All we can say is that philosophy began to ferment in India during the period filled by Brahmanas and Upanishads, nay, even in some of the Vedic hymns, that the existence of Upanishads, though not necessarily our own, is recognised in the Buddhist Canon, and lastly, that the name of Suttas, as a component part of the Buddhist Canon, must be later than that of the earliest Brahmanic Sutras, because in the meantime the meaning of the word had been changed from short mnemonic sentences to fully developed discourses. Possibly Sutra was originally meant for the text to be elucidated in a sermon, so that the long Buddhistic sermons came to be called Suttas in consequence.

BRIHASPATI-SUTRAS

That some of the earlier philosophical Sutras were lost, is shown in the case of the Brihaspati-Sutras. These are said to have contained the doctrines of the out and out materialists, or sensualists, the Laukayatikas or Charvakas, who deny the existence of everything beyond what is given by the senses. They are referred to by Bhaskaracharya at, Brahma-Sutras III, 3, 53, and as he gives an extract, it is likely that they still existed in his time, though no MS. of them has been found as yet in India. The same applies to such Sutras as the Vaikhanasa-Sutras, possibly intended for the Vanaprasthas, and the Bhikshu-Sutras, quoteu by Panini, and intended, it would seem, for Brahmanic, and not yet for Buddhistic mendicants. It is a sad truth which we have to learn more and more, that of the old pre-Buddhistic literature we have but scanty fragments, and that even these may be, in some cases, mere reproductions of lost originals, as in the case of the Samkhya-Sutras. We know now that such Sutras could have been produced at any time, and we should not forget that even at present, in the general decay of Sanskrit scholarship, India still possesses scholars who can imitate Kalidasa, to say nothing of such poems as the Mahabharata and Ramayana, and so successfully that few scholars could tell the difference. It is not long ago that I received a Sanskrit treatise written in Sutras with a commentary, the work of a living scholar in India, which might have deceived many a European scholar of Sanskrit literature. If that is possible now, if, as in the case of the Kapila-Sutras, it was possible in the fourteenth century, why should not the same have taken place during the period of the Renaissance in India, nay, even at an earlier time? At all events, though grateful for what has been preserved, and preserved in what may seem to us an almost miraculous manner, we should not imagine that we possess all, or that we possess what we possess in its original form.

BOOKS OF REFERENCE

I shall mention here some of the most important works only, from which students of philosophy, particularly those ignorant of Sanskrit, may gain by themselves a knowledge of the six recognised systems of Indian philosophy. The titles of the more important of the original Sanskrit texts may be found in Colebrooke's 'Miscellaneous Essays,' vol. ii, and in the Catalogues, published since his time, of the various collections of Sanskrit MSS. in Europe and India.

For the Vedanta-philosophy of Badarayana the most useful book is Thibaut's English translation of the text of the Sutras and Samkara's commentary.

Of books written in German, Deussen's translation of the same work, 1887, preceded as it was by his 'System des Vedanta,' 1883, can be thoroughly recommended.

Of the Samkhya-system we have the Sutras translated by Ballantyne in 1882-1885, the 'Aphorisms of the Samkhya

Philosophy of Kapila,' with illustrative extracts from the, Commentaries.

In German we have the Samkhya-Pravachana-Bhashya, Vijnana-bhikshu's 'Commentarzu den Samkhya-Sutras,' ubersetzt von R. Garbe, 1889. Also Aniruddha's Commentary and the original parts of Vedantin Mahdeva's commentary on the Samkhya-Sutras, by Richard Garbe, 1892.

'Der Mondschein der Samkhya Wahrheit,' Vachaspatimisra's Samkhya-tattva-kaumudi, ubersetzt von R. Garbe, 1892, is also a very useful work.

The Samkhya Karika by Iswarakrishna, translated from the Sanskrit by H. T. Colebrooke, also the Bhashya or commentary by Gaurapada; translated and illustrated by an original comment by H. H. Wilson, Oxford, 1837, may still be consulted with advantage.

Other useful works are:

John Davies, 'Hindu Philosophy. The Sankhya Karika of Iswarakrishna,' London, 1881.

'Die Samkhya-Philosophie, nach den Quellen,' von R. Garbe, 1894.

Of the Purva-Mimamsa or simply Mimamsa, which deals chiefly with the nature and authority of the Veda with special reference to sacrificial and other duties, we have the Sutras with Sabarasvamin's commentary published in the original; but there is as yet no book in English in which that system may be studied, except Professor Thibaut's translation of Laugakshi Bhaskara's Arthasamgraha, a short abstract of that philosophy, published in the Benares Sanskrit Series, No. 4.

The Vaiseshika system of philosophy may be studied in an English translation of its Sutras by A. E. Gough, Benares, 1873;

also in a German translation by Roer, 'Zeitschrift der Deutschen Morgenlandischen Gesellschaft,' vols. 21 and 22, and in some articles of mine in the same Journal of the German Oriental Society, i849.

The Nyaya-Sutras of Gotama have been translated, with the exception of the last book, by Ballantyne, Allahabad, 1850-57.

The Yoga-Sutras are accessible in an English translation by Rajendralala Mitra, in the Bibliotheca Indica.

DATES OF THE PHLLOSCPHICAL SUTRAS

If we consider the state of philosophical thought in India such as it is represented to us in the Brahmanas and Upanishads, and afterwards in the canonical books of the Buddhists, we cannot wonder that all attempts at fixing the dates of the six recognised systems of philosophy, nay, even their mutual relationship, should hitherto have failed. It is true that Buddhism and Jainism were likewise but two philosophical systems out of many, and that it has been possible to fix their dates. But if in their case we know something about their dates and their historical development, this is chiefly due to the social and political importance which they acquired during the fifth, the fourth, and the third centuries B. C., and not simply to their philosophical tenets. We know also that there were many teachers, contemporaries of Buddha, but they have left no traces in the literary history of India.

Nor should we forget that, though the date of the Buddhist Canon may be fixed, the date of many of the texts which we now possess and accept as canonical is by no means beyond the reach of doubt.

In the Buddhist annals themselves other teachers such as Jnatiputra, the Nirgrantha, the founder of Jainism, Purana

Kasyapa, Kakuda Katyayana, Ajita Kesakambali, Samjaya Vairattiputra, Gosaliputra, the Maskarin, are mentioned by the side of Gautama, the prince of the clan of the Sakyas. One of these only became known in history, Jnatiputra, the Nirgrantha or gymnosophist, because the society founded by him, like the brotherhood founded by Buddha, developed into a powerful sect, the Jainas. Another, Gosali with the bamboo stick, originally an Ajivaka, then a follower of Mahavira, became likewise the founder of a sect of his own, which, however, has now disappeared. Jnatiputra or Nataputta was actually the senior of Buddha.

Though it seems likely that the founders of the six systems of philosophy, though not the authors of the Sutras which we possess, belonged to the same period of philosophical and religious fermentation which gave rise to the first spreading of Buddha's doctrines in India, it is by no means clear that any of these systems, in their literary form, are presupposed by Buddhism. This is owing to the vagueness of the .quotations which are hardly ever given verbatim. In India, during the mnemonic period of literature, the contents of a book may have become considerably modified, while the title remained the same. Even at a much later time, when we see Bhartrihari (died 650 A. D.) referring to the Mimamsaka, Samkhya, and Vaiseshika Darsanas, we have no right to conclude that he knew these Darsanas exactly as we know them, though he may well have known these philosophies after they had assumed their systematic form. Again, when he quotes Naiyayikas, it by no means follows that he knew our Gotama-Sutras, nor have we any right to say that our Gotama-Sutras existed in his time. It is possible, it is probable, but it is not certain. We must therefore be very careful not to rely too much on quotations from, or rather allusions to, other systems of philosophy.

MNEMONIC LITERATURE

It has now been generally admitted, I believe, that whenever writing has once become popular, it is next to impossible that there should be no allusion to it in the poetical or prose compositions of the people. Even as late as the time of Samkara, the written letters are still called unreal (Anrita) in comparison with the audible sounds, as classified in the Pratisakhyas, which are represented by them (Ved. Sutras II, 1, 14,). There is no allusion to writing in the hymns, the Brahmanas and Upanishads; very few, if any, in the Sutras. The historical value of these allusions to writing which occur in the literature of the Buddhists depends, of course, on the date which we can assign, not to the original authors, but to the writers of our texts. We must never forget that there was in India during many centuries a purely mnemonic literature, which continued down to the Sutra-period, and which was handed down from generation to generation according to a system which is fully described in the Pratisakhyas. What would have been the use of that elaborate system, if there had been manuscripts in existence at the same time?

When that mnemonic literature, that Smriti, came for the first time to be reduced to writing, this probably took place in something like the form of Sutras. The very helplessness of the Sutra-style would thus become intelligible. Letters at that time were as yet monumental only, for in India also monumental writing is anterior to literary writing, and to the adoption of a cursive alphabet. Writing material was scarce in India, and the number of those who could read must have been very small. At the same time there existed the old mnemonic literature, invested with a kind of sacred character, part and parcel of the ancient system of education, which had so far answered all purposes and was not easy to supplant. Much of that mnemonic literature has naturally been lost, unless it was reduced to writing at the proper time. Often the name may have survived, while the body of a work was entirely changed. Hence when we see the Samkhya mentioned by name in the Buddhist texts, such as the Visuddhi-magga, it is impossible to tell whether even at that time there existed a work on the Samkhya-philosophy in the form of Sutras. It is clear at all events that it could not have been our Samkhya-Sutras, nor even the Samkhya-karikas which seem to have superseded the ancient Sutras early in the sixth century, while our present Sutras date from the fourteenth.

It might be possible, if not to prove, at all events to render probable the position assigned here to Buddha's teaching as subsequent to the early growth of philosophical ideas in their systematic and more or less technical form, by a reference to the name assigned to his mother, whether it was her real name or a name assigned to her by tradition. She was called Maya or Mayadevi. Considering that in Buddha's eyes the world was Maya or illusion, it seems more likely that the name was given to his mother by early tradition, and that it was given not without a purpose. And if so this could only have been after the name of Avidya (nescience) in the Vedanta, and of Prakriti in the Samkhya-philosophy had been replaced by the technical term of Maya. It is well known that, in the old classical Upanishads, the name of Maya never occurs; and it is equally significant that it does occur in the later and more or less apocryphal Upanishads. In the Svetasvatara, for instance, I, 10, we read, *Mayam tu Prakritim vidyat*, 'Let him know that Prakriti is Maya or Maya Prakriti.' This refer's it would seem, to the Samkhya system in which Prakriti acts the part of Maya and fascinates the Purusha till he turns away from her and she ceases to exist, at all events as far as he is concerned. But whether in Samkhya or Vedanta, Maya in its technical meaning belongs certainly to a secondary period, and it might therefore be argued that Maya, as the name of Buddha's mother, is not likely to have found a place in the Buddhistic legend during the early period of Indian philosophy, as represented in the early Upanishads, and even in the Sutras of these two prominent schools.

There was, no doubt, a certain amount of philosophical mnemonic composition after the period represented by the old Upanishads, and before the systematic arrangement of the philosophical Sutras, but whatever may have existed in it, is for ever lost to us. We can see this clearly in the case of the Brihaspati-philosophy.

THE BRIHASPATI-PHILOSOPHY

Brihaspati is no doubt a very perplexing character. His name is given as that of the author of two Vedic hymns, X, 71, X, 72, a distinction being made between a Brihaspati Angirasa and a Brihaspati Laukya (Laukayatika?). His name is well known also as one of the Vedic deities. In Rv. VIII, 96, 15, we read that Indra, with Brihaspati as his ally, overcame the godless people. He is afterwards quoted as the author of a law-book, decidedly modern, which we still possess. Brihaspati is besides the name of the planet Jupiter, and of the preceptor or Purohita of the gods, so that Brihaspati-purohitas became a recognised name of Indra, as having Brihaspati for his Purohita or chief priest and helper. It seems strange, therefore, that the same name, that of the preceptor of the gods, should have been chosen as the name of the representative of the most unorthodox, atheistical, and sensualistic system of philosophy in India. We may possibly account for this by referring to the Brahmanas and Upanishads, in which Brihaspati is represented as teaching the demons his pernicious doctrines, not for their benefit, but for their own destruction. Thus we read in Maitrayana Up. 7, 9:

'Brihaspati, having become or having assumed the shape of Sukra, brought forth that false knowledge, for the safety of Indra and for the destruction of the Asuras (demons). By it they show that good is evil and that evil is good, and they say that this new law, which upsets the Veda and the other sacred books, should be studied (by the Asuras, the demons). That being so, it is said, Let no man (but the demons only) study that false knowledge, for it is wrong; it is, as it were, barren. Its reward lasts only as long as the pleasure lasts, as with one who has fallen from his station (caste). Let that false doctrine not be attempted, for thus it is said:

1. Widely divergent and opposed are these two, the one known as false knowledge, the other as knowledge. I (Yama) believe Nachiketas to be possessed of a desire for knowledge; even many pleasures do not tempt him away.
2. He who knows at the same time both the imperfect knowledge (of ritual) and the perfect knowledge (of Self), crosses death by means of the imperfect, and obtains immortality by means of the perfect knowledge.
3. Those who are wrapt up in imperfect knowledge fancy themselves alone wise and learned, they wander about floundering and deceived, like the blind led by a man who is himself blind.'

Arid again:

'The gods and the demons, wishing to know the Self, went once into the presence of Brahman (their father Prajapati). Having bowed before him, they said; "O blessed one, we wish to know the Self, do thou tell us!" Thus, after considering, he thought, these demons believe in a difference of the Atman (from themselves), and therefore a very different Self was taught to them. On that Self these deluded demons take their stand, clinging to it, destroying the true boat of salvation, and praising untruth. What is untrue they see as true, like jugglery. But in reality, what is said in the Vedas, that is true. What is said in the Vedas, on that the wise take their stand. Therefore let no Brahman study what is not in the Vedas, or this will be the result (as in the case of the demons).'

This passage is curious in several respects. First of all, it is a clear reference of one Upanishad to another, namely, to the Chhandogya, in which this episode of Brihaspati giving false instruction to the demons is more fully detailed. Secondly, we see an alteration which was evidently made intentionally. In the Chhondogya Upanishad it is Prajapati himself who imparts false knowledge of the Atman to the Asuras, while in the Maitrayana Upanishad Brihaspati takes his place. It is not unlikely that Brihaspati was introduced in the later Upanishad in order to take the place of Prajapati, because it was felt to be wrong that this highest deity should ever have misled anyborly, even the demons. In the Chhandogya the demons who believed in the Anyata (otherness) of the Atman, that is to say, in the possibility that the Atman could be in some place different from themselves, were told to look for it in the person seen in the pupil of the eye, or in the image in a looking-glass, or in the shadow in the water. All this would, however, refer to a visible body only. Then Prajapati goes on to say that the Atman is what moves about full of pleasures in a dream, and as this would still be the individual man, he declares at last that Atman is what remains in deep sleep, without however losing its own identity.

If then in the Upanishads already Brihaspati was introduced for the purpose of teaching wrong and unorthodox opinions, we may possibly be able to understand how his name came to cling to sensualistic opinions, and how at last, however unfairly, he was held responsible for them. That such opinions existed even at an earlier time, we can see in some of the hymns in which many years ago I pointed out these curious traces of an incipient scepticism. In later Sanskrit, a Barhaspatya, or a follower of Brihaspati, has come to mean an infidel in general. Among the works mentioned in the Lalita-vistara as studied by Buddha a Barhaspatyam is mentioned, but whether composed in Sutras or in metre, does not appear. Besides, it is well known that the Lalita-vistara is rather a broken reed to rest upon for chronological purposes.

If we may trust, however, to a scholar of Bhaskara on the Brahma-Sutras, he seems to have known, even at that late time, some Sutras ascribed to Brihaspati, in which the doctrines of the Charvakas, i.e., unbelievers, were contained. But although such Sutras may have existed, we have no means of fixing their date as either anterior or posterior to the other philosophic Sutras. Panini knew of Sutras which are lost to us, and some of them may be safely referred to the time of Buddha. He also in quoting Bhikshu-Sutras and Nata-Sutras, mentions the author of the former as Parasarya, of the latter as Silalin. As Parasarya is a name of Vyasa, the son of Parasara, it has been supposed that Panini meant by Bhikshu-Sutras, the Brahma-Sutras, sometimes ascribed to Vyasa, which we still possess. That would fix tlieir date about the fifth century B.C., and has been readily accepted therefore by all, who wish to claim the greatest possible antiquity for the philosophical literature of India. But Parasarya would hardly have been chosen as the titular name of Vyasa; and though we should not hesitate to assign to the doctrines of the Vedanta a place in the fifth century, B.C., nay, even earlier, we cannot on such slender authorIty do the same for the Sutras themselves.

When we meet elsewhere with the heterodox doctrines of Brihaspati, they are expressed in verse, as if taken from a Karika rather than from Sutras. They possess a peculiar interest to us, because they would show us that India, which is generally considered as the home of all that is most spiritual and idealistic, was by no means devoid of sensualistic philosophers. But though it is difficult to say how old such theories may have been in India it is certain that, as soon as we get any coherent treatises on philosophy, sensualistic opinions crop up among them.

Of course the doctrines of Buddha would be called sceptical and atheistic by the Brahmans, and Charvaka as well as Nastika are names freely applied to the Buddhists. But the doctrines of Brihaspati, as far as we know them, go far beyond Buddhism, and may be said to be hostile to all religious feelings, while Buddha's teaching was both religious and philosophical, though the lines that separate philosophy and religion in India are very faint.

There are some tenets of the followers of Brihaspati which seem to indicate the existence of other schools of philosophy by their side. The Barhaspatyas speak as if being *inter pares*, they differ from others as others differed from them. Traces of an opposition against the religion of the Vedas (Kautsa) appear in the hymns, the Brahmanas, and the Sutras, and to ignore them would give us an entirely false idea of the religious and philosophical battles and battle-fields of ancient India. As viewed from a Brahmanic point of view, and we have no other, the opposition represented by Brihaspati and others may seem insignificant, but the very name given to these heretics would seem to imply that their doctrines had met with a world-wide acceptance (Laukayatikas). Another name, that of Nastika, is given to them as saying No to everything except the evidence of the senses, particularly to the evidence of the Vedas, which, curiously enough, was called by the Vedantists Pratyaksha, that is, self-evident, like sense-perception.

These Nastlkas, a name not applicable to mere dissenters, but to out and out nihilists only, are interesting to us from a historical point of view, because in arguing against other philosophies, they prove, *ipso facto*, the existence of orthodox philosophical systems before their time. The recognised schools of Indian philosophy could tolerate much; they were tolerant, as we shall see, even towards a qualified atheism, like that of the Samkhya. But they had nothing but hatred and contempt for the Nastikas, and it is for that very reason, and on account of the strong feelings of aversion which they excited, that it seemed to me right that their philosophy should not be entirely passed over by the side of the six Vedic or orthodox systems.

Madhava, in his 'Sarvadarsana-samgraha' or the Epitome of all philosophical systems, begins with an account of the Nastika or Charvaka system. He looks upon it as the lowest of all, but nevertheless, as not to be ignored in a catalogue of the philosophical forces of India. Charvaka is given as the name of a Rakshasa, and he is treated as a historical individual to whom Brihaspati or Vachaspati delivered his doctrines. The name of Charvaka is clearly connected with that of Charva, and this is given as a synonym of Buddha by Balasastrin in the Preface to his edition of the Kasika. He is represented as a teacher of the Lokayata or world-wide system, if that is the meaning originally intended by that word. A short account of this system is given in the 'Prabodha-Chandrodaya' in the following words: 'The Lokayata system in which the senses alone form an authority, in which the elements are earth, water, fire, and wind (not Akasa or ether), in which wealth and enjoyment form the ideals of man, in which the elements think, the other world is denied, and death is the end of all things.' This name Lokayata occurs already in Panini's Gana Ukthadi. It should be noted, however, that Hernakandra distinguishes between Barhaspatya or Nastika, and Charvaka or Lokayatika, though he does not tell us which he considers the exact points on which the two are supposed to have differed.

The Buddhists use Lokayata for philosophy in general. The statement that the Lokayatas admitted but one Pramana, i.e., authority of knowledge, namely, sensuous perception, shows clearly that there must have been other philosophical systems already in existence. We shall see that the Vaiseshika acknowledged two, perception (Pratyaksha) and inference (Anumana); the Samkhya three, adding trustworthy affirmation (Aptavakya); the Nyaya four, adding comparison (Upamana); the two Mimamsas six, adding presumption (Arthapatti) and privation (Abhava). Of these and others we shall have to speak hereafter. Even what seems to us so natural an idea as that of the four or five elements, required some time to develop, as we see in the history of the Greek and yet such an idea was evidently quite familiar to the Charvakas. While other systems admitted five, i.e., earth, water, fire, air, and ether, they admitted four only, excluding ether, probably because it was invisible. In the Upanishads we see traces of an even earlier triad of elements. All this shows the philosophical activity of the Hindus from the earliest times, and exhibits to us the Charvakas as denying rather what had been more or less settled before their time, than as adding any new ideas of their own.

So it is again with regard to the soul. Not only philosophers, but every Arya in India had a word for soul, and never doubted that there was something in man different from the visible body. The Charvakas only denied this. They held that what was called soul was not a thing by itself, but was simply the body over again. They held that it was the body that felt, that saw and heard, that remembered and thought, though they saw it every day rotting away and decomposing, as if it never had been. By such opinions they naturally came in conflict with religion even more than with philosophy. We do not know how they accounted for the evolution of consciousness and intellect out of mere flesh, except that they took refuge with a simile, appealing to the intoxicating power that can be developed by mixing certain ingredients, which by themselves are not intoxicating, as an analogy to the production of soul from body.

Thus we read:

'There are four elements, earth, water, fire, and air,

And from these four elements alone is intelligence produced—

Just like the intoxicating power from Kinwa, etc., mixed together;

Since in "I am fat," "I am lean," these attributes abide in the same subject,

And since fatness, etc., resides only in the body, it alone is the soul and no other,

And such phrases as "my body" are only significant metaphorically.'

In this way the soul seems to have been to them the body qualified by the attribute of intelligence, and therefore supposed to perish with the body. Holding this opinion, it is no wonder that they should have considered the highest end of man to consist in sensual enjoyment, and that they should have accepted pain simply as an inevitable concomitant of pleasure.

A verse is quoted:

'The pleasure which arises to men from contact with sensible objects,

Is to be relinquished as accompanied by pain—such is the warning of fools;

The berries of paddy, rich with the finest white grains,

What man, seeking his true interest, would fling them away, because covered with husks and dust.'

From all this we see that, though fundamental philosophical principles are involved, the chief character of the Charvaka system was practical, rather than metaphysical, teaching utilitarianism and crude hedonism in the most outspoken way. It is a pity that all authoritative books of these materialistic philosophers should be lost, as they would probably have allowed us a deeper insight into the early history of Indian philosophy than the ready-made manuals of the six Darsanas on which we have chiefly to rely. The following verses preserved by Madhava in his Epitome are nearly all we possess of the teaching of Brihaspati and his followers:

'Fire is hot, water cold, and the air feels cool;

By whom was this variety made? (we do not know), therefore it must have come from their own nature (Svabhava).'

Brihaspati himself is held responsible for the following invective:

'There is no paradise, no deliverance, and certainly no Self in another world,

Nor are the acts of the Asramas (stations in life) or the castes, productive of rewards.

The Agnihotra, the three Vedas, the three staves (carried by ascetics) and smearing oneself with ashes,

They are the mode of life made by their creator for those who are devoid of sense and manliness.

If a victim slain at the Jyotishtoma will go to heaven,

Why is not his own father killed there by the sacrificer?

If the Sraddha-offering gives pleasure to beings that are dead,

Then to give a *viaticum* to people who travel here on earth, would be useless.

If those who are in heaven derive pleasure from offerings,

Then why not give food here to people while they are standing on the roof?

As long as he lives let a man live happily; after borrowing money, let him drink Ghee,

How can there be a return of the body after it has once been reduced to ashes?

If he who has left the body goes to another world,

Why does he not come back again perturbed by love of his relations?

Therefore, funeral ceremonies for the dead were ordered by the Brahmans,

As a means of livelihood, nothing else is known anywhere.

The three makers of the Vedas were buffoons, knaves, and demons.

The speech of the Pandits is unintelligible, like Jarphari Turphari.

The obscene act there (at the horse sacrifice) to be performed by the queen has been

Proclaimed by knaves, and likewise other things to be taken in hand.

The eating of flesh was likewise ordered by demons.'

This is certainly very strong language; as strong as any that has ever been used by ancient or modern materialists. It is well that we should know how old and how widely spread this materialism was, for without it we should hardly understand the efforts that were made on the other side to counteract it by establishing the true sources or measures of knowledge, the Pramanas, and other fundamental truths which were considered essential both for religion and for philosophy.

The idea of orthodoxy, however, is very different in India from what it has been elsewhere. We shall find philosophers in India who deny the existence of a personal god or Isvara, and who, nevertheless, were tolerated as orthodox as long as they rccognised the authority of the Veda, and tried to bring their doctrines into harmony with Vedic texts. It is this denial of the authority of the Veda which, in the eyes of the Brahmans, stamped Buddha at once as a heretic, and drove him to found a new religion or brotherhood, while those who followed the Samkhya, and who on many important points did not differ much from him, remained secure within the pale of orthodoxy.

Some of the charges brought by the Barhaspatyas against the Brahmans who followed the Veda are the same which the followers of Buddha brought against them. Considering therefore, that on the vital question of the authority of the Veda the Samkhya agrees, however inconsistently, with orthodox Brahmanism and differs from the Buddhists, it would be far easier to prove that Buddha derived his ideas from Brihaspati than from Kapila, the reputed founder of the

Samkhya. **If we are right in the description we have given of the unrestrained and abundant growth of philosophical ideas in ancient India, the idea of borrowing, so natural to us, seems altogether out of place in India.** A wild mass of guesses at truth was floating in the air, and there was no controlling authority whatever, not even, as far as we know, any binding public opinion to produce anything like order in it. Hence we have as little right to maintain that Buddha borrowed from Kapila as that Kapila borrowed from Buddha. No one would say that the Hindus borrowed the idea of building ships from the Phenicians, or that of building Stupas from the Egyptians. In India we move in a world different from that which we are accustomed to in Greece, Rome, or Modern Europe, and we need not rush at once to the conclusion that, because similar opinions prevail in Buddhism and in the Samkhya-philosophy of Kapila, therefore the former must have borrowed from the latter, or as some hold, the latter from the former.

Though we can well imagine what the spirit of the philosophy of the ancient Indian heretics, whether they are called Charvakas or Barhaspatyas, may have been, we know, unfortunately, much less of their doctrines than of any other school of philosophy. They are to us no more than names, such as the names of Yajnavalkya, Raikva, or any other ancient leaders of Indian thought mentioned in the Upanishads, and credited there with certain utterances. We know a few of the conclusions at which they arrived, but of the processes by which they arrived at them we know next to nothing. What we may learn from these utterances is that a large mass of philosophical thought must have existed in India long before there was any attempt at dividing it into six well-defined channels of systematic philosophy, or reducing it to writing.

Even when the names of certain individuals, such as Jaimini, Kapila, and others, are given us as the authors of certain systems of philosophy, we must not imagine that they were the original creators of a philosophy in the sense in which Plato and Aristotle seem to have been so.

•••

2

The Bases of Indian Philosophy

While in most countries a history of philosophy is inseparable from a history of philosophers, in India we have indeed ample materials for watching the origin and growth of philosophical ideas, but hardly any for studying the lives or characters of those who founded or supported the philosophical systems of that country. Their work has remained and continues to live to the present day, but of the philosophers themselves hardly anything remains to us beyond their names. Not even their dates can be ascertained with any amount of certainty. In Greece, from the earliest times, the simplest views of the world and of the destinies of man, nay, even popular sayings, maxims of morality and worldly wisdom, and wise laws of every kind, even though they contained nothing very original or personal, were generally quoted as the utterances of certain persons or at least ascribed to certain names, such as the Seven Sages, so as to have something like a historical background.

We have some idea of who Thales was, and who was Plato, where and when they lived, and what they did; but of Kapila, the supposed founder of the Samkhya philosophy, of Patanjali, the founder of the Yoga, of Gotama and Kanada, of Badarayana and Jaimini, we know next to nothing. Whether any of these Indian philosophers lived at the same time and in the same place, whether they were friends or enemies, whether some were the pupils and others the teachers, all this is unknown to us, nor do I see any chance of our ever knowing more about them than we do at present.

It is quite true that every literary composition, whether in prose or in poetry, presupposes an individual author, that no poem makes itself, and no philosophical system is elaborated by the people at large. But on the other hand, no poet makes himself, no philosopher owes everything to himself. He grows from a soil that is ready made for him, and he breathes an intellectual atmosphere which is not of his own making. The Hindus seen to have felt this indebtedness of the individuals to those before and around them far more strongly than the Greeks, who, if they cannot find a human author, have recourse even to mythological and divine personages in order to have a pedestal, a name, and on authority, for every great thought and every great invention of antiquity. The Hindus are satisfied with giving us the thoughts, and leave us to find out their antecedents as best we can.

SMRITAM

The Hindu have divided the whole of their ancient literature into two parts, which really mean two periods, Srutam, what was heard, and was not the work of men or any personal being, human or divine, and Smritam, what was remembered and has always been treated as the work of an individual, whether man or god.

What we call philosophy in its systematic form, is from an Indian point of view, not revealed, Srutam, but belongs to Smriti or tradition. We possess it in carefully composed and systematically eleborated manuals in short Ephorisms or Sutras as in metrical Karikas, ascribed to authors of whom we hardly know anything, and followed by large commentaries or independent treatises which are supposed to contain the outcome of a continuous tradition going back to very ancient times. In the Sutras each system of philosophy is complete, and elaborated in its minutest details. There is no topic within the sphere of philosophy which does not find a clear or straightforward treatment in these short Sutras. They represent the last result of a long continued study of philosophy, carried on for centuries in the forests and hermitages of India.

Writing for literary purposes was unknown in India before the rise of Buddhism. We hear nothing as yet of paper, ink and reeds but only of oral and even musical repetition. The very name of a Buddhist Council was Samgiti or Mahasamgiti, i.e., singing together. It is actually mentioned that the Southern Canon was not reduced to writing till the first century B.C. under king Vattagamani. about 80 B.C.

But there must have been, nay, there was one period previous to the Sutras, during which we can watch something like growth, like life and strife, in Indian philosophy, and that is the last stage of the Vedic period, as represented to us in the Upanishads. This period is in fact the most valuable, though of systematised philosophy, it contains, as yet, little or nothing. As we can feel that there is electricity in the air, and that there will be a storm we feel on reading the Upanishads that there is philosophy in the Indian mind, and that there will be thunder and lightening to follow soon. Nay, I should even go a step further. In order to be able to account for what seem to us mere sparks of thought, mere guesses at truth, we are driven to admit a long familiarity with philosophic problems before the time that gave birth to the Upanishads.

The Upanishads contain too many technical terms, such as Brahman, Atman, Dharma, Vrata, Yoga, Mimamsa and many more, to allow us to suppose that they were the products of one day or of one generation. Even if the later systems of philosophy did not so often appeal themselves to the Upanishads as their authorities, we could easily see for ourselves that, though flowing in very different directions, like the Ganges and the Indus, these systems of philosophy can all be traced back to the same distant heights from which they took their rise. And as India was fertilised, not only by the Ganges and Indus, but by ever so many rivers and rivulets, all pointing to the snowy mountains in the north, we can see the Indian mind also being nourished through ever so many channels, all starting from a vast accumulation of religious and philosophic thought of which we seem to see the last remnants only in our Upanishads.

During that distant period philosophy was not yet separated from religion; but the earliest religion, at least, among the speakers of Aryan languages, seems always to have been not only the first religion, but the first philosophy also, of the races that had taken possession of India, as well as of the best soil of Asia and Europe. If it is the object of philosophy to discover the causes of things, *rerum cognoscere causeas*, what was the creation of the earliest mythological gods but an attempt to explain the causes of light of fire, of dawn, of day and night, of rain and thunder, by postulating agents for every one of them, and calling them Days or Agni, light or fire, Ushas, dawn, the Asvins, day and night, Indra, the sky-god, and calling all of them Devas, the Bright, of *dii* the gods? Here are the first feeders of the idea of the Godhead, whatever tributaries it may have received afterwards.

INTELLECTUAL LIFE IN ANCIENT INDIA

In certain chapters of the Brahmanas and in the Upanishads we see a picture of the social and intellectual life of India at that early time, which seems fully to justify the saying that **India has always been a nation of philosophers. The men of ancient India, as they are there represented to us, if by tradition only, are different from Greeks and Romans and from ourselves.** That in very early times kings and nobles and sages in India should have been absorbed in philosophical questions seems no doubt strange to us, because the energies of the people of Europe, as far back as we know anything about them, have always been divided between practical and intellectual pursuits, the former, in ancient times, considerably preponderating over the latter. But why should not a different kind of life have been possible in a country which, without much effort on the part of its cultivators yielded in abundance all that was necessary for the support of life? Thus, we read at the beginning of the Svetasvatara Upanishad: 'Whence are we born? Whereby do we live, and whither do we go? O ye who know Brahman, (tell us) at whose command we abide here, whether in pain or in pleasure? Should time or nature, or necessity, or chance, or the elements be considered as the cause, or He who is called Purusha, the man, that is, the Supreme Spirit?'

KSHATRIYAS AND BRAHMINS

It might be thought that all this was due to the elevating influence of an intellectual aristocracy, such as we find from very early times to the present day in India, the Brahmins. But this by no means is the case. The so-called Kshatriyas or military nobility take nearly as active a part in the intellectual life of the country as the Brahmins themselves.

In ancient times neither Kshatriyas nor Vaisyas were excluded from taking part in those religious and philosophical struggles, which seem to have occupied India far more than wars of defence or conquest. Nay, **women also claimed a right to be heard in their philosophical assemblies. The Kshatriyas never surrendered their right to take part in the discussions of the great problems of life and death,** and they occasionally asserted it with great force and dignity. Besides, the strong reaction against priestly supremacy came at last from them, for we must not forget that Buddha also was a Kshatriya, a prince of Kapilavastu, and that his chief opposition, from a social and political point of view, was against the privileges of teaching and sacrificing, claimed by the Brahmins as their exclusive property, and against the infallible and divine character ascribed by them to their Vedas.

THE EVIDENCE OF THE UPANISHADS, JANAKA, AJATASATRU

We read of an ancient King Janaka, whose fame at the time when the Upanishads were composed had already spread far and wide. He was a king of the Videhas, his capital was Mithila. We read of him as taking part in metaphysical discussions, as presiding over philosophical councils, as bestowing his patronage on the most eminent sages of his kingdom, as the friend of Yajnavalkya, one of the most famous philosophical teachers. When performing a great sacrifice, a disputation in which philosophers and even women, such as Gargi, take an active part, to the victor the king promised a reward of a thousand cows with ten padas of gold fixed to their horns. As Yajnavalkya claimed these cows on account of his superior knowledge, the other Brahmins present propounded a number of questions which he was expected to answer in order to prove his superiority. The first question is how a man who offers a sacrifice can be freed thereby from the fetters of death. Then follow questions such as, While death swallows the whole world, who is the deity that shall swallow death?

What is the soul? What contains the worlds? These and other questions were answered by Yajnavalkya in a manner that would seem satisfactory to ourselves. **What is important to us is that such questions should have been asked at all, that they should have formed the staple of public discussion at that early time. There is no other country in the world where in such ancient times such disputations would have been thought of,** unless it were in Egypt. Neither Menelaos nor Priam would have presided over them, neither Achilles nor Ulysees would have shone in them.

Do we know of any other country where at that early time such religious congresses would have been thought of, and royal rewards bestowed on those who were victorious in these philosophical tournaments?

We have a record of another disputation between a king Ajatasatru and the Brahmin Balaki, and here again it is the king who has to teach the Brahmin not vice versa.

When he has convinced Balaki of the insufficiency of the information which this learned Brahmin had volunteered to impart to him, the proud Brahmin actually declares himself the pupil of the king.

BUDDHA

Out of the midst of this whirlpool of philosophical opinions there rises the form of Buddha, calling for hearing, at first, not as the herald of any brand new philosophy, which he has to teach, but rather as preaching a new gospel to the poor.

There was one, not a mere name, but a real power in the history of India, a man who made a new epoch in the growth of Indian philosophy, and still more of Indian religion and ethics. Like several of the philosophers in the Upanishads, he was a Kshatriya and the very fact of his making himself a popular teacher and religious reformer attracted attention. And as the Brahmins had always been not only the teachers of the people, but likewise the counsellors of princes, we find Buddha also not only patronised, but consulted by the kings of his own time.

As in the Upanishads, so in the Tripitaka also kings appear as friends and patrons of a philosopher, such as Buddha, long before he had become recognised as the founder of a new religion, that they take a prominent part in public assemblies, convened for discussing the great problems of religion and philosophy, or afterwards for settling the canon of their religious texts. The best known are Bimbisara, king of Magadha, and Prasenajit, king of Kosala.

But though Buddhism and the Upanishads share many things in common which point back to the same distant antiquity, Buddhism in its practical working produced a complete social revolution in India. Though it did not abolish caste, as has sometimes been supposed, it led to a mixture of classes which had formerly been kept more carefully distinct. Anybody, without reference to his birth, could join the Buddhist fraternity, if only he was of good report and free from certain civil disabilities. He could then become an itinerant (Parivrajaka) friar, without any of that previous discipline which was required from a Brahmin.

BUDDHIST PILGRIMS, HIUEN-TSANG

Some centuries later we have another and independent source of information as to the intellectual state of India, and this also is in perfect accordance with what we have hitherto learnt about India as the home of philosophers. Beginning with the fourth century of our era, that is, at the time when what I call the Renaissance of Sanskrit literature and national independence began, Chinese Buddhists, who made their pilgrimages to India as to their Holy Land, described to us the state of the country such as they saw it. Those who came early, such as Fa-hian, saw Buddhism flourishing in the fifth century, those who came later in the sixth and seventh centuries, witnessed already the evident signs of its decline. The most important among them was Hiuen-tsang who visited India from 620 to 645. He describes the Buddhist monasteries scattered all over the country, the schools of the most illustrious teachers whose lectures he attended and their public assemblies, particularly those that took place at the court of Siladitya Harshavardhana, 610-650.

Every year he assembled the Sramanas from different kingdoms, and made them discuss in his presence the most important points of Buddha's doctrine. Hiuen-tsang was invited by the king to be present at one of these great assemblies, on the southern bank of the Ganges. Twenty kings were gathered there, each bringing with him both Sramanas and Brahmins.

From the time of the Upanishads to the time of Hiuen-tsang's sojourn in India, one dominant interest pervaded the whole country, the interest in the great problems of humanity here on earth. While in other countries the people at large cared more for their national heroes, as celebrated in their epic poetry on account of their acts of bravery or cunning, India under the sway of its Vedic poets, most of them of a priestly rather than a warrior origin, remained true to its character.

If after these preliminary remarks we look for the real beginnings of philosophy on the soil of India, we shall find them in a stratum where philosophy is hardly differentiated as yet from religion that is in the Vedas. No one has ever doubted that in the Veds we have the earliest monument of Aryan language and thought, and in a certain sense, of Aryan literature which, in an almost miraculous way, has been preserved to us, during the long night of centuries, chiefly by means of oral tradition. **The Vedas are to us unique and priceless guides in opening before our eyes tombs of thought richer in relics than the royal tombs of Egypt,** and more ancient and primitive in thought than the oldest hymns of Babylonian or Accadian poets.

Whatever may be the date of the Vedic hymns, whether 1500 or 15,000 B.C., they have their own unique place and stand by themselves in the literature of the world. They tell us something of the early growth of the human mind of which we find no trace anywhere else. Every word in them is an authentic document in the history of the greatest empire, the empire of the human mind, as established in India in the second millennium B.C.

THE PHILOSOPHICAL BASES OF THE VEDIC GODS

Let us begin with the simplest beginnings. What can be simpler than the simple conviction that the regularly recurring events of nature require certain agents? Animated by this conviction the Vedic poets spoke not only of rain (Indu), but of a rainer (Indra), not only of fire and light as a fact, but of a lighter and burner, an agent of fire and light, a Dyaus (*Zeus*) and an Agni (*ignis*). We may smile at such thoughts, but they were natural thoughts. One of these agents they called Savitar the enlivener, as distinguished yet inseparable from Surya, the heavenly, the Sun, Greek Helios. Soma, from the same root Su, was likewise at first what enlivens, i.e., the rain, then the moon which was supposed to send dew and rain, and lastly, the enlivening draught, used for sacrificial purposes and prepared from a plant called Soma. In this way both the religion and the mythology of the Vedic sages have a philosophical basis, and deserve our attention, if we wish to undrestand the beginnings not only of Indian mythology and religion, but of Indian philosophy also. 'No one', as Deussen truly says, 'can or should in future talk about these things who does not know the Rigveda. The process on which originally all gods depended for their very existence, the personification of, or the activity attrributed to the great natural phenomena, while more or less obscured in all other religions, takes place in the Rigveda as it were in the full light of day. **This was the beginning of philosophy, the first applicaiton of the law of causality.**

THREE CLASSES OF VEDIC GODS

We know now by what very simple process the Vedic Aryans satisfied their earliest craving for causes, how they created their gods, and divided the whole drama of nature into three acts and the actors into three classes, those of the sky, those of mid-air, and those of the earth. To the first belong Dyaus, the agent of the sky. To mid-air belong Indra, the agent of the atmosphere in its change between light and darkness, the giver of rain. To the earth belong Prithivi herself, Agni, the agent of fire; Sarasvati and other rivers; sometimes the Dawn also. These gods were the first philosophy, the first attempt at explaining the wonders of nature.

OTHER CLASSIFICATIONS OF GODS

If we call this creation and likewise classification of the Devas or gods, the first philosophy of the human race, we can clearly see that it was not artificial or the work of one individual only, but was suggested by nature herself. Earth, air, and sky, or again, morning, noon, and night, spring, summer, and winter are triads clearly visible in nature, and therefore, under different names and forms, mirrored in ancient mythology in every part of the world. Though the Devas are known in the Rigveda and the Avesta as thirty-three, I doubt whether there is any physical necessity for this number. It seems rather due to a taste very common among uncivilised tribes of playing with numbers and multiplying them to any extent.

I look upon all these attempts at a classification of the Vedic gods as due once more to the working of a philosophical or systematising spirit.

THE VISVA OR ALL-GODS

The first step in this direction seems to be represented by the Visve or the Visve Devas. Visva is different from Sarva, all. It means the gods together, not simply all the gods. What is important in these Visve is that they represent the first attempt at comprehending the various gods as forming a class. They ought not to be ignored by those who are interested in the progress of the ancient mythological religions from given multiplicity to postulated unity, as an essential character of the godhead.

They arrived at the conviction that above the great multitude of gods there must be one supreme personality, and, after a time, they declared that there was behind all the gods that one (Tad Ekam) of which the god were but various names.

The sages call that one in many ways, they call it Agni, Yama, Matrisvan. (Rv. I, r64, 46.)

That One breathed breathlessly by itself, other than it there nothing since has been. (Rv. X, 129, 2.)

PRAJAPATI

Distinguishing as much as possible, between what has been called tentative monotheism, which is religion, and tentative monism, which is philosophy, we can discover traces of the former in the famous hymn X, 121, which, I called the hymn to the Unknown God. Here the poet asks in every verse to whom, to what Deva, he should offer his sacrifice, and says towards the end whether it should be, 'he who alone was god constantly represented as supreme, but this is very different from the distinct demand here made by the poet for a god that should be above all other gods. The idea of oneness is really involved in the idea of God as a supreme and unlimited being. Here, in the demand for and in the supply of a supreme deity, we can watch a slow and natural progress. At first, for instance, when (Rv. VIII, 89) Indra was to be praised for his marvellous deeds, it was he who had made the sun to shine. He was called Satakratu, the all-powerful and all-wise, or Abhibhu, the conqueror. At the end the poet sums up by saying: 'Thou art the maker of all things, thou art the great Visvadeva.'

VISVAKARMAN

In such adjectives as Satakratu, and still more in Visvakarman, the maker of all things, we see the clear germs that were to grow into the one supreme deity. As soon as Visvakarman was used as a substantive, the Brahmins had what they wanted, they had their All-maker, their god above all gods, the god whose friendship the other gods were eager to secure (VIII, 89, 3).

SEARCH FOR A SUPREME DEITY

The same hymns yearning for one supreme deity which led the Vedic priests to address their hymns to the Visve Devas or to Visvakarman as the maker of all things, induced them likewise to give a more personal character to Prajapati.

BRAHMAN, ATMAN, TAD EKAM

We have now to take another step in advance. By the side of the stream of thought which we have hitherto followed, we see in India another powerful movement which postulated from the first more than a god above, yet among other gods. In the eyes of more thoughtful men everyone of the gods, called by a personal and proper name, was limited *ipso facto*, and therefore not fit to fill the place which was to be filled by an unlimited and absolute power, as the primary cause of all created things. No name that expressed ideas connected with the male or famale sex, was considered as fit for such a being, and thus we see that as early as the Vedic hymns it was spoken of as Tad Ekam, That One, as neither male nor female, that is, as neuter. We come across it in the hymn of Dirghatamas where, after asking who he was that established these six spaces of the world, the poet asks, 'Was it perhaps the One (neuter), in the shape of the Unborn (masc.)?'

This One, or the Unborn, is mentioned also in X, 82, 6, where we read 'The One is placed in the name of the unborn where all beings rested.' The same postulated Being is most fully described in hymn X, 129, I, the Nasadiya Hymn.

There are several passages in this hymn which, in spite of much labour spent on them by eminent scholars, remain obscure. The poet himself is evidently not quite clear in his own mind, and he is constantly oscillating between a personal and impersonal or rather superpersonal cause from whence the universe emanated. But the step from a sexual to a sexless god, from a mythological to a metaphysical one, had evidently been made at that early times, and with it the decisive step from mythology to philosophy had been taken. These startling outbursts of philosophic thought seem indeed to require the admission of a long continued effort of meditation and speculation before so complete a rupture with the old conception of physcial gods could have become possible. It must have required considerable boldness, when surrounded by millions who never got tired of celebrating the mighty deeds achieved by such Devas as Agni, Indra, Soma, Savitri, or Varuna, to declare that these gods were nothing but names of a higher power which was at first without any name at all, called simply Tad Ekam, That One, and afterwards addressed by such dark names as Brahman and Atman.

That One Being was free from the character of a mere Deva, entirely free from mythology, from parentage and sex, and if endowed with personality at all, then so far only as personality was necessary. This was very different from the vulgar personality ascribed by the Greeks to their Zeus ar Aphrodite, nay, even by many Jews and Christians to their Jehovah or God. Such names as Brahman and Atman, which afterwards became so important as the two main supports of Vedanta philosophy, or Purusha, the name of the transcendent soul as used in the Samkhya system, do not spring into life without a long previous incubation.

BRAHMAN, ITS VARIOUS MEANINGS

If then we find Brahman used as another name of what before was called Tad Ekam, That One, if late on we meet with such questions as–

Was Brahman the first cause? Whence are we born? By what do we live? Whither are we hastening? By whom constrained do we obtain our lot in life whether of happiness or of misery, O ye knowers of Brahman? Is time, is the nature of things, is necessity, is accident, are the elements, or its Purusha to be considered the source?

ATMAN

The next word we have to examine is Atman. It is next in importance to Brahman only, and the two together may be called the two pillars on which rests nearly the whole of the edifice of Indian philosophy, more particularly of the Vedanta and Samkhya systems.

As early as the time of the Apastamba Sutras, that is, at the end of the Vedic period, we read: 'The Brahmin who is wise and recognises all things to be in the Atman, who does not become bewildered when pondering on it, and who recognises the Atman in every created thing, he shines indeed in heaven...'(I, 8, 23, I) And in the same Sutras, we find a definition of Brahman, as the cause of the world, which presupposes, as clearly as possible, the prevalence of Vedantic ideas at the time of the auther of this Sutra.

The etymology of Atman is extremely obscure; there can be little doubt that in the Veda Atman, in several places, still means breath, as in Rv. X, 16, 3, words addressed to a dead person, 'May the eye go to the sun, the breath (Atma) to the wind.' It then came to mean vital breath, life, and like, the spirit or breath, was frequently used in the sense of what we call soul. From soul there is but a small step to Self. We have thus seen three words growing up in the hymns and Brahamanas of the Veda, Prajapati, Brahman, and Atman, each of which by itself represents a whole philosophy or a view of the world.

A belief in that Prajapati, as a personal god, was the beginning of monotheistic religion in India, while the recognition of Brahman and Atman, as one, constituted the foundation of all the monistic philosophy of the country.

GROWTH OF PHILOSOPHICAL IDEAS

All these ideas, metaphysical, cosmological, and otherwise, burst forth in India in great profusion and confusion, and without any preconceived system.

Earliest philosophy existed for a long time without being fixed by writing, that there was neither control, authority, nor public opinion to protect it. Every Asrama or settlement was a world by itself, even the simplest means of communication, such as high-roads or rivers, being often wanting. **The wonder is that, in spite of all this, we should find so much unity in the numerous guesses at truth** preserved to us among these Vedic ruins. We learn from the Brahmanas and Upanishads of the intellectual life of India, to **admit an infinite number of intellectual centres of thought, scattered all over the country,** in which either the one or the other view found influential advocates.

If in the period of the Brahmanas and Upanishads we have to find our way through religious and philosophical thoughts, as through clusters of thickly tangled creepers, the outlook becomes brighter as soon as we approach the next period, which is characterised by persistent attempts at clear and systematic thought. We must not imagine that even then we can always discover in the various systems of philosophy a regular historical growth. The Sutras or aphorisms which we possess of the six systems of philosophy, each distinct from the other, cannot possibly claim to represent the very first attempts at a systematic treatment; they are rather the last summing up of what had been growing up during many generations of isolated thinkers.

It is the multiplicity and variety of these paths that form the chief interest of the history of philosophy, and the fact that to the present day these six different systems of philosophy have held their own in the midst of a great multitude of philosopic theories, propounded by the thinkers of India, shows that we must try to appreciate their characteristic peculiarities.

These philosophers are:

1. Badarayana, called also Vyasa Dvaipayana or Krishna Dvaipayana, the reputed author of the Brahma Sutras, called also Uttra Mimamsa Sutras, or Vyasa Sutras.
2. Jaimini, the author of the Purva Mimamsa Sutras.
3. Kapila, the author of the Samkhya Sutras.
4. Patanjali, also called Sesha or Phanin, the author of the Yoga Sutras.
5. Kanada, also called Kanabhuj, Kanabhakshaka, or Uluka, the author of the Vaiseshika Sutras.
6. Gotama, also called Akshapada, the author of the Nyaya Sutras.

It is easy to see that the philosophers to whom our Sutras are ascribed, cannot be considered as the first originators of Indian philosophy. These Sutras often refer to other philosophers, who, therefore, must have existed before the time when the Sutras received their final form.

LITERARY REFERENCES IN THE UPANISHADS

It is of considerable importance to remember that of the technical names **of the six systems of philosophy, two only occur in the classical Upanishads, namely, Samkhya and Yoga or Samkhya-Yoga.** Vedanta does not occur, except in the Svetasvatara, Mundaka and some of the later Upanishads. Mimamsa occurs in the general sense of investigation, Nyaya and Vaiseshika are altogether absent, nor do we meet with such words as Hetuvidya, or Anvikshiki, nor with the names of the reputed founders of the six systems, except those of the two Mimamsas, Badarayana and Jaimini. The names of Patanjali, or Kanada, are absent altogether, while the names of Kapila and Gotama, when they occur, refer, it would seem, quite different personalities.

SAMKHYA-SUTRAS

The Samkhya-Sutras, as we possess them, are very chary of references. They clearly refer to Vaiseshika and Nyaya, when they examine the six categories of the former and the sixteen Padarthas of the latter, whenever they refer to the Anus or atoms, we know that they have the Vaiseshika philosophy in their minds; and once the Vaiseshikas are actually mentioned by name.

VEDANTA-SUTRAS

The Vedanta Sutras contain more frequent references, but they too do not help us much for chronological purposes. Badarayana refers more or less clearly to the Buddhists, the Jainas, Pasupatas, and Pancharatras, all of whom he is endeavouring to refute. It is out of a floating mass of philosophical and religious opinion, which was common property in India, that the regular systems slowly emerged.

COMMON PHILOSOPHICAL IDEAS

There existed in India a large common fund of philosophical thought which, like language, belonged to no one in particular, but was like the air breathed by every living and thinking man. Thus only can it be explained that we find a number of ideas in all, or nearly all, the systems of Indian philosophy which all philosophers seem to take simply for granted, and which belong to no one school in particular.

The best known of these ideas is that which is known under the name of Metempsychosis. To a Hindu **the idea that the souls of men migrated after death into new bodies of living beings, of animals, nay, even of plants, is so self-evident that it was hardly ever questioned.** As early as the period of the Upanishads we hear of human souls being reborn both in animal and in vegetable bodies. To me it seems that such a theory was so natural that it might perfectly well have arisen independently among different races.

IMMORTALITY OF THE SOUL

The idea of the immortality of the soul also should be included in what was the common property of all Indian philosophers. This idea was so completely taken for granted that we look in vain for any eleborate arguments in support of it. Mortality with the Hindus is so entirely restricted to the body which decays and decomposes before our very eyes, that such an expression as immortality of the Self, sounds almost tautological in Sanskrit.

PESSIMISM

All Indian philosophers have been charged with pessimism, and in some cases such a charge may seem well founded but not in all. People who derived their name for good from a word which originally meant nothing but being or real, Sat, are not likely to have looked upon what is as what ought not to be. Indian philosophers are by no means dwelling for ever on the miseries of life. They are not always whining and protesting that life is not worth living. That is not their pessimism. They simply state that they received the first impulse to philosophical reflection from the fact that there is suffering in the world. Considering that the aim of all Indian philosophy was the removal of suffering, which was caused by nescience, and the attainment of the highest happiness, which was produced by knowledge, we should have more right to call it eudaemonistic than pessimistic.

KARMAN

The next idea that seems ingrained in the Indian mind, and therefore finds expression in all the systems of philosophy, is a belief in Karman, deed, that is, the continuous working of every thought, word, and deed through all ages. All works, good or bad, must bear and do bear fruit, is a sentiment never doubted by any Hindu, whether today or thousands of years ago. And the same eternity which is claimed for works and their results is claimed for the soul also, only with this difference, that while works will cease to work when real freedom has been obtained, the soul itself continues after the obtainment of freedom or final beatitude.

INFALLIBILITY OF THE VEDA

One more common element presupposed by Indian philosophy might be pointed out in the recognition of the supreme authority and the revealed character ascribed to the Veda.

THREE GUNAS

The theory of the three Gunas also, which has been claimed as originally peculiar to the Samkhya philosophy, seems to have been quite familiar to most Hindu philosophers. The impulse to everything in nature, the cause of all life and variety, is ascribed to the three Gunas. Guna means quality, the component constituents of nature. In the most general sense they represent no more than thesis, antithesis, and something between the two such as cold, warm, and neither cold nor warm; good, bad, and neither good nor bad; and so on through every part of physical and moral nature.

•••

3

Uttara-Mimamsa or Vedanta

If now we pass on to a consideration of the six orthodox systems of philosophy, and begin with the Vedanta, we have to take as our chief guides the Sutras of Badarayana, and the commentary of Samkara. We know little of Badarayana, the reputed author of the Sutras.

In India, he has been identified with Vyasa, the collector of the Mahabharata, but withoutt sufficient evidence, nor should we gain much by that identificaiton, as Vyasa of the Mahabharata also is hardly more than a name to us. This Vyasa is said by Samkara, to have lived at the end of the Dvapara and the beginning of the Kali age, and to have had intercourse with the gods. But though we call him the author of the Mahabharata, Samkara, in the whole of his commentary on the Vedanta Sutras, never mentions that the Vyasa of the epic was the author of the book on which he is commenting, though he mentions Badarayana as such. All we can say is that, whatever the date of the Bhagavad-gita is, and it is a part of the Mahabharata, the age of the Vedanta Sutras and of Badarayana must have been earlier.

Though the name of Vedanta does not occur in the old Upanishads, we can hardly doubt that it was the Vedantic thoughts, contained in the Upanishads, which gave the first impulse to more systematic philosophical speculations in India. Several scholars have tried to prove that Samkhya ideas prevailed in India at an earlier time than the Vedantic ideas. But though there certainly are germs of Samkhya theories in the Upanishads, **they are but few and far between, while the strictly Vedantic concepts meet us at every step in the hymns,** the Brahmanas, the Aranyakas and in the Sutras, Vedanta is clearly the native philosophy of India.

If we ask for the fundamental doctrines of the Vedanta the Hindus themselves have helped us and given us in a few words what they themselves consider as the quintessence of that system of thought:

'In one half verse I shall tell you what has been taught in thousands of volumes: Brahman is true, the world is false, the soul is Brahman and nothing else.'

And again:

'There is nothing worth gaining, there is nothing worth enjoying, there is nothing worth knowing but Brahman alone, for he who knows Brahman, is Brahman.'

We have another and still shorter abstract of the Vedanta in the famous words addressed by Uddalaka Aruni to his son Svetaketu: *'Tat tvam asi,'* 'Thou art That.' These words, however, convey little meaning without the context in which they occur, that is to say, unless we know what is meant by the Tat, that, and by the Tvam, thou. The Tat is what we saw shadowed forth in the Upanishads as the Brahman, as the cause of the world, the Tvam is the Atman, the self in its various meanings, from the ordinary I to the divine Soul or Self, recognised in man; and it is the highest aim of the Vedanta to show that these two are in reality one. **This fearless synthesis seems to me the boldest and truest synthesis in the whole**

history of philosophy. Even Kant, who clearly recognised the Tat or it, that is, the *Ding an sich* behind the objective world, never went far enough to recognise the identity of the Tat, the objective *Ding an sich* and the Tvam, the *Ding and sich* on the subjective side of the world. Such a synthesis of the subjective with the objective Self would even now rouse the strongest theological, if not philosophical, protests, whereas the theologians of India discuss it with perfect equanimity, and see in it the truest solution of the riddle of the world.

Their idea of the Supreme Cause of the universe went far beyond what is meant by God, the creator and ruler of the world, Prajapati. That being was to them a manifestation only of the Supreme Cause of Brahman, it was Brahman as phenomenal, and it followed that, as, Brahman, as they held, was indeed the cause of everything, the All in All, man also could be nothing but a phenomenon of Brahman. The idea therefore that it would be blasphemy to make the creature equal to the creator so far as their substance was concerned, never presented itself to their minds. Their Tat was something behind or above the purely personal creator, it was the absolute divine essence, the Godhead, manifested in a subjective and personal creator, and present likewise in all its phenomenal manifestations, including gods and men.

With us unfortunately such questions can hardly be discussed in a calm philosophical sprit, because theology steps in and protests against them as irreligious and blasphemous, just as the Jews declared it blasphemy in Christ to teach that He was equal to God, nay, that He and the Father were one, *Tat tvam asi.* On this point even our philosophy may have something to learn which has often been forgotten in modern Christianity.

The teachers of the Vedanta, while striving to resuscitate in man the consciousness of the identity of the Tat and the Tvam, and, though indirectly, of man and God, seem to be moving in the most serene atmosphere of thought, and in their stiff and algebraic Sutras they were working out these mighty problems with unfaltering love of truth, and in an unimpassioned and truly philosophic spirit. These Upanishads represent the soil which contained the seeds of philosophy which sprang up and had their full growth in the great systems of philosophy of a later age.

If now we turn to the philosophy elaborated by Badarayana, we find no longer rhapsodies, but a carefully reasoned system, contained in 555 short paragraphs, the so-called Vedanta Sutras. We read there in the first Sutra and as a kind of title, 'Now then a desire to know Brahman,' or as Deussen translates Jignasa, 'Now then research of Brahman.'

In real life, the first step would have been to study the Purva Mimamsa, or what is called Dharma, law, virtue, etc., and that only after having gained a knowledge of Dharma particularly of the sacrificial Dharma, would there arise a desire to know Brahman. In that case the Mimamsa might be looked upon as one body, the Purva Mimamsa forming the first, the Uttara Mimamsa the second part, and we should have to consider the practice of virtue and the performance of sacrificial acts as a necessary preliminary to a study of the Vedanta philosophy.

But Brahman cannot be known like all other things, by being defined as So and So, it can be explained negatively as Not so and Not so and can thus be cleared from many doubts which arise from the various utterances about it in the Upanishads. When we read, however, that food is Brahman, that Manas is Brahman, that the sun is Brahman, nay, that Narayana is Brahman, there is surely room enough for trying to determine what Brahman really is, or at least what he or it was to Badarayana and his predecessors.

The best answer, however, to all these questions is that given in the Sutra, 'That *from* which the origin etc. (origin, subsistence, and dissolution) of this world proceed, the full sense of this Sutra, according to the commentator, is: 'That omniscient, omnipotent cause from which proceed.' the origin, subsistence and dissolution of the world, which world is differentiated by names and forms, contains many agents and enjoyers, and is the abode of fruits or effects, caused by former actions, these fruits having their definite places, times and causes, and the nature of whose arrangement cannot be conceived by the mind–that cause is Brahman.'

If it be asked, how this is known, the commentator insists very strongly that such knowledge is not to be gained by sense perception or by inference, but simply by the Veda (Upanishads), passages of which have been collected and properly arranged in the Sutras. If in some places he admits as a second source of knowledge Sakshatkara, or manifestation, that can only be meant for intuition, but strictly speaking, such intuition also presupposes a previous working of the organs of sensuous perception, while the object of such Sakshatkara, i.e., Brahman, can at first be supplied by the Veda only. In support therefore of our Sutra which is intended to give a general idea of Brahman, a passage is quoted from the Taitt. Up. III, I, where Varuna explains to his son that 'that from which these beings are born, that by which, when born they live, that into which at their death they re-enter, try to, know that that, is Brahman.'

APPEALS TO THE VEDA

And here we should mark a curious feature of orthodox Indian philosophy. Though the Vedanta appeals to the Veda, it appeals to it, not as having itself grown out of it as belonging to it, but rather as an independent witness looking back to it for sanction and confirmation. The same applies, though in a less degree, to other systems also. They all speak as if they had for several generations elaborated their doctrines independently and after they had done so, they seem to come back to get the approval of the Veda, or to establish their conformity with the Veda, as the recognised highest authority. This shows that a certain time must have elapsed after the final redaction of the Upanishads and the return, as it were, of their offspring, the Sutras, to their original home. How this came about, we cannot tell, because we have no historical documents, but that there had been something very important intervening between the old Upanishads and the first attempts at systematising Vedanta and Samkhya doctrines in the form of Sutras is very clear by the manner in which the Sutras appeal to the Veda.

It is characteristic of the Vedanta Sutras that they pay much smaller attention to the Pramanas, the sources and authorities of knowledge, than the other systems. These questions of Pramana are often referred to in the commentaries, but not so much in the text. We must be satisfied with the expressed view of Badarayana that the evidence for what the Vedanta teaches is neither perception nor inference, but the Word (Sabda) alone, such as we find it in our manuscripts, or rather in the oral tradition of the Veda.

WORK-PART AND KNOWLEDGE-PART OF THE VEDA

Of course a distinction has to be made, and has been made by Badarayana between the knowledge-part, the Jnana-kanda, chiefly the Upanishads, and the Karma-kanda, the work-part, the hymns and Brahmanas. Both are called Veda or Sruti, revelation, and yet the work-part does not exist for the true philosopher, except in order to be discarded as soon as he has understood the knowledge-part. Samkara is bold enough to declare that the whole Veda is useless to a man who has obtained knowledge, or Mukti or freedom. A man who has neglected the Vedas and disregarded the rules of the four Asramas, in fact, a man who has lost caste, may still be allowed to study the Vedanta as the fountain of all true knowledge, and thus become liberated. The hymns and Brahmanas refer in fact to the phenomenal world, they presuppose the existence of a manifold creation, of an enjoyer of what is to be enjoyed, of good works and their fruits. But all this is not real, but phenomenal; it belongs to the realm of Avidya, Nescience, and vanishes as soon as true wisdom or Vidya has been obtained. It is to be observed in the world, such as it is as a lower stage, but as essential in leading on to a higher stage.

VIDYA AND AVIDYA

If then the highest truth contained in the Veda is the Tat Tvam Asi, that is, Thou, the Jivatman, art is (the Paramatman or Brahman), and if, as we are told, there is but one Brahman and nothing beside it, the Vedanta philosopher is at once met by the question: How then are we to account for the manifold Thous, the many individuals, and the immense variety of the objective world? If the Veda is true, our view of the world cannot be true at the same time. It can therefore be due only to what is called Avidya, Nescience, and it is the very object of the Vedanta philosophy to expel and annihilate this Avidya, and replace it by Vidya.

SUBJECT AND OBJECT

This Avidya is the next point that has to be discussed. Samkara, in the introduction to his commentary, has some important remarks on it: 'As it is well knwon,' he says, 'that object and subject, which fall under the concepts of We and You (or as we should say, of the Ego and Non-Ego), are in their very essence opposed to each other, like darkness and light, and that the one can never therefore take the place of the other, it follows further that their attributes also can never be interchanged.' This means that object and subject mutually exclude each other, so that what is conceived as object can never in the same act of thought be conceived as subject and *vice versa*. We can, for instance, never say or think: We are you, or You are we, nor ought we ever to substitute subjective for objective qualities. 'Therefore,' he continues, 'we may conclude that to transfer what is objective, that is, what is perceived as You or Non-ego with its qualities, to what is subjective, that is, what perceives as We, the Ego, which consists of thought, or *vice versa* to transfer what is subjective to what is objective, must be altogether wrong.' A subject can never be anything but a subject, the object always remains the object. 'Nevertheless,' he adds, 'it is a habit in human nature (a necessity of thought as we might call it), to say, combining what is true and what is false, "I am this," "this is mine." This is a habit caused by a false apprehension of subject and predicate, and by not distinguishing one from the other, but transferring the essence and the qualities of the one upon the other.

It is clear that Samkara here uses subject and object not only in their simple logical sense, but that by subject he means what is real and true, in fact the Self, while object means with him what is unreal and phenomenal, such as the body with its organs, and the whole visible world. In 'I am', the verb has a totaly different character from what it has in 'thou art' of 'he is'. Such statements therefore as 'I am strong' or 'I am blind' arise from a false apprehension which, though it is inseparable from human thought, such as it is, has slowly to overcome and at last to be destroyed by the Vedanta philosophy.

This distinction between subject and object in the sense of what is real and what is phenomenal is very important, and stamps the whole of the Vedanta philosophy with its own peculiar character.

It follows in fact from this fundamental distinction that we should never predicate what is phenomenal or objective of what is real and subjective, or what is real and subjective of what is phenomenal and objective; and it is in causing this mistake that the chief power of Avidya or Nescience consists. I should even go so far as to say that this warning might be taken to heart by our own philosphers also, for many of our own fallacies arise from the same Avidya and are due in the end to the attribution of phenomenal and objective qualities to the subjective realities which we should recognise in the Divine only, and as underlying the Human Self and the phenomenal world.

It must not be supposed, however, that the Avidya or Nescience which makes the world what we make it and take it to be, is simply our own individual ignorance, our being unacquainted with the truths of Vedanta. It should rather be looked upon as inborn in human nature, or, from an Indian point of view, as the result of accumulated thoughts and deeds before the mountains were brought forth. It has truly been called a general cosmical Nescience, inevitable for a time, as darkness is with light. So far as in true reality we are Brahman, our Nescience might indeed be called the

Nescience of Brahman, if for a time only; and if we remember that it can be annihilated, we can understand why it was said to be nought, for, according to a general principle of the Vedanta, nothing that is real can ever be annihilated, so that nothing that is liable to annihilation has a right to be called real.

THE PHENOMENAL REALITY OF THE WORLD

But it is very curious to find that though Samkara looks upon the whole objective world as the result of Nescience, he nevertheless allows it to be real for all practical purposes (Vyavahararartham). Thus we read, 'The entire complex of phenomenal existence is considered as true so long as the knowledge of Brahman and the Self of all has not arisen, just as the phantoms of a dream are considered to be true until the sleeper wakes...' Hence, as long as true knowledge does not present itself, there is no reason why the ordinary course of secular and religious activity should not go on undisturbed, and more particularly, why all the commands of the Veda even of the work-part should not be obeyed.

But apart from this concession, the fundamental doctrine of Samkara remains always the same. There is Brahman and nothing else; and to this Brahman as the subject nothing must be ascribed that is peculiar to the individual living soul. The individual soul is, no doubt, Brahman for the simple reason that there is nothing but Brahman, but Brahman is not the individual soul, which in its present state is personal, that is, conditioned, and phenomenal.

CREATION OF CAUSATION

If with these ideas, taken as granted, we approach the problem of what we call the creation or the making of the world, it is clear that creation in our sense cannot exist for the Vedantist. As long as creation is conceived as a making or fashioing of matter, it does not exist for Badarayana; only so far as it is a calling forth out of nothing does it approach the ideas of the Vedantist. Creation with Badarayana would be nothing but the result of Nescience, and yet Brahman is again and again represented as the cause of the world, and not only as the efficient, but as the material cause as well, so far as such foreign terms can be applied to the reasoning of the Vedanta. Here lies our great difficulty in rendering Hindu philosophy intelligible.

The terms used by them seem to be the same as those which we use ourselves, and yet they are not. It is easy to say that Karana is cause and Karya effect, that the created world is the effect, and that Brahman is the cause. But the Vedantists have elaborated their own theory of cause and effect. According to them, cause and effect are really the same thing looked at from two points of view, and the effect is always supposed to be latent in the cause. Hence, if Brahman is everything, and nothing exists besides Brahman, the substance of the world can be nothing but Brahman. Divyadasa, a living Vedantist, seems therefore to draw a quite legitimate inference when he says that the univese with all its sins and miseries must have existed latent in Brahman, just as steam existed latent in water before it was heated, though it does not become evident as vapour till fire is brought near to water.

Creation is not real in the highest sense in which Brahman is real, but it is real in as far as it is phenomenal, for nothing can be phenomenal except as the phenomenon of something that is real.

In some of the later Upanishads this Nescience or Ignorance assumes a more independent character and even a new name, Maya. Thus we read in the Svet. Up. IV, 10: 'Know Prakriti (nature) as Maya (magic) and the great Lord as the Mayin (magician).' Though this is not pure Vedanta, it shows us, at all events, the way by which the ignorance of the individual, became the cause of what we call objective reality and led at the same time to the admission of an active and creative Lord, the personal Brahma or Isvara; how Avidya in fact became a Sakti or *potentia*, somehow or other related to Brahman itself.

But before there arises this Maya of objective nature, belonging as it were to Brahman himself, there was the Maya of the internal or subjective world. This was originally the only Maya, and deceived by the Maya or Avidya the Atman or pure Self was covered up (Upahita) or blinded, or conditioned by the so-called Upadhis, the conditions or impositions, if we may say so, in both senses.

The Upadhis are:

1. The Mukhyaprana, the vital spirit (unconscious);
2. The Manas, the central organ of perception, ready to receive what is conveyed to it by the separate senses, and to react on them by will; Manas being that which, as we say, perceives, feels, thinks and wills;
3. The Indriyas, the five senses, both afferent (Upalabdhi) and efferent (Adhyavasaya), The five afferent senses are the senses of hearing, touch, sight, taste, scent. The five efferent or acting senses are the senses of speaking, grasping, going, evacuating and generating;
4. the material organic body.

   To these is sometimes added–
5. The objective environment, or the objects or meanings of the senses (Artha).

All these are not the Atman. That there is in man something that can be called Atman or Self requires no proof, but if a proof were wanted it would be found in the fact that no one can say, 'I am not, (I being the disguised Atman), for he who would say so, would himself be not, or would not be. The question then is, What is really I or what is there real behind the I? The Upadhis, conditions, are to be treated as Not-self.

We can understand how this startling idealism or monism—for it is not nihilism, though our philosophy has no better name for it—led to two distinct, yet closely united views of the world. All that we should call phenomenal, comprehending the phenomena of our inward as well as of our outward experience was unreal, as the phenomenal was considered impossible without the noumenal, that is, without the real Brahman, it was in that sense real also, that is, it exists, and can only exist, with Brahman behind it. And this led to the admission by the strict Advaitists or Monists of two kinds of knowledge well known under the names of Apara, the lower, and Para, the higher knowledge.

THE HIGHER AND THE LOWER KNOWLEDGE

The higher knowledge consists in the distinction and thereby the freedom of the Self (Atman) from all its Upadhis, and this not for this life only, but for all eternity. This is the true Moksha or freedom which implies knowledge of the identity of the Atman with Brahman, and deliverance from birth and rebirth in the constant evolution (Samsara) of the world. The lower knowledge is likewise founded on the Veda, but chiefly on its work portion (Karmakanda), and teacher, not how Brahman is to be known, but how it or he is to be worshipped in its or his phenomenal state, that is, as a personal Lord and Creator, or even under the name of any individual deity. This worship

(Upasana) being enjoined in many parts of the Veda, is recognised as obligatory on all who have not yet the comfort that in worshipping a personal god, they are really worshipping Brahman the true Godhead, though in its phenomenal aspect only, and they are promised, as a reward of their worship, happiness on earth and in heaven, nay, by way of preparation a slow advance (Kramamukti) towards complete Moksha or freedom.

In this sense it has been truly said that Samkara did not attack or destroy idolatry, though with him it was always symbolism rather than idolatry.

THE TWO BRAHMANS

It sometimes seems as if Samkara and Badarayana had actualy admitted not only two kinds of knowledge but two Brahmans also, Sagunam and Nirgunam, with or without qualities, but this would agains apply to a state of Nescience or Avidya only. The true Brahman, however, remains always Nirgunam or unqualified, whatever we may think about him.

In full reality Brahman is as little affected by qualities as our true Self is by Upadhis (conditions) but the same Nescience which clouds us for a time, *clouds ipso facto* Brahman also, Atman (Jivatman) and Brahman being substantially one. If the qualified Brahman makes us, we, the qualified Atman, make Brahman, as our maker. Only we must never forget that all this is illusion, so that in truth we can predicate nothing of Brahman but Na, na, i.e., No, no; he is not this, he is not that. He is, that is all we can say, and is more than everything else.

If in the later Upanishads Brahman is called Sach-chid-ananda, 'being, perceiving, and blessed,' then these three predicates are in reality but one, for he or it could not be without perceiving itself (*esse est percipere*), and he or it could not perceive himself or itself except as independent, perfect, unaffected and untrammelled by anything else (Advitiya). Having no qualities, this highest Brahman cannot of course be known by predicates. It is subjective, and not liable to any objective attributes. If it knows, it can only know itself, like the sun that is not lighted, but lights itself.' Our knowledge of Brahman also can only be consciousness of Brahman as our own subjective Atman or Self.

It seems only a concession to the prejudices or let us say, the convictions of the people of India, that an ecstatic perception of Brahamn was allowed as now and then possible in a state of trance, such as the Yogins practised in ancient, and even in modern times, though, strictly speaking, this perception also could only be perception of the Atman as identical with Brahman.

We shall thus understand the distinction which the Vedantists and other Indian philosopher also make between the Brahman, το, ντως ον and the Brahman as Isvara, the personal God, worshipped under differnt names , as creator, preserver, and dissolver of the universe. This Isvara exists, just as everthing else exists, as phenomenally only, not as absolutely real. Most important acts are ascribed to him, and whatever he may appear to be, he is always Brahman.

PHILOSOPHY AND RELIGION

It is interesting to see how this very bold philosophy of the Vedanta was always not only tolerated, but encouraged and patronised by religion and by its recognised representatives. Nor did the Vedanta as a philosophy interfere with popular religion; on the contrary, it accepted all that is taught about the gods in the hymns and in the Brahmanas. They were even considered as a necessary preliminary to higher knowledge.

KARMAN

The individual souls, so far as they can claim any reality, date, we are told, from all eternity, and not from the day of their birth on earth. They are clothed in their Upadhis (conditions) according to the merit or demerit which they have acquired by their former, though long-forgotten, acts. Here we perceive the principal moral element in the ancient Vedanta, so far as it is meant for practical life; and this doctrine of Karman or deed, has remained to the present day, and has leavened the whole of India. The whole world, such as it is, is the result of acts; the character and fate of each man are the result of his acts in this or in a former life, possibly also of the acts of others. This is with them the solution of what we venture to call the injustice of God. A man who suffers and suffers, as we say, unjustly, seems to them but paying off a debt or laying up capital for another life. A man who enjoys health and wealth is made to feel that he is spending more than he has earned and that he has therefore to make up his debt by new efforts. It can be the result of former acts only, whether, in this life, the doer of them is aware of them or not.

THE STHULA AND SUKSHMA-SARIRA

The conditions of Upadhis consists of Manas, mind, Indriyas, senses, Pranas, vital spirits, and the Sarira, body, as determined by the outward world. What is peculiar in it is the admission of a central organ receiving and arranging what has been conveyed to it by the separate organs of sense. We have no word corresponding to it, though with proper limitations we may continue to translate it by *mens* or mind. It would represent perception as uniting and arranging the great mass of sensations, but it includes besides Upalabdhi, perception, Adhyavasaya, determination also, so far as it depends on a previous interaction of percepts. Hence a man is said to see by the mind but he may also be said to decide and act by the mind (Manas).

By the side of the vital spirit, the Mukhya Prana, we find a fivefold division into Prana, Upana, Vyana, Samana, and Udana, meaning originally forth-, off-, through-, with-, and out-breathing, but afterwards defined differently and without much reference to any physiological data.

What is more interesting is the distinction between the Sthula and Sukshma-sarira, the coarse and the fine body, the former the visible outward body; the latter invisible and consisting of Mukhya Prana, vital spirit, Manas, mind, and Indriyas, organs of sense. This body is supposed to remain after death, while the outer body is dissolved into its material elements. The thin or subtle body, though transparent or invisible, is nevertheless accepted as material; and it is this Sukshma-sarira, which is supposed to migrate after death from world to world, but for the most part in an unconscious state.

THE FOUR STATES

Here again we come across an original idea of Indian philosophy, the doctrine of the four states, the state of being awake, the state of dreaming, the state of deep and dreamless sleep to which is added as the fourth, the state of death. In the first state the Atman is supposed to be perceiving and acting by means of the Manas and the Indriyas. In the second the Indriyas cease to act, but the Manas remains active, and the Atman, joined to the Manas, moves through the veins of the body and sees dreams made out of the remnants of former impressions (Vasanas). The third state arises from a complete separation of Atman from Manas and Indriyas. While these are absorbed in the vital spirit, which remains in ful activity, the

Atman in the heart is supposed to have for a time become one with Brahman, but to return unchanged at the time of awakening. In the fourth or disembodied state Atman with the Sukshma-sarira is supposed to escape from the heart through a vein in the head or through the hundred veins of the body, and then to take, according to merit and knowledge, different paths into the next life.

We are told there that, in the case of persons who have fulfilled their religious or sacrificial duties and have lived a good life, but have not yet reached the highest knowledge, the subtle body in which the Atman is clothed migrates, carried along by the Udana through the Murdhanya Nadi, the capital vein, following either the path of the fathers (Pitriyana) or the path of gods (Devayana) The former is meant for good people, the latter for those who are good and have already reached the lower, if not the highest knowledge. The former leads on to smoke, night the waning moon, the waning year, the world of the fathers, the ether, and lastly, the moon. In the moon the departed souls remain for a time enjoying the rewards of their good deeds, in company with the Pitris and then descend again, supported by the remnant of unrewarded merit due to their goods works, to the ether, wind, smoke, cloud, rain, and plants.

Little is said in the Upanishads of those who, owing to their evil deeds, do not even rise to the moon and descend again. But Badarayana tries to make it clear that the Upanishads know of a third class of beings who reap the fruits of their evil actions in Samyamana (abode of Yama) and then ascend to earth again.

But while evildoers are thus punished in different hells, as mentioned in the moon and then return again to the earth, those who have been pious and have also reached at least the lower knowledge of Brahman follow a different road. After leaving the body, they enter the flame, the day, the waxing moon, the waxing year (northern precession), the year, the world of the Devas, the world of Vayu, air, the sun, the moon, and then lighting; but all these, we are told, are not abodes for the soul, but guides only who, when the departed has reached the lightning, hand him over to a person who is said to be not-a-man. This person conducts him to the world of Varuna, then to that of Indra, and lastly to that of Prajapati or the qualified Brahma. Here the souls are supposed to remain till they realise true knowledge of the Samyagdarsana, which does not mean universal, but through and complete knowledge, that knowledge which, if obtained on earth, at once frees a man from all illusion. Finally, the souls when fully released, share in all the powers of Brahman except those of creating and ruling the universe. They are not supposed ever to return to the world of Samsara.

All this is hardly to be called philosophy, and which naturally vary according to different schools, help us much towards a real insight into the Vedanta. But it would have been unfair to leave out what, though childish is a characteristic feature of the Vedanta philosophy, and must be judged from a purely historical point of view.

FREDDOM IN THIS LIFE

What is of importance to remember in these ancient fancies is that the enlightened man may become free or obtain Mukti even in this life (Jivanmukti). This is indeed the real object of the Vedanta-philosophy, to overcome all Nescience, to become once more what the Atman always has been, namely, Brahman, and then to wait till death removes the last Upadhis or fetters, which though they fetter the mind no longer, remain like broken chains hanging heavy on the mortal body. The Atman having recovered its Brahmahood, is even in this life so free from the body that it feels no longer any pain, and cannot do anything, whether good or bad.

It is hardly necessary to say or to prove that the Vedanta philosophy even in its popular form, holds out no encouragement to vice. Far from it. No one can even approach it who has not previously passed through a course of discipline, whether as a student (Brahmacharin) or as a householder (Grihastha). In order to make this quite clear there has been a word called the Mohamudgara, the Hammer of Folly, and is ascribed to Samkara. Though not strictly philosophical it served to show the state of mind in which the true Vedantist is meant to maintain himself.

To sum up, the Vedanta teaches that in the highest sense Creation is but Self-forgetfulness, and Eternal Life remembrance or Self-consciousness. And while to us such high abstractions may seem useless for the many, it is all the more surprising that, with the Hindus, the fundamental ideas of Vedanta have pervaded the whole of their literature, have leavened the whole of their language, and form to the present day the common property of the people at large.

RAMANUJA

There are schools of Vedantists who try to explain the Sutras of Badarayana in a far more human spirit. The best known is the school of Ramanuja, who lived in the twelfth century. While Samkara's system is Advaita, i.e., absolute Monism, that of Ramanuja has been called Visishta-Advaita, the doctrine of unity with attributes of Monism with a difference. Of course with Ramanuja also Brahman is the highest reality, ommnipotent, omniscient, but this Brahman is at the same time full of compassion or love. This is a new and very important feature in Ramanuja Brahman, as compared with the icy self-sufficiency ascribed to Brahman by Samkara. Even more important and more humanising is the recognition that souls as individuals possess reality, that Chit and Achit, what perceives and what does not perceive soul and matter, form as it were the body of Brahmans are in fact modes (Prakara) of Brahman. Sometimes Chit is taken for the Supreme Spirit as a conscious cause, Achit for the unconscious effect or matter; but there is always Isvara as a third, the Lord; and this originally Brahma, is later on identified without much ado with Vishnu, so that Ramanuja's sect is actually called Sri-Vaishnava. It assumed no doubt the greatest importance as a religious sect, as teaching people how to live rather than how to think.

Brahman, whether under the name of Isvara, Vishnu, or Vasudeva, or Bhagavat, is with Ramanuja as with Samkara both the efficient and the material cause of all that exists, and he is likewise the lord and ruler of the world. But here mythology comes in at once. From this Brahman, according to Ramanuja, spring Samkarshana, the individual soul (Jiva), from Samkarashana Pradyumna, mind (Manas) and from Pradyumna Aniruddha or the Ego (Ahankara). Brahma, here called Vasudeva, is not without qualities, as Samkara holds, but possesses Jnana (knowledge), Sakti (energy), Bala (strength), Aisvarya (supreme power), Virya (vigour), and Tejas (energy) as his Gunas or qualities.

I am well aware that the view of the world, of God, and of the soul, as propounded by the Vedantists, whether in the Upanishads or in the Sutras and their commentaries, has often been declared strange and their commentaries, of the name of philosophy, at all events utterly unsuited to the West, whatever may have been its value in the East. I have nothing to say against this criticism, nor have I ever tried to make propaganda for Vedantism, least of all in England. But I maintain that it represents a phase of philosophic thought which no student of philosophy can afford to ignore, and which in no country can be studied to greater advantage than in India. And I go even a step further. I quite admit that, as a popular philosophy, the Vedanta would have its dangers that it would fail to call out and strengthen the manly qualities required for the practical side of life, and that it might raise the human mind to a height from which the most essential virtues of social and political life might dwindle away into mere phantoms. At the same time I make no secret that all my life I have been very fond of the Vedanta. Nay, I can fully agree with Schopenhauer, and quite understand what he meant when he said–'In the whole world there is no study, except that of the original (of the Upanishads), so beneficial, and so elevating as that of the Oupnekhat (Persian translation of the Upanishads). It has been the solace of my life, it will be the solace of my death.'

Schopenhauer was the last man to write at random, or to allow himself to go into ecstasies over so-called mystic and inarticulate thought. And I am neither afraid nor ashamed to say that I share his enthusiasm for the Vedanta, and feel indebted to it for much that has been helpful to me in my passage through life.

And while some of the most important doctrines of the Vedanta, when placed before us in the plain and direct language of the Vedanta Sutras, may often seem very startling to us, it is curious to observe how, if clothes in softer language, they do not jar at all on our ears, nay, are in full harmony with our own most intimate convictions. Thus, while the idea that our own self and the Divine Self are identical in nature might seem irreverent, if not blasphemous, one of our own favourite hymns contains the prayer:

And that a higher gift than grace
Should flesh and blood refine
God's Presence and His very Self,
And Essence all-divine!

This is pure Vedanta. We also speak without hesitation of our body as the temple of God, and of the voice of God within us; nay, we repeat with St. Paul that we live, and move, and have our being in God, yet we shrink from adopting the plain and simple language of the Upanishads that the Self of God and man is the same.

Again, the unreality of the material world, though proved point by point Berkeley seems to many a pure fancy; and yet one, of our most popular poets, the very type of manliness and strength, both mental and physical speaks like a Vedantist of the shadows among which we move:

For more than once when I
Sat all alone, revolving in myself
The word that is the symbol of Myself,
The mortal limit of the Self was loosed,
And passes into the Nameless, as a cloud
Melts into Heaven. I touched my limbs—the limbs
Were strange, not mine—and yet no shade of doubt,
But utter clearness, and thro' loss of Self
The gain of such large life as matched with ours
Were Sun to spark—unshadowable in words,
Themselves but shadows of a shadow-word.

•••

4

Purva-Mimamsa

We would now treat of the other Mimamsa, the Purva-Mimamsa, that is, the Former Mimamsa, as it is called, in connection with the one we have examined. The Hindus admit a Purva-Mimamsa and an Uttara-Mimamsa. They look upon the Vedanta as the Uttara- or later Mimamsa, and on that of Jaimini as the Purva or prior. It meant no more than that the Purva-Mimamsa, having to do with the Karmakanda, the first or work-part of the Veda, comes first and the Uttara-Mimamsa, being concerned with the Jnanakanda, comes second, just as an orthodox Hindu at one time was required to be a Grihastha or householder first, and then only to retire into the forest and lead the contemplative life of a Vanaprashta or a Samnyasin. We shall see, however, that this prior Mimamsa, if it can be called a philosophy at all, is inferior in interest to the Vedanta and could hardly be understood without the previous existence of such a system as that of Badarayana. It is clear that while Badarayana endeavoured to introduce order into the Upanishads, and to reduce their various guesses to something like a system, Jaimini undertook to do the same for the rest of the Veda, the so-called Karmakanda or work-portion; that is all that had regard to sacrifice, as described chiefly in the Brahmanas. Sacrifice was so much the daily life of the Brahmins that the recognised name for sacrifice was simple Karman, i.e., work. That work grew up in different parts of India, just as we saw philosophy springing up, full of variety, not free even from contradictions. Every day had its sacrifice, and in some respects these regular sacrifices may be called the first calender of India. They depended on the seasons or regulated the seasons and marked the different divisions of the year.

There were some rites that lasted the whole year or even several years. And as philosophy existed, independent of the Upanishads, and though Badarayana attempted to make peace with the Upanishads, we must consider that sacrifices also existed for a long time without the Brahmanas, such as we possess them; that they grew up without being restrained by generally binding authorities of any kind; and that at a later time only, after the Brahmanas had been composed and had acquired some kind of authority, the necessity began to be felt of reconciling variant opinions and customs, as embodied in the Brahamans and elsewhere, giving general as well as special rules for the performance of every kind of ceremony.

We can hardly imagine that there ever was a time in India when the so-called priests, settled in distant localities, did not know how to perform their own sacrificial duties for who were the authors of them, if not the priests? But when the Brahmins once existed, a new problem had to be solved: how to bring the Brahmins into harmony with themselves and with existing family and local customs, and also how to discover in them a meaning that should satisfy every new generation. This was achieved by means of what is called Mimamsa, investigation, examination, consideration. There is little room for real philosophy in all this, but there are questions such as that of Dharma or duty including sacrificial duties, which offer an opportunity for discussing the origin of duty and the nature of its rewards; while in accounting for seeming contradictions and in arriving at general principles concerning sacrificial acts, problems would naturally turn up which, though often in themselves valueless, are generally treated with considerable ingenuity. In this way the work of Jaimini secured for itself a place by the side of the works ascribed to Badarayana, Kapila and others and was actually raised to the rank of one of the six clasical philosophies of India.

While Badarayana begins his Sutras with 'Athato Brahmajignasa.' "Now therefore the desire of knowing Brahman, Jaimini apparently in imitation of it, begins with Athato Dharmajignasa, 'Now therefore the desire of knowing Dharma or duty.'

Dharma, here translated by duty, refers to acts of prescriptive observance, chiefly sacrifices.

This Dharma or duty is enjoined in the Brahmanas, and these together with the Mantras are held to constitute the whole of the Veda, so that whatever is not Mantra as Brahmana, whatever is not Brahmana, is Mantra. The Brahmanas are said to consist of Vidhis, injunctions, and Arthavadas, glosses. The injunctions are meant either to make us do a thing that had not been done before, or to make us know a thing that had not been known before. Subsequently, the Vidhis are divided into Utpatti-vidhis, original or general injunctions, such as Agnihotram Juhoti where he performs the Agnihotra and Viniyoga-vidhi, showing the manner in which a sacrifice is to be performed. The latter comprises injunctions as to the details such as Dadhna Juhoti, where he performs the sacrifice with sour milk, etc. Then follow the Prayoga-vidhis which settle the exact order of sacrificial performances and there is lastly a class of injunctions which determine who is fit to perform a sacrificial act. They are called Adhikara-vidhis.

The hymns or formulas which are to be used at a sacrifice though they are held to possess also a transcendental or mysterious effect, the Apurva, are conceived by Jaimini as mainly intended to remind the sacrificer of the gods who are to receive his sacrificial gifts.

He likewise lays stress on what he calls Namadheya or the technical name of each sacrifice such as Agnihotras Dasapurnamasa, Udbhid, etc. These names are found in the Brahmanas, and they are considered important, as no doubt they are, in defining the nature of a sacrifice. The Nishedhas or probihitions require no explanation. They simply state what ought not to be done at a sacrifice.

Lastly, the Arthavadas are passages in the Brahmanas which explain certain things; they vary in character, being either glosses, comments, or explanatory statements.

CONTENTS OF THE PURVA-MIMAMSA

Perhaps I cannot do better than give the principal contents of Jaimini's Sutras, as detailed by Madhava in his Nyaya-Mala-vistara. The Mimamsa consists of twelve books. In the first book is discussed the authoritativeness of those collections of words which are severally meant by the terms injunction (Vidhi), explanatory passage (Arthavada), hymn (Mantra), tradition (Smriti), and name (Namadheya). In the second we find certain subsidiary discussions, as, e.g., on Apurva, relative to the difference of various rites in refutation of erroneously alleged proofs, and difference of performance as in obligatory and voluntary offerings. In the third are considered revelation (Sruti), 'sign' or sense of passage (Linga), 'context' (Vakya) etc. and their respective weight, when in apparent opposition to one another; then the ceremonies called Pratipatti-Karmani, things mentioned by the way, Anarabhyadhita, things accessory to several main objects, as Prayajas, and the duties of the sacrificer.

In the fourth the chief subject is the influence of the principal and subordinate rites on other rites, the fruit produced by the Juhu when made of the *Butea frondosa* and the dice-playing etc. which forms part of the Rajsuya-sacrifice. In the fifth the subjects are the relative order of diffeent passages of the Sruti etc. the order of different parts of a sacrifice, as the seventeen animals at the Vajapeya the multiplication and non-multiplication of rites and the respective force of the words of the Sruti the order of mention etc. as determining the order of performance. In the sixth we read of the persons qualified to offer sacrifices, their obligations the substitutes for prescibed materials supplies for lost or injured offerings expiatory rites, the Sattra-offerings, things proper to be given and the different sacrificial fines. In the seventh is treated the mode of transference of the ceremonies of one sacrifice to another by direct command in the Vaidic texts and others as inferred by name or sign. In the eighth, transference by virtue of the clearly expressed or obscurely expressed sign or by the predominant 'sign' and cases also where no transference takes place.

In the ninth, the discussion begins with the adaptation (Uha) of hymns, when quoted in a new connection, the adaptation of Saman and Mantras, and collateral questions connected therewith. In the tenth the occasions are discussed where the non-performance of the primary rite involves the preclusion; and non-performance of the dependent rites, and occasions when rites are precluded, because other rites produce their special results, also Graha-offerings, certain Samans and various other things, as well as different kinds of negation. In the eleventh we find the incidental mention and subsequently the fuller discussion of Tantra, where several acts are combined into one, and Avapa, or the performing an act more than once. In the twelfth there is the discussion on Prassanga, when the rite is performed with one chief purpose, but with an incidental further reference, on Tantra, cumulation of concurrent rites (Samuchchhaya), and option.

It is easy to see from this table of contents that neither Plato nor Kant would have felt much the wiser for them. There are passages, however, which appeal to philosophers, such as for instance, the chapter on the Pramanas or the authoritative sources of knowledge, on the relation between word and thought, and similar subjects.

PRAMANAS OF JAIMINI

Thus, if we turn our attention first to the Pramanas, the measures of knowledge or the authorities to which we can appeal as the legitimate means of knowledge as explained by the Purva-Mimamsa, we saw before that the Vedantists did not pay much attention to them, though they were acquainted with the three fundamental Pramanas–sense-perception, inference, and revelation. The Purva-Mimamsa, on the contrary, devoted considerable attention to this subject and admitted five: (I) Sense-perception, Pratyaksha, when the organs are actually in contiguity with an object; (2) Inference (Anumana), i.e. the apprehension of an unseen member of a known association (Vyapti) by the perception of another seen member; (3) Comparison (Upamana), knowlege arising from resemblance; (4) Presumption (Arthapatti), such knowledge as can be derived of a thing not itself perceived, but implied by another; (5) Sabda, verbal information derived from authoritative sources. One sect of Mimamsakas, those who follow Kumarila Bhatta, admitted besides, (6) Abhava, not-being, which seems but a subdivision of inference, as if we infer dryness of the soil from the not-being or absence of clouds and rain.

All these sources of information are carefully examined, but it is curious that Mimamsakas should admit this large array of sources of valid cognition, considering that for their own purposes, for establishing the nature of Dharma or duty, they practically admit but one, namely, scripture or Sabda. Duty, they hold cannot rest on human authority, because the 'ought' which underlies all duty, can only be supplied by an authority that is more than human or more than fallible, and such an authority is nowhere to be found except in the Veda. This leaves, of course, the task of proving the superhuman origin of the Veda on the shoulders of Jaimini; and we shall see hereafter how be performs it.

HAS THE VEDA A SUPERHUMAN ORIGIN?

This discussion leads on to another and more important one, whether the Veda has supreme authority, whether it is the work of man, or of some inspired person, or whether it is what we should call revealed. If it were the work of a person, then, like any other work, it could not establish a duty, nor could it promise any rewards as a motive for the performance of any duty; least of all, a reward in heaven, such as the Veda promises again and again to those who perform Vedic sacrifices. It follows therefore either that the Veda has no binding authority at all, or that it cannot be the work of a personal or human author.

Let us see how the Mimamsa deals with this problem of the Apaurusheyatva, i.e., the non human origin of the Vedas. Inspiration in the ordinary sense of the word would not have satisfied these Indian orthodox philosophers for as they truly remark, this would not exclude the possibility of error, because, however true the message might be, when given, the human recipient would always be a possible source of error, as being liable to misapprehend and misinterpret such a message. Even the senses, as they point out, can deceive us, so that we mistake mother-of-pearl for silver; how much more easily then may we misapprehend the meaning of revealed words.

I quote from Madhava's introduction to his commentary on the Rigveda:

Some people, he says, and he means of course the Purvapakshins the recognised objectors uphold approximation towards the Vedas, that is to say they hold that as the Raghuvamsa of Kalidasa and other poems are recent, so also are the Vedas. The Vedas, they continue, are not without a beginning or eternal, and hence we find men quoted in them as the authors of the Vedas. As in the case of Vyasa's Mahabharata and Valmiki's Ramayana, Vyasa, Valmiki etc. are known to be their human authors; thus in the case of the Kathaka, Kauthuma, Taittiriya and other sections of the Veda, Katha, etc., are given us as the names of the authors of these branches of the Veda; and hence it follows that the Vedas were the work of human authors.

And if it were suggested that such names as Katha etc. were meant for men who did no more than had down the oral tradition like teachers, the Purvapakshin is ready with a new objection, that the Vedas must be of human origin, becase we see in the Vedas theselves the mention of temporal matters. Thus we read of a Babara Pravanani, of a Kusuruvinda Auddalaki, etc. The Vedas therefore, could not have existed in times anterior to these persons mentioned in them, and hence cannot be prehistoric, pre-temporal, or eternal. It is seen from this that what is claimed for the Veda is not only revelation communicated to historical persons, but existence from all eternity, and before the beginning of all time. We can understand therefore why in the next Sutra, which is the Siddhanta or final conclusion, Jaimini should appeal to a former Sutra in which established that relation of words to their meanings is eternal.

Jaimini wishes us first of all to keep in mind that the words of the Vedas themselves are superhuman or supernatural, nay, that sound itself is eternal; and thus fortified he next proceeds to answer the objections derived from such names as Kathaka, or Babara Pravahani. This is done by showing that Katha did not compose, but only handed down a certain portion of the Veda, and that Babara Pravahani was meant not as the name of a man, but as a name of the wind, Babara imitating the sound, and Pravahana meaning 'carrying along.'

Then follows a new objection taken from the fact that impossible or uneven things occur in the Veda; for instance, we read that trees or serpents performed sacrifices, or that an old ox sang foolish songs fit for the Madras. Hence it is argued once more that the Veda must have been made by human beings. But the orthodox Jaimini answers 'No' for if it had been made by man, there could be no injunction for the performances of sacrifices like the Jyotishtoma, as a means of attaining Svarga or paradise, because no man could possibly know either the means, or their effect.

Such injunctions as 'Let a man who desires paradise, sacrifice with the Jyotishtoma' are not like a speech of a madman; on the contrary, they are most rational in pointing out the object (paradise), in suggesting the means Soma, etc. and in mentioning all the necessary subsidiary acts as Dikshaniya etc. We see, therefore, that the commands of the Veda are not unintelligible or absurd. And if we meet with such passages as that the trees and serpents performed certain sacrifices, we must recognise in them Arthavadas or glosses, conveying in our case indirect laudations of certain sacrifices, as if to say, 'if even trees and serpents perform them, how much more should intelligent beings do the same!'

As therefore, no flaws that might arise from human workmanship can be detected in the Veda, Jaimini concludes triumphantly that its superhuman origin and its authority cannot be doubted. This Mimamsa method of discussing questions has been adopted in other branches of learning also, for instance, by the highest legal authorities in trying to settle contested questions of law. We meet with it in other systems of philosophy also as the recognised method of discussing various opinions before arriving at a final conclusion.

There are some curious subjects discussed by Jaimini such as what authority can be claimed for tradition as different from revelation, how far the recognised customs of certain countries should be followed or rejected, what words are to be considered as correct or incorrect; or again how a good or bad act, after it has been performed, can in spite of the lapse of time, produce good or bad results for the performer. All this is certainly of interest to the student of Indian literature, but hardly to the student of philosophy, as such.

•••

5

The Samkhya

We must now return and enter once more into the densely entangled and almost impervious growth of thought from which all the high roads leading towards real and definite systems of philosophy have emerged, branching off in different directions.

As springing from the great mass of philosophic thought accumulated in the Upanishads the Samkhya, like the Vedanta-philosophy, was probably at first considered as neither orthodox nor unorthodox. It was simply one out of many attempts to solve the riddle of the world, and even the fact that it did not appeal to a personal Lord or creator, was evidently at first not considered sufficient to anathematise it as unorthodox or un-Vedic.

I venture to call the Tattva-samasa the oldest record that has reached us of the Samkhya philosophy and I prefer to follow them in the account I give of that philosophy. These Samasa-Sutras, are hardly more than a table of contents, a mere Samkhyam or Pari-samkhya.

A certain Brahman, we are told, overcome by the three kinds of pain, took refuge with the great Rishi Kapila, the teacher (not necessarily the originator) of the Samkhya, and having declared his family, his name and his clan in order to become his pupil, he said: 'Reverened Sir, What is here on earth the highest (the *summum bonum*)? What is truth? What must I do to be saved?'

Kapila said, 'I shal tell thee.' Then follow the topics which are twnety-five in number:

I. The eight Prakritis (primary and productive elements),

1. The Prakriti as Avyakta (the non-differentiated or undeveloped principle);
2. The Buddhi (intellect), of eight kinds;
3. The Ahamkara (the subject) of three kinds (Vaikarika, Taijas, Bhutadi);

4-8. The five Tanmatras (essences) of sound, touch, colour, savour, odour.

II. The sixteen Vikaras (modifications),

9-13. The five Buddhindriyas (perceptive organs);

14-18. The five Karmendriyas (active organs);

19. Manas (central) organ or mind);

20-24. The Mahabhutas (material) elements);

III. 25. The Purusha (Spirit or Self).

The twenty-five Tattvas.

IV. The Traigunya (triad of forces).

V. The Sankara (evolution).

VI. The Pratisankara (dissolution).

VII. The Adhyatma
VIII. The Adhibhuta
IX. The Adhidaivata
— refrerring to the thirteen instruments, i.e., to Buddhi, Ahamkara. Manas, and the ten Indriyas.

X. The five Abhibuddhis (apprehensions, five acts of Buddhi of the Indriyas).

XI. The five Karmayonis (sources of activity).

XII. The five Vayus, winds or vital spirits.

XIII. The five Karmatmans, kinds of Ahamkara.

XIV. Avidya (Nescience), fivefold, with sixty-two subdivisions.

XV. Asakti (weakness), twenty-eightfold (nine Atushtis and eight Asiddhis).

XVI. Tushti (contentment), ninefold.

XVII. Siddhi (perfections), eightfold.

XVIII. Mulikarthas (cardinal facts), eight.

XIX. Anugrahasarga (benevolent creation).

XX. Bhutasarga (creation of material elements), four.

XXI. Bandha (bondage), threefold.

XXII. Moksha (freedom), threefold.

XXIII. Pramana (authorities), threefold.

XXIV. Duhkha (pain), threefold.

The commentator begins by asking, 'Now what are the eight Prakritis? and he answers, again in technical terms: which will have to be explained: I. 1. The Avyakta (chaos), 2. Buddhi (light or perception), 3. Ahamkara (subjectivity), or 4–8. the five Tanmatras (transcendental elements).

The Avyakta: He then continues: 1. Here then the Avyakta, neuter (the undeveloped), is explained. As in the world various objects such as water-jars, cloths, vases, beds, etc. are manifest, not so is the Avyakta manifest. It is not apprehended by the senses, such as the ear, etc. And why? Because it has neither beginning, middle, nor end, nor has it any parts. It is inaudible, itangible, invisible, indestructible, eternal without savour and odour. This Avyakta is subtle, without attributes, without beginning or end, producing (Prasuta), but alone of all the eight Prakritis unproduced (Aprasuta), without parts, one only, but common to all. And these are its synonyms: Pradhana (principal), Brahman, Pura (abode), Dhruva (unchanging), Pradhanaka (chief), Akshara (indestructible), Kshetra (field, object), Tamas (darkness), Prasuta (productive).

Buddhi: 'And what is called Buddhi (intellect)? Buddhi is Adhyavasaya (ascertainment). It is that through which there is in regard to a cow, etc. the conviction (Pratipatti), "This is so and so, not a horse; this is a post not a man." Such is Buddhi, the most wonderful phase of Prakriti.'

The Buddhi or the Mahat must here be a phase in the cosmic growth of the universe, like Prakriti in the beginning, and the senses and the other organs of the soul.

There are eight manifestations of this Buddhi (intellect): (1) Dharma, virtue, (2) Jnana, knowledge, (3) Vairagya dispassionateness, (4), Aisvarya, superhuman power.

(1) Dharma, virtue, is the opposite of Adharma, vice, and is enjoined by Sruti and Smriti, revelation and tradition. It is not opposed to, nay, it is in harmony with the practice of the best people, and has happiness for its outward mark.

(2) Jnana or knowledge, the opposite of Ajnana or ignorance, is explained as the understanding of the twenty-five subjects (Tattvas), the states of thought (Bhava), and the elements (Bhuta).

(3) Vairagya, dispassionateness, is the opposite of passion and consists in not being dependent on or influenced by external objects, such as sound etc.

(4) Aisvarya, superhuman power, is the opposite of powerlessness, and consists of the eight qualities such as Animan, extreme minuteness, i.e., being able to assume the smallest form and weight etc.

These four kinds of intellect (Buddhi) are classed as

Sattvika. Their opposites are classed as Tamasa, dark or bad. Through virtue, as a means, there takes place going upward, through knowledge there arises liberation, through dispassionateness men are absorbed in Prakriti (Prakritilaya?) through superhuman power there comes unfettered movement. Thus has Buddhi in its eight forms been described.

Ahamkara: Ahamkara is Abhimana, assumption or misconception and this consists in the belief that I am in the sound, i.e., I hear, I feel, I see, I taste, and I smell, I am lord and rich, I am Isvara, I enjoy, I am devoted to virtue, by me a man was slain, I shall be slain by powerful enemies, etc.

Here we must distinguish between Ahamkara, as a cosmic power, and Ahamkara as a condition presupposed in any mental act of an individual thinker. Ahamkara was so familiar in the sense of Egoism that, like Buddhi it was taken in its ordinary rather than in its technical Samkhya sense. I quite admit that this is a somewhat bold proceeding, but how to get without it at a proper understanding of the ancient Samkhya, the rival of the Vedanta, I cannot see.

We must remember that Ahamkara whatever it may mean in later times is in the Samkhya something developed out of primordial matter, after that matter has passed through Buddhi. Buddhi cannot really act without a distinction of the universe into subject and object, without the introduction of the Ego or I, which is impossible without a Non-Ego, or something objective. After that only do we watch the development of what is objective in general into what is objectively this or that (the Tanmatras). While the creation of what is subjective and objective is the only possible meaning of the cosmic Ahamkara, its psychological interpretation is far more easy.

Thus we are told that there are three or four modifications of the Ahamkara, (1) the Vaikarika dominated by the Sattva-guna, helps to do good works; (2) the Taijasa, dominated by the Rajasguna, helps to do evil works; (3) the Bhutadi, dominated by the Tamas-guna helps to do hidden works; (4) the Sanumana Ahamkara is responsible for unintentional good; (5) the Niranumana, for unintentional evil works. Ahamkara is herc treated as simply a moral agent, dominated by the Gunas.

Five Tanmatras: If it is asked, what are the five Tanmatras (substances) the five substances or essences as emanating from Ahamkara are, the essence of sound, contact, colour, savour, and odour.

The essences of sound are perceived in sounds only. Differences of sound, such as acute, grave, circumflexed and the notes of the gamut, such as Shadja, C, Rishabha, D, Jandhara, E, Madhyama, F, Panjama, G, Dhaivata, A Nishada, B, are perceived; but there is no difference in the essence of sound.

The essences of touch are perceived in touch only. Differences of touch, such as soft, hard, rough, slippery, cold, and hot, are perceived, but there is no difference in the essence of touch.

The essences of colour are perceived in colour only. Differences of colour, such as white, red, black, green, yellow, purpole, are perceived, but there is no difference in the essence of colour.

The essences of savour are perceived in savour only. Differences of savour, such as pungent, bitter, astringent, corrosive, sweet, acid, salt, are perceived, but there is no difference in the essence of savour.

The essences of odour are perceived in odour only. Differences of odour, such as sweet and offensive, are perceived, but there is no difference in the essence of odour.

Sixteen Vikaras: The sixteen Vikaras or evolutions are: the eleven sense organs (including manas), and the five elements.

Five Buddhindriyas: The ear, the skin, the eyes, the tongue, and the nose, constitute the five Buddhindriyas, or perceptive organs. The ear perceives as its object sound, the skin touch, the eye colour, the tongue savour, the nose odour.

Five Karmendriyas: The five Karmendriyas or organs of action, voice, hands, feet, the organ of excretion, and the organ of generation, perform each its own work. The voice utters words, the hands work, the feet perform movement, the organ of excretion evacuation, the organ of generation pleasure.

Manas: Manas, mind, both perceptive and active, performs its acts of doubting and ascertaining.

Five Mahabhutas: The Mahabhutas, or gross elements, are earth, water, light, air, and ether.

Here the earth, we are told, helps the other four, by being their support. Water helps the other four by moistening. Light helps the other four by ripening. Air helps the other four by drying. Ether helps the other four by giving space.

Earth is possessed of five qualities, sound, touch, colour, savour, and odour. Water is possessed of four qualities, sound, touch, colour, and savour. Light is possessed of three qualities, sound, touch, and colour. Air is possessed of two qualities, sound and touch. Ether has one quality, sound.

Purusha: Purusha is without beginning, it is subtle, omnipresent, perceptive, without qualities, eternal, seer, experiencer, not an agent, knower of objects, spotless, not producing. Why is it called Purusha? Because of its being old (Puranat), because it rests in the body (Puri sayate), and because it serves as Purohita (Director). These are, of course, fanciful etymologies; and we can hardly doubt that we have, in the name of Purusha, a recollection of the Vedic Purusha, one of the many names of the supreme deity, by the side of Visvakarman, Hiranyagarbha, Prajapati, etc. Like Brahman when conceived as Atman, Purusha also was probably used both for the divine and for the human side of the same power. It is the multiplicity only of the Purusha which is peculiar to the Samkhya philosophy.

The synonyms of Purusha are Atman, Self, Puman, male, Pumgunajantuivah, male living creature, Kshetragna, knower of objects or of the body, Nara, man, Kavi, poet, Brahman, Akshara, indestructible, Prana, spitit, Yahkah, anybody, Sat, He.

Thus have the twenty-five substances been described, the eight Prakritis, the sixteen Vikaras, and the Purusha. He who knows these twenty-five substances, whatever stage of life he may be in, and whether he wear matted hair, a topknot, or be shaven, he is liberated, there is no doubt.

IS PURUSHA AN AGENT?

Now follow a number of special questions, which seemed to require fuller treatment. The first is, Is the Purusha an agent, or is he not? If Purusha were an agent, he would do good actions only, and there would not be the three different kinds of action. The three kinds of action are:

(1) Good conduct, called virtue (Dharma), which consists in kindness, control and restraint (of the organs), freedom from hatred, reflection, displaying of supernatural powers.

(2) But passion, anger, greed, fault-finding, violence, discontent, rudeness, shown by change of countenance, these are called indifferent conduct.

(3) Madness, intoxication, lassitude, nihilism, devotion to women, drowsiness, sloth, worthlessness, impurity, these are called bad conduct.

Whenever this triad is perceived in the world it is clear that agency belongs to the Gunas, and it follows that Purusha is not the agent.

'Deceived by passion and darkness, and taking a wrong view of these Gunas which belong to Prakriti, not to himself, a fool imagines that he himself is the agent, though in reality he is unable by himself to bend even a straw. Nay, he becomes an agent, as it were, foolish and intoxicated by vain imagination and saying, All this was made by me and belongs to me.'

IS PURUSHA ONE OR MANY?

Now comes the important question, Is that Purusha one or many? The answer to this question divides the Samkhya from the Vedanta philosophy. The Samkhya answer is that the Purusha is clearly many, because of the variety in the acts of pleasure, pain, trouble, confusion and purifying (of race), health, birth and death; also on account of the stages in life (Asrama) and the difference of caste (Varna). If there were but one Purusha, as the Vadantins hold, then if one were happy, all would be happy; if one were unhappy, all would be unhappy, and so on in the case of people affected by trouble, confusion of race, purity of race, health, birth and death. Hence there is not one Purusha, but many, on account of the manifoldness indicated by form, birth, abode, fortune, society or loneliness. Thus Kapila, Asuri, Panjasikha and Patanjali, and all other

Samkhya teachers describe Purusha as many. But teachers who follow the Vedata, such as Harihara, Hiranya-garbha, Vyasa and others, describe Purusha as one.

Traigunya: We meet, with some more remarks about the three Gunas, Sattva, explained as virtue, purity, goodness; Rajas, explained as dust, mist, passion, movement; and Tamas, darkness, as ignorance.

The triad consists of Goodness, Passion, and Darkness. Goodness (Sattva) is of endless variety, such as calmness, lightness, complacency, attainment of what is wished for, contentment, patience, joy, etc.

Passion (Rajas) is of endless variety, such as grief, distress, separation, excitement, attainment of what is evil, etc. In short, it consists of pain.

Darkness (Tamas) is of endless variety, such as covering, ignorance, disgust, misery, heaviness, sloth, drowsiness, intoxication, etc. In short, it consists of trouble or madness.

Goodness is all that is bright, passion all that excites, and darkness all that is not bright.

These Gunas act a very prominent part in Indian philosophy, and have quite entered into the sphere of popular thought.

Sanchara and Pratisanchara: Sanchara is evolution, Pratisanchara dissolution or re-involution. Evolution is as follows: From the Avyakta (undeveloped Prakriti) before explained, when superintended by the high and omnipresent Purusha (Spirit), Buddhi (intellect) arises, and this is of eight kinds. From this Buddhi, the substance of intellect, arises Ahamkara (conceit of I, or subjectivity). Ahamkara is of three kinds, Vaikarika, modified, that is, modified of Sattva; Taijasa, luminous, as under the influence of Rajas producing the

Buddhindriyas; and Bhutadi (first of elements). From the modified or Vaikarika Ahamkara, which under the influence of Tamas produces the gross material elements, spring the gods and the senses; from the first of elements, Bhutadi, the Tanmatras (essences); from the luminous, Taijasa, both. From the Tanmatras, essences, are produced the material elements. Dissolution is as follows: The material elements are dissolved into the essences, Tanmatras, the essences and senses into Ahamkara, Ahamkara into Buddhi (intellect), Buddhi into Avyakta (the undeveloped), all being different forms of Prakriti. The Undeveloped is nowhere dissolved, because it was never evolved out of anything. Know both Prakriti and Purusha as having no beginning.

Adhyatma, Adhibhuta, and Adhidaivata: What is meant by Adhyatma (subjective), Adhibhuta (objective), and Adhidaivata (pertaining to deity)? Intellect is subjective, what is to be perceived is objective, Brahma is deity. Ahamkara is subjective, what is to be received and perceived by it is objective, Rudra is the deity. Manas, mind, is subjective, what is to be conceived is objective, Chandra, moon, is the deity. The ear is subjective, what is to be heard is objective, Akasa, ether, is the deity. The skin is subjective, what is to be touched is objective, Vayu, wind, is the deity. The eye is subjective, what is to be seen is objective, Aditya, the sun, is the deity. The tongue is subjective, what is to be tasted is objective, Varuna is the deity. The nose is subjective, what is to be smelled is objective, Earth is the deity. The voice is subjective, what is to be uttered is objective, Agni, fire, is the deity. The two hands are subjective, what is to be grasped is objective, Indra is the deity. The feet are subjective, what has to be gone over is objective, Vishnu is the deity. The organ of excretion is subjective, what is to be excreted is objec-tive, Mitra is the deity. The organ of generation is subjective, what is to be enjoyed is objective, Prajapati, lord of creatures, is the deity. Thus in the case of each of the thirteen instruments is there what is subjective, what is objective, and the deity.

'Whoever has properly learnt the substances, the forms of the qualities (Gunasvarupani), and the deity (Adhidaivatam) is freed from evil and released from all his sins; he experiences the qualities (Guans), but is not united to them.'

Abhibuddhis: Abhibuddhis (apprehensions) are Vyavasaya, ascertainment, Abhimana, conceit, Ichchha, desire, Kartavyata, determination to act or will, Kriya, action.

The apprehension that this has to be done by me is ascertainment; an act of the intellect. Abhimana, conceit, is dirceted towards the perception of the nature of Self and not-Self, it is Ahamkara, an act of the intellect. Ichchha, desire, is wish, an idea of the mind, an act of the intellect. Kartavyata, the will of doing such acts as hearing, etc., performed by the senses that have sound, etc., for their objects, is an act of the intellect pertaining to the Buddhindriyas. Kriya, the act of the intellect, such as speaking, etc., pertaining to the Karmendriyas, is action.

Karmayonis: What are the five Karmayonis? They are Dhriti, energy, Sraddha, faith or faithfulness, Sukha, bliss, Avividisha, carelessness, Vividisha, desire of knowledge.

The character of Dhriti or energy is when a man resolves and carries out his resolution. Sraddha, faith or faithfulness, is said to consist in study of the Veda religious studentship, sacrificing and causing sacrifices to be performed, penance, giving and receiving proper gifts, and making Homa-oblations.

But Sukha or bliss arises when a man, in order to obtain blessedness, devotes himself of knowledge, sacrifices and penance, being always engaged in penitential acts.

Avividisha or carelessness consists in the heart's being absorbed in the sweetness of sensual pleasures.

Vividisha or desire of knowledge is the source of knowledge of thoughtful people. What has to be known is the oneness (belonging to Prakriti), the separateness (of Purusha and Prakriti) etc., Prakriti being eternal, and not-percipient, subtle, with real products, and not to be disturbed; and this is Vividisha. It is a state of belonging to Prakriti destroying cause and effect.

Vayus: What are the Vayus (winds)? They are Prana, Apana, Samana, Udana, and Vyana, i.e., the winds in the bodies of those who have bodies. The wind called Prana is superintended by mouth and nose, and is called Prana because it leads out or moves out. Apana is superintended by the navel, and is called Apana because it leads away and moves downward. Samana is superintended by the heart, and is called Samana because it leads equally and moves equally. Udana is superintended by the throat. It is called Udana because it goes upward and moves out. Vyana is the all-pervader.

Karmatmans: The five Karmatmans, the Ego as active are Vaikarika, Taijasa, Bhutadi, Sanumana, and Niranumana. The Vaikarika, modifying, is the doer of good works. The Taijasa, luminous, is the doer of bad works. The Bhutadi, first of elements, is the doer of hidden works. If associated with inference (Sanumana), the Ahamkara is the doer of what is good and reasonable; if not associated with inference (Niranumana) it is the doer of what is not good and not reasonable.

Avidya: The fivefold Avidya (Nescience) is Tamas, darkness, Moha, illusion, Mahamoha, great illusion, Tamisra, gloom, Andhatamisra, utter gloom. Here darkness and illusion are again each eightfold, great illusion is tenfold, gloom and utter gloom are eighteenfold. Tamas, darkness, is the misconception that Self is identical with things which are not Self, namely, with Prakriti, Avyakta, Buddhi, Ahamkara, and the five Tanmatras. Moha, illusion, is the misconception arising from the obtainment of supernatural powers, such as minute-ness and the rest. Mahamoha, great illusion, is when one supposes oneself to be liberated in the ten states with regard to the objects of sound, colour, etc., whether heard or seen, etc. Gloom is unrestrained hatred, directed against the eightfold superhuman powers, such as minuteness, etc., and against the tenfold world of sense causing threefold pain. Utter gloom is that distress which arises at the time of death after the eightfold human power has been acquired, and the tenfold world of sense has been conquered.

Asakti: The twenty-eightfold Asakti weakness, is faults of the eleven organs of sense and the seventeen faults of the intellect. First, with regard to the organs of sense, there is deafness in the ear, dullness in the tongue, leprosy in the skin, blindness in the eye, loss of smell in the nose, dumbness in the voice, crippledness in the hands, lameness in the feet, constipation in the organ of excretion, impotence in the organ of generation, madness in the mind; these are defects of the eleven organs. The seventeen defects of the intellect are the opposites of the Tushtis, contentments, and of the Siddhis, perfections.

Atushti and Tushti: First then the opposites of the Tushtis or the contentments. They are Ananta, the conviction that there is no Pradhana (Prakriti); Tamasalina, consisting in recognising the Atman in the Mahat (Buddhi, intellect); Avidya, the non-recognition of the Ego (Ahamkara); Avrishti, the denial that the Tanmatras, essences, are the causes of the elements; Asutara, occupation in acquiring the objects of the senses; Asupara, occupation in their preservation; Asunetra, occupation for wealth, without seeing that it is liable to be lost; Asumarichika, addiction to enjoyment; Anuttamambhasika, engaging in enjoyment without seeing the evil of injury (to living beings).

Asiddhis and Siddhis: Next follow the opposites of Siddhi, perfection, which are also called Asiddhis, non-perfections: Atara, when diversity is mistaken for phenomenal unity; Sutara, when, after hearing words only, the opposite is understood, as, for instance, when after hearing that a man who knows the various principles (tattvas) is liberated, a man understands the opposite, that such a man is not liberated; Ataratara, ignorance, when a man, though devoted to hearing and studying, does not succeed in knowing the twenty-five principles, owing either to his obtuseness or to his intellect being impaired by false doctrines. If a man, though overcome by mental suffering, is not anxious to know, being careless as to transmigration, so that knowledge is no pleasure to him, this is Apramoda. Thus the next pair also of Apramudita (mutually not delighted) and Apramodamana (mutually not delighting) should be considered. Ignorance of a man of undecided mind even with regard to what has been taught to him by a friend is Arasya. But failure of an unfortunate man in obtaining knowledge, either because of bad instruction or disregard on the part of the teacher, is Asatpramuditam. Thus have the eight Asiddhis been explained, and the twenty-eightfold Asakti (weakness) is finished.

Tushtis and Siddhis: Next follow the Tushtis and Siddhis themselves, but as their oppsites have already been exmained we may dispense with their enumeration here. The nine Tushtis or contentments are: Ambhas, water, Salila, Ogha, Vrishti, Sutara, Supara, Sunetra, Sumarichika and Uttama Sattviki. The eight Siddhis are: Tara, Sutara, Tarayanti, Pramoda, Pramudita, Pramodamana, Ramyaka and Satpramudita.

Mulikarthas: The Mulikarthas or eight cardinal facts, are the most important subjects established by the Samkhya. They are with regard to Prakriti or Pradhana, its reality (Astitva), its oneness (Ekatva), its having an object or an intention (Arthavattva), and its being intended for someone else (Pararthya). They are with regard to Purusha, his being different from Prakriti (Anyatva), his not being an agent (Akartritva), and his being many (Bahutva). They are with regard to both Prakriti and Purusha, their temporary union and separation, while Sthiti, durability, is said to refer of the Sukshma-and Sthula-sarira, the gross and the subtle bodies. Astitva, reality, might seem to belong to both Prakriti and Purusha, but it is meant as the reality of Prakriti only, which the Samkhya is chiefly concerned with establishing as against the Vedantins who deny it with regard to all that is objective, keeping it for the subject only, whether he is called Purusha or Atman. The commentator, however, connect Astitva with Purusha as well as with Prakriti. The highest reality of the Purusha or the Atman has of course never been doubted by Samkhya or Vedanta philosophers, but that is more than mere Astitva.

Anugraha-sarga: The Tattva-samasa goes on to explain the Anugraha-sarga, the creation of benevolence, which is explained as the production of external objects from the five Tanmatras or subtle essences for the sake of the Purusha.

Bhuta-sarga: After this follows the Bhuta-sarga in fourteen divisions. The divine creation has eight divisions, consisting of good and evil spirits and gods, such as Pisachas, Rakshasas, Yakshas, Gandharvas, Indra, Prajapati, and Brahma. The animated creation consists of domestic animals, birds, wild animals, reptiles, and immovable things or plants. The human creation consists of one, of man only, from Brahmins down to Chandalas. Domestic animals are from cows down to mice; birds from Garuda down to gnats; wild animals from lions down to jackals; reptiles from Sesha (world-serpent) down to worms; immovable things from the Parijata-tree (in paradise) down to grass. This is the threefold creation, consisting of gods, men, and animals, the animals, i.e., living beings, forming again five classes.

Bandha, Bondage: The threefold bondage (Bandha) consists in, the eight Prakritis, in the sixteen Vikaras, and in Dakshina (gifts to priests). There are eight Prakritis, as described before; and as ong as a man considers these as the highest, he is absorbed in Prakriti and bound by Prakriti. The bondage of the sixteen Vikaras applies both to ascetics and to men of the world, if they are subdued by the senses, which are Vikaras, if they are devoted to objects of sense, if their organs of sense are not in subjection, if they are ignorant and deluded by passions.

Dakshina-bondage, Gifts to Priests: The priestly bondage applies to those, whether householders, students, mendicants or anchorets. This last bondage seems to me very important. What would have become of the Brahmins without their Dakshinas or fees, the very name of a Brahman being Dakshiniya, one to be fee'd? In the Aitareya-Brahmana already we read of Yatis who condemned sacrifices, but they are said to have been thrown to the jackals. That this feeing of a priest should have been considered one of the three bondages shows at all events that the followers of Kapila were above superstition, and looked upon sacrifice and priestcraft as hindrances rather that as helps to true freedom and Moksha of the spirit.

Moksha: This Moksha, the highest aim of Kapila's philosophy, is again of three kinds, according as it arises from increase of knowledge, from the quieting of the passions of the senses or lastly, from the destruction of the whole. From these arises the destruction of all that is commonly considered as merit and demerit; and from the destruction of merit and demerit there arises final beatitude consisting in complete detachment from the world, and in concentration of the Purusha in himself.

Pramanas: The three Pramanas which follow have been examined before. All systems of philosophy in India admit Pratyaksha or perception of the senses as the first of Pramanas. Anumana, inference, is illustrated by the usual examples, such as inference of rain from the rising of clouds. Whatever cannot be proved by either sense or inference has to be accepted as Apta-vachana, as, for instance, the existence of Indra, the king of the gods, the Northern Kurus, Meru, the golden mountain, the Apsaras, or nymphs of Svarga etc.

Duhkha: The last paragraph points back to the first. We saw how a Brahmin was introduced who, overcome by threefold pain, took refuge with the great Rishi Kapila. The threefold pain is Adhyatmika, Adhibhautika, and Adhidaivika. Adhyatmika is pain arising from the body, whether produced by wind, bile, or phlegm, etc., and from the mind (Manas), such as is due to desire, anger, greed, folly, envy, separation from what is liked, union with what is disliked, etc. Adhibhautika is pain that arises from other living beings, such as thieves, cattle, wild beasts, etc. Adhidaivika is pain that is caused by divine agents, as pain arising from cold, heat, wind, rain, thunderbolts, etc., all under the direction of the Vedic devas. If a Brahmin is affected by this threefold pain, a desire to know the reason arises in him, as a desire for water arises in a thirsty man. Freedom from pain, or final beatitude, is to be gained, from a study of the Tattva-samasa. Whoever knows the philosophy is not born again. This is the doctrine of the great sage Kapila.

NATURE OF PAIN

Here we come across something like a really human sentiment. We can well understand why pain, not only as actual suffering, but as an apparent anomaly or imperfection in the universe, should have opened man's eyes to the fact that there was something wrong or limited in his nature, and in the world in which he found himself; and it is quite intelligible that this consciousness of his limitation should have acted as the first impulse to an inquiry for the cause of it. This would naturally lead either to a religious or to a philosophical solution, and it certainly did so in India. A religion must have existed already before this question of the origin of suffering could well have been mooted: but religion seems rather to have increased the difficulty of the questioner than solved it. The gods or god, were generally supposed to be good and just. How then could they be the authors of human suffering?

Here then it was that philosophy was called in, nay, was first brought to life, and the answer which it gave as to the origin of suffering or, in a wider sense, the origin of evil, was that all that seemed wrong in the world must have been the effect of causes, of deeds done, if not in this, then in a former life. No deed (Karman) good or bad, small or great, could ever be without its effect, its reward or punishment. This was the fundamental principle of their ethics, and an excellent principle it was. It was but another version of what we mean by eternal punishment, without which the world would fall to pieces.

Then there arose a new question which could not well be suppressed, Whether it was beyond the power of man ever to put an end to the unbroken and irresistible sequence of the effects of the deeds of himself and of his fellow creatures; whether, in fact, the cycle of life and death, or what was called Samsara, would go on for ever. And here the bold answer was, Yes, the Samsara can be stopped, man's former acts can be shaken off and annihilated, but by one means only, by means of knowledge or philosophy. In order to achieve this, man must learn what he really is. He must learn that he is not the body, for the body decays and dies, he is not even what is meant by the Ego, the Ego also has been formed by surroundings or circumstancess, and will vanish again like everyting else.

Then what remains? There remains behind the body, and behind the Ego, or the individual person, what is called the Purusha or the Atman, the Self, and that Self is to be recognised either as identical with what was in earlier times conceived and called the Divine, the Eternal, the Unconditioned, namely, Brahman, or as Purusha, perfect, independent, and absolute in itself, blissful in its independence and in the complete aloofness from everything else. The former was the view of the Vedanta, the latter is the view of the Samkhya philosophy.

Both may have had the same roots, but they differ in their later growth.

Whatever we may think of these two solutions of the world's great riddle, we cannot but admire their originality and their daring, particularly if we compare them with the solutions proposed by other philosohiesa, whether of ancient or modern times. None of them seems to me to have so completely realised what may be called the idea of the soul as the Phoenix, consumed by the fire of thought and rising from his own ashes, soaring towards regions which are more real than anything that can be called real in this life. Such views cannot be criticised as we criticise ordinary systems of religion or morality. They are visions, if you like, but they are visious which, to have seen is like having been admitted to the vision of another world; of a world that must exist, however different in its eternal silence from what we and from what the ancient seers of India imagined it to be.

The most curious thing is that such views could be held by the philosophers of India without bringing them into conflict with the representatives of the ancient religion of the country. It is true that the Samkhya philosophy was accused of atheism, but that atheism was very different from what we mean by it. It was the negation of the necessity of admitting an active or limited personal god, and hence was carefully distinguished in India from the atheism of Nastikas or nihilists, who denied the existence of anything transcendent, of anything beyond our bodily senses, of anything divine. To call the Samkhya atheistic, and the Vedanta not, would be philosophically most unfair, and it does the Indian priesthood great credit that they treated both systems as orthodox, or at all events as not prohibited, provided always that the students had, by a previous severe discipline, acquired the strength and fitness necessary for so arduous a task.

SAMKHYA, AVIVEKA

The Samkhya takes what seems a very differen attitude towards the problem of the world. It we call the Vadanta monistic, the Samkhya is decidedly dualistic. It accepts the whole objective universe as real, and calls it Prakriti, a word often translated as Nature, but in reality untranslatable, because the idea which it represents has never arisen in our philosophy. Prakriti may be called the undeveloped matter, containing in itself the possibilities of all things. By itself it has no consciousness, it simply grows or develops into consciousness when seen by Purusha. And it develops not only into an objective or material world, but at the same time, into what we should call the subjective or intellectual world, supplying the instruments of perception and thought, both what perceives and what is perceived. The question whence it came is never asked, as little as we could ask that question with regard to Brahman. It is, it has been, and it has had no beginning. But in order to account for to world of experience, it is supposed that this undeveloped Prakriti is always operative, and always passing through a process of evolution.

Prakriti is at work so long only as it is perceived by a Purusha or a true Self. If we call Prakriti matter, the Samkhya philosopher saw clearly enough that dead, dull, inert matter alone would not account for the world. Therefore he makes Prakriti, under the eye of a Purusha, develop into Buddhi, the lighting up of Prakriti or dull matter by intelligence. In this stage Prakriti is called Mahat, the great, possibly in order to indicate its importance in the great development of the universe. As a cosmic force, Buddhi is that which gives light as the essential condition of all knowledge, and is afterwards developed into the senses, the powers of light and thought, two ideas often comprehended by the root Budh, to awaken or to perceive. Budh means literally to awake. And as a sleeping person is dull and inert to the world, but begins to perceive as soon as he is awake, Prakriti also is inert till it is awakened (Prabuddha), and thus becomes Buddhi, perceiving or perception.

ATMAN AND PURUSHA

There is one Brahman in the Vedanta, but there are many Purushas in the Samkhya. According to the former, there is but one Atman or Self, as it were, one sun reflected in the countless waves of the world-ocean; according to the latter there are many Purushas, as many as there are divine, human, animal, and vegetal souls, and their plurality is conceived as eternal, not as phenomenal only. This is due, as it seems to me, to a want of accurate reasoning on the part of the Samkhyas. It is fair to point out what the reason of this aberration may have been. From a higher point of view the Purusha of Kapila is really the same as the Brahman or the Atman of the Vedanta, the absolute subject. Kapila has certainly brought forward every possible argument in support of the plurality of individual Purushas, but he has forgotten that every plurality presupposes an original unit, many Purushas, from a metaphysical point of view, necessitate the admission of one Purusha, Vijnana-Bhikshu was right that Kapila did not differ so much from Badarayana as it would seem, because, if the Purushas were supposed to be many, they would not be Purushas, and being Purusha they would by necessity cease to be many.

GROSS AND SUBTLE BODY

The idea of a subtle body by the side of our gross body is very natural; and we know that among the Greeks also

Pythagoras claimed a subtle ethereal clothing for the souls apart from its grosser clothing when united with the body.

Both Samkhyas and Vedantists agreed in admitting the necessity of a subtle body in order to make the process of migration after death intelligible. In the Vedanta the name of that body, or vehicle, for the journey is Sukshma-sarira, the subtle body. The Vedantists look upon this thin and transparent vehicle of the soul as a seminal or potential (Vija or Sakti) body, which at death leaves the coarse material body, without being injured itself.

In the Samkhya philosophy the Sukshma-sarira appears as Linga-sarira, or the sign-body. The subtle or inner body, is formed of eighteen elements, of Buddhi, Ahamkara, Manas, the five Taumatras or Sukshma-bhutas, and the ten senses. It forms what we should call our personality, and causes the difference in the characters of individuals, being itself what it has been made to be by former works. All fitness for reward and punishment attaches to it, not to the Purushas and if determines by means of its acquired dispositions the gross bodies into which it has to enter from life to life, till final freedom is obtained by the Purusha; and not only the gross body, but the subtle body also is reabsorbed in Prakriti.

•••

6

The Yoga

The relation of the Yoga to the Samkhya philosophy is not easy to determine, but the Bhagavad-gita goes so far as to say that children only, not learned people, distinguish between Samkhya and Yoga at all, as it were between faith (knowledge) and works. We find the Samkhya and Yoga represented, each in its own Sutras, which are ascribed to different authors, Kapila and Patanjali. Yoga, in the sense of ascetic practices and meditations, may no doubt have existed in India in very ancient times, and this is probably what the author of the Bhagavad-gita meant.

It is much the same with the other philosophies, and we are left in no doubt as to whether the three couples, Samkhya and Yoga, Nyaya and Vaiseshika, nay, even Purva-and Uttara-Mimamsa, were amalgamations of systems which had originally an independent existence, or whether they were differentiations of former systems. Samkhya and Yoga might easily have formed one comprehensive system, because their divergence with regard to the existence of an Isvara, or Lord, was not so essential a point to them as it seems to us. The Nyaya and Vaiseshika show clear traces of a common origin; while the two Mimamsas, seem to sanction, by their names at least, the suspicion of their former unity.

MEANINGS OF THE WORD YOGA

In the Bhagavad-gita Yoga is defined as Samatva, equability. It has been repeated again and again that Yoga, from Yuj, to join, meant originally joining the deity, or union with it. A moment's consideration, however, would have shown that such an idea could never have entered the mind of a Samkhya, for the simple reason that there was nothing for him that he could have wished to join. Even the Vedantist does not really join Brahman. The soul is always Brahman, even though it does not know it, and it only requires the removal of ignorance to become what it always has been.

YOGA, NOT UNION, BUT DISUNION

A false interpretation of the term Yoga as union has led to a total misrepresentation of Patanjali's philosophy. Rajendralal Mitra was quite right when he wrote: 'Professor Weber, in his History of Indian Literature, has entirely misrepresented the case. He says, "One very peculiar side of the Yoga doctrine–and one which was more and more developed as time went on–is the Yoga practice" that is, the outward means, such whereby this absorption into the supreme Godhead is sought to be attained. "The idea of absorption," he continues rightly, "into the supreme Godhead forms no part of the Yoga theory." "Patanjali, like Kapila," he adds, "rests satisfied with the isolation of soul, and does not pry into the how and where the soul abides after separation."'

That native scholars were well aware of the double meaning of Yoga, we may see from a verse in the beginning of Bhogadeva's commentary on the Yoga-Sutras, where he states that, with a true Yogin, Yoga, joining, means really Viyoga, separation, or Viveka, discrimination between Purusha and Prakriti, subject and object, in the Samkhya: *Pumprakrityor viyogopi yoga ityudito yaya,* 'By which (teaching of Patanjali) Yoga (union) is said to be Viyoga (separation) of Purusha and Prakriti.'

PATANJALI, VYASA

The Sutras of the Yoga-philosophy are ascribed to Patanjali, who is also called Phanin or Sesha, the divine serpent.

In India we must learn to be satisfied with the little we know, not of the chronology of years, but of the chronology of thought; and taking the Yoga, in its systematic for, i.e., in the Patanjali-Sutras, as post-Buddhistic, we can best understand the prominence which it gives both to the exercises and to the arguments in support of the existence of an Isvara or Divine Lord. This marked opposition became intelligible and necessary as directed against Kapila as well as against Buddha; and in reading the Yoga-Sutras it is often difficult to say whether the author had his eye on the one or the other.

But though the Sutras are post-Buddhistic, there can be no doubt that not only the general outlines of the Samkhya, but likewise all that belongs to the Karmayoga or work-yoga was known before the rise of Buddhism.

THE YOGA PHILOSOPHY

The Yoga-Sutras, or the Yoganusasana, called also by the same name which was given to the Samkhya-Sutras, Samkhya-pravachana, both being considered as expositions of the old Samkhya, may have been contained originally in some such text-book as the Tattva-samasa. Vijnana-Bhikshu, who is chiefly known by his Yoga-varttika, is the author also of the Yoga-sara-samgraha.

MISCONCEPTION OF THE OBJECTS OF YOGA

It was almost impossible that the Yoga-philosophy, as should not have suffered from its close association with the Samkhya. All its metaphysical antecedents were there. Yoga is indeed, as the Brahmans, say Samkhya, only modified, particularly in one point, namely, in its attempt to develop and systematise an ascetic discipline by which concentration of thought could be attained, and by admitting devotion to the Lord God as part of that discipline.

The Patanjala-bhashya dwells very strongly on the difference between the liberated soul and the Lord; for 'the liberated or isolated souls,' it says, 'attain their isolation by rending asunder the three bonds, whereas in regard to Isvara there never was and never can be such bondage. The emancipated implies bondage, but this can never be predicated of the Lord.'

Patanjali seems to me to come very near to the Homoiousia of man with God, though he does not go quite as far as the Vedantin who claims for the Atman perfect Homoiousia with Brahman. His Isvara may be *primus inter pares*, but as one of the Purushas, he is but one among his peers. He is a little more than a god, but he is certainly not what we mean by God.

WHAT IS ISVARA?

As Kapila had declared that the existence of such a being as Isvara did not admit of proof, Patanjali proceeds to offer what he calls his proofs. 'In Him the seed of the omniscient (or omniscience) attaines infinity.' It would be difficult to discover in this anything like a proof without the help of the commentary. But Bhoja explains that what is meant here is that there are different degrees of all excellences, such as omniscience, greatness, smallness, and other Aisvaryas, and that therefore there must be for all of them a point beyond which it is impossible to go. This Niratisaya point, this *non plus ultra* of excellence, is what is claimed for Isvara or the Lord. What he means is that where there is a great and greater, there must also be a greatest, and this is Isvara.

Nor does he flinch in trying to answer the questions which follow: how this Isvara, without any inducement, could have caused that union and separation of himself and Prakriti which, as we saw, is only another name for creation. The answer is that the inducement was his love of beings, arising from his mercifulness, his determination being to save all living beings at the time of the Kalpa pralayas and Maha pralayas, the great destructions and reconstruction of the world.

Next Patanjali proceeds to explain the majesty of Isvara by saying,

'He is the superior (Guru) even of the former ones, being himself not limited by time.'

Next follow his name,

'His name is Pranava.'

Pranava might etymologically mean breathing forth or glory. It is assigned as a name to the sacred syllable Om, possibly a relic of a time beyond our reach. It is said to have been the name of Isvara from all eternity. Patanjali continues by telling us that repetition of the syllable Om and reflection on its meaning are incumbent on the student of Yoga. And this, as Bhoja adds, as a means to concentrate our thoughts, and to attain to Samadhi, the chief end of the whole Yoga-philosophy. In that sense he adds,

'Thence also obtainment of inward-turned thought, and absence of obstacles.'

Inward-turned thought (Pratyakchetana) is explained as a turning away of our senses from all outward objects, and turning them back upon the mind. The obstacles to Samadhi are mentioned in the next Sutra,

Disease, languor, doubt, carelessness, idleness, worldlines, error, not having a settled standpoint, and not keeping it.

With them arise pain, distress, tremor of limbs, and disturbance of the regular inbreathing and out-breathing.

'To prevent all this, there is constant fixing of the mind on one subject (Tattva).'

How subordinate a position is occupied in Patanjali's mind by the devotion to Isvara. It is but one of the many means for steadying the mind, and thus realising that Viveka or discrimination between the true man (Purusha) and the objective world (Prakriti). This remains in the Yoga as it was in the Samkhya, the *summum bonum* of mankind.

The Isvara, with the Yogins, was originally no more than one of the many souls, or rather Selves or Purushas, but one that has never been associated with or implicated in metempsychosis, supreme in every sense, yet of the same kind as all other Purushas. The idea of other Purushas obtaining union with him could therefore never have entered Patanjali's head. According to him, the highest object of the Yogin was freedom, aloneness, aloofness, or self-centredness. As one of the useful means of obtaining that freedom, or of quieting the mind previous to liberating it altogether, devotion to Isvara is mentioned, but again as one only out of many means, and not even as the most efficacious of all. In India this belief in one Supreme Being may have been a strong point in favour of Patanjalis's system, but from a philosophical point of view, they are mere side issues. We must remember that Kapila had committed himself to no more than that it is impossible to prove the existence of Isvara, this Isvara not being synonymous with God, in the highest sense of the word, but restricted to a personal creator and ruler of the world. In the Vedanta philosophy the questions of the real existence of a personal Isvara never arises, though we know how saturated that philosophy is with a belief in the existence of Brahman, the absolute Divine Essence of which the active or personal Isvara or the Lord is but a passing manifestation. The Samkhya, in attempting to explain the universe, has no need to call in the assistance of a personal Isvara. His system is therefore without a creator but if we called it therefore atheistic, we should have to apply the same name to Newton's system of the world and Darwin's theory of evolution, though we know that both Newton and Darwin were thoroughly religious men. Darwin himself went so far as to maintain most distinctly that his system of nature required a Creator who breathed life into it in the beginning. Kapila might easily have used the very words of Darwin, and this is very much what Patanjali actually did in his Yoga-Sutras.

If now we turn to the Yoga-Sutras of Patanjali we find that the first book, the Samadhi-pada, is devoted to an explanation of the form and aim of Yoga, and of Samadhi, meditation or absorption of thought; the second, Sadhana-pada, explains the means of arriving at this absorption; the third, Vibhuti-pada, gives an account of the supernatural powers that can be obtained by absorption and ascetic exercises; while the fourth, the Kaivalya-pada, explains Kaivalya to be the highest object of all these exercises, of concentration of thought, and of deep absorption and ecstasy. Kaivalya, from Kevala, alone, means the isolation of the soul from the universe and its return to itself, and not to any other being, whether Isvara, Brahman, or any one else.

That this is the right view of the case is confirmed by the remarks made by Vijnana-Bhikshu in his Yoga-sara-samgraha. Here we are told that even when there is some imperfection in the employment of the above means the two results (absorption and liberation) can be brought very near by the grace of the Parama-Isvara, the Highest Lord, and secured by devotion to Him.

By Parama-Isvara or the Highest Lord is here meant that particular Purusha (Self) who was never touched by the five troubles, nescience and the rest, nor by virtue or vice and their various developments, or by any residue (results of former deeds) in general. He is evidently quite convinced that, however different the roads followed by the Vedantins and Samkhya-yogins may be, the Divine idea of both schools is much the same.

TRUE OBJECT OF YOGA

It is clear throughout the whole chapter on Isvara that devotion to him is no more than one of the means, for the attainment of liberation, the highest goal of the Yoga. But it is not that highhest goal itsefl, but only a means towards it, nor could it be accepted as the most important feature of the Yoga. The really important character of the Yoga consists in its teaching that, however true the Samkhya philosophy may be, it fails to accomplish its end without those practical helps which the Yoga-philosophy alone supplies. The human mind, though fully enlightened as to its true nature, woul soon be carried away again by the torrent of life if there were no manes of making the mind as firm as a rock. Now this steadying of the mind, this Yoga, is what Patanjali is chiefly concerned with.

The principal acts and functions of the mind are described as right notion, wrong notion, fancy, sleep, and remembering, and they may be either painful or not.

Now all these actions or functions have to be restrained, and in the end to be suppressed, and this is said to be effected by exercises (Abhyasa) and freedom from passions (Vairagya).

MEDITATION WITH OR WITHOUT AN OBJECT

Patanjali next proceeds to explain an important distinction between the two kinds of meditative absorption (Samadhi), which he calls Samprajnata and Asamprajnata. This seems to mean that there is one kind of meditation when our thoughts are directed and fixed on a definite object, and another when there is no definite object of meditation left. We are told that what is called conscious meditation may have for its object either one or the other of the twenty-four Tattvas or the Isvara. The twenty-four Tattvas are called unconscious, the twenty-fifth or Purusha is conscious. When meditation (Bhavana) has something definite for its object it is called not only Prajnata, known, or, as referred to the subject, knowing, but also Savija, literally with a seed, on which it can fix, and from which it can develop.

Those who in their Samadhi do not go beyond the twenty-four Tattvas, without seeing the twenty-fifth, the Purusha, but at all events identify themselves no longer with the body, are called Videhas, bodyless; others who do not see the Purusha yet, but only existence, are called Prakritilayas, absorbed in Prakriti.

OTHER MEANS OF OBTAINING SAMADHI

The benefits arising from this devotion to the Lord are not essentially different from those that are to be obtained from other Upayas or means of attaining Samadhi. Nor is this devotion even the last or the highest Upaya, for Patanjali goes on immediately after to mention other means equally conducive to concentrated meditation or absorption in the thought of one object. Expedients, such as the expulsion and retention of the breath, follow next, the Pranayamas, which we can well believe, may have been really useful. We approach here to the pathological portion of the Yoga, the so-called Hatha or Kriya-yoga, a subject certainly far more important than has generally been supposed, but a subject for students of pathology rather than of philosophy.

Next to the moderation or restraint of the breathing, follow descriptions of how the mind, by being directed to the tip of the nose, cognises a heavenly odour, and the same with all the other senses. We are next told of the perception of an inward luminous and blessed state, which produces a steadiness and contentedness of the mind when directed towards objects which no longer appeal to the passions.

All these are means towards an end, and there can be no doubt that they have proved efficacious; only, as so often happens, the means have evidently encroached in this case also, on the aims, and to such an extent that Yoga has often been understood to consist in these outward efforts rather than in that concentration of thought which they were meant to produce, and which was to lead on to Kaivalya or spiritual separateness and freedom. This true Yoga is often distinguished as Raja-yoga or royal Yoga from the other called Kriya-yoga or working Yoga.

Samadhi (here called Samapatti) may be either Savitarka or Savichara; he now explains that when meditation is mixed with uncertainties as to word, meaning, or knowledge, it is called Savitarka. Thus, supposing that our meditation was centred on a cow, the question would be whether we should meditate on the sound cow, Go, or on the meaning of it that is the genus cow, or the idea or picture conveyed by it. Such a meditation would be called Savitarka. Its opposite is Nirvitarka when all memory vanishes and the meaning alone, without any form, remains, and becomes, one in form with the object.

After Samadhi, the next division is into Savichara and Nirvichara. They are defined as having reference to subtle objects, essences, and the senses, and thus we learn that the former, the Savitarka samadhi, had to deal with material objects only. Subtle objects include Prakriti also, and there is nothing subtle beyond it, for the Purusha is neither subtle nor non-subtle.

If we look upon the Nirvichara samadhi as the highest then there would follow contentment or peace of the Self (Atman). Knowledge in this state is called Ritambhara, right or truth-bearing, quite different from the knowledge which is acquired by inference or by revelation. And from this knowledge springs a disposition which overcomes all former dispositions and renders them superfluous.

There is still something beyond knowledge, and that is what was called before Aprajnata samadhi, meditation without any object, or pure ecstasy. This restores the Purusha to his own nature.

It is quite possible that some of my readers will be disappointed by my having suppressed fuller details about these matters, but it seems to me that they really have nothing to do with philosophy in the true sense of the word; and those who take an interest in them may easily consult texts such as the second and third books of the Yoga-Sutras, and better still the Hathaprayoga.

VIBHUTIS, POWERS

The third chapter is devoted to a description of certain powers which were supposed to be obtainable by the Yogin. They are called Vibhutis, or Mahasiddhis, Riddhis, or Aisvaryas. The eight Yogangas or accessories of Yoga are: restraints (Yama), subduing (Niyama), postures (Asana), regulation of breathing (Prana-yama), abstraction (Pratyahara), firmness (Dharana), contemplation (Dhyana), and absorption (Samadhi), three only are chosen as constituting Samyama, firmness, Dharana, Dhyana, and Samadhi, the other five being treated as merely outward helps.

SAMYAMA AND SIDDHIS

The Samyama, which comprises the three highest helps to Yoga, is called internal. It is this Samyama, which leads on to the Siddhis, or perfections. These are at first by no means miraculous, though they become so afterwards, nor are they the last and highest goal of Yoga-philosophy. Patanjali, before explaining these Siddhis, endeavours to show that everything exists in three forms, as not yet, as now, and as no more, and that it is possible from knowing one to know the other states. Thus a jar is not yet, when it exists only as clay; it is now, when it is the visible jar, and it is no more, when it has been broken up and reduced to dust again. So in all things, it is said, the future may be known from the present and the present accounted for by the past. When we are told that a Yogin by means of Samyama knows what is to come and what is past, it sounds very much like a claim of the gift of prophecy. Because a man has learned to understand the meanings and percepts indicated by words, a Yogin by applying Samyama to this gift, is supposed to be able to understand the language of birds and other animals. We get more and more into superstitions, which have little claim on the attention of the philosopher. Then follow other miraculous gifts all ascribed to Samyama, such as knowledge of former existences, a knowledge of another's mind, or thought-reading, a power of making oneself invisible, a fore-knowledge of one's death. More of these Siddhis are mentioned such as the soul entering another body, ascension to the sky effulgence, unlimited hearing, lightness like that of cotton, conquest of all elements, conquest of the organs, conquest of time, omniscience, etc. They form an essential part of the Yoga-philosophy, and it is certainly noteworthy, even from a philosophical point of view, that we find such vague and incredible statements side by side with specimens of the most exact reasoning and careful observation.

The general drift of the Yoga remains always the same, it is to serve as a Taraka, as a ferry, across the ocean of the world, as a light by which to recognise the true independence of the subject from any object; and as a preparation for this, it is to serve as a discipline for subduing all the passions arising from worldly surroundings.

There remains with me a strong conviction that Indian philosophers are honest in their reasonings, and never they use empty words. But there remains much to be done, and I can only hope that if others follow in my footsteps, they will in time make these old bones to live again. These ancient sages should become fellow-workers and fellow-explorers with ourselves in unknown continents of thought, and we ought not to be afraid to follow in their track. They always have the courage of their convictions, they shrink from no consequences if they follow inevitably from their own premises. Indian philosophers are truthful, and Patanjali says in so many words that truth is better than sacrifice. They may err, as Plato has erred and even Kant, but they are not *decepti deceptores*, they do not deceive or persuade themselves, nor do they try to deceive others.

•••

7

The Nyaya

We now come to two systems, Nyaya and Vaiseshika, which are very dry and unimaginative, and much more like what we mean by scholastic systems of phiosophy, businesslike expositions of what can be known, either of the world which surrounds us or of the world within, that is, of our faculties or powers of perceiving, conceiving, or reasoning on one side, and the objects which they present to us, on the other.

We possess a separate body of Nyaya-Sutras and another a Vaiseshika-Sutras, and these with their reputed authors, Gotama and Kanada, have long been accepted as the original sources whence these two streams of the ancient philosophy of India proceeded. It seems likely that there existed at first an as yet undifferentiated thought, bearing on things that can be known, the Padarthas, i.e., *omne scibile*, and on the means of acquiring such knowledge, from which at a later time, the two systems branched off.

NYAYA PHILOSOPHY

Though Nyaya has always been translated by logic, we must not imagine that the Nyaya-Sutras are anything like our treatises on formal logic. There is, no doubt, a greater amount of space allowed to logical questions in these than in any of the other systems of Indian philosophy; but originally the name of Nyaya would have been quite as applicable to the Purva-Mimamsa, which is actually called Nyaya in such works, for instance, as Sayana's Nyaya-mala-vistara. Nor is logic the sole or chief end of Gotama's philosophy. Its chief end, like that of the other Darsanas, is salvation, the *summum bonum* which is promised to all. This *summum bonum* is called by Gotama literally that which has nothing better, the *non plus ultra* of blessedness. Even Brahmahood must not be an object of desire, for such desire would at once produce a kind of bondage, and prevent that perfect freedom from all fear or hope, which is to follow by itself, but should never be yearned for. This perfect state of freedom, or resignation, can, according to Gotama, be realised in one way only, namely, by knowledge, and in this case, by a knowledge of the sixteen great topics of the Nyaya-philosophy.

The Apavarga (bliss) of the Nyaya and Vaiseshika systems seems entirely negative, and produced simply by the removal of false knowledge.

MEANS OF SALVATION

The means by which the Nyaya-philosophy undertakes to secure Apavarga, are: The Sixteen Topics or Padarthas: (1) Pramana, means of knowledge; (2) Prameya, objects of knowledge; (3) Samasya, doubt; (4) Prayogana, purpose; (5) Drishtanta, instance; (6) Siddhanta, established truth; (7) Avayava, premises; (8) Tarka, reasoning; (9) Nirnaya, conclusion; (10) Vada, argumentation; (11) Jalpa, sophistry; (12) Vitanda, wrangling, cavilling; (13) Hetvabhases, fallacies; (14)

Chhal, quibbles; (15) Jati, fales analogies; (16) Nigrahasthana, unfitness for arguing.

This may seem a very strange list of the topics to be treated by any philosophy, particularly by one that claims the title of Nyaya or logic. In reality the chapters on Pramana or means of knowledge, and Prameya, objects of knowledge, comprehend the whole of philosophy.

MEANS OF KNOWLEDGE

The four Pramanas, according to Gotama, are Pratyaksha, sensuous perception, Anumana, inference, Upamana, comparison, and Sabda, word.

Perception comes first, because inference can only begin to do its work after perception has prepared the way, and has supplied the material to which inference can be applied. Comparison is no more than a subordinate king of inference, while the Sabda or the word, particularly that of the Veda, depends again, as we should say, on a previous inference by which the authority of the word, more particularly the revealed word, has first been established. Imperfect as this analysis of our instrument of knowledge may seem, it seems to me highly creditable to Indian philosophers that they sould have understood the necessity of such an analysis on the very threshold of any system of philosophy. How many misuderstandings might have been avoided if all philosophers had recognised the necessity of such an introductory chapter. If we must depend for all our knowledge, first on our senses, then on our combina-tory and reasoning faculties, the question whether revelation falls under the one or the other, or whether it can claim an independent authority, can far more easily be settled than if such questions are not asked *in limine*, but turn up casually whenever transcendental problems come to be treated.

OBJECTS OF KNOWLEDGE

The objects of knowledge, as given by the Nyaya, comprehend *omne scibile,* such as body, soul, organs of sense, qualities, cognition, mind, will, fault, death, enjoyment, pain, and final freedom. Doubt and purpose mark the first steps towards philosophical discussion, instances and established truths supply materials, while premise and reasoning lead on to the conclusion which disputants wish to reach. We have rules for dialectic rather than for logic. We are taught how to meet the artifices of our antagonists in a long argumentation, how to defend truth against unfair antagonists.

If we deny the name of logic to such problems, we should be perfectly justfied, though a glance at the history of Greek philosophy would show us that, before logic became an independent branch of philosophy it was likewise mixed up with dialectic and with questions of some more special interest, the treatment of which led gradually to the elaboration of general rules of thought, applicable to all reasoning, whatever its subject may be.

Padartha, object. Nothing shows so well the philosophical character of the Sanskrit language as this very word Padartha, which has been translated by Category. It means in ordinary Sanskrit simply a thing, but literally it meant Artha, the meaning, the object, Pada, of a word. What we should call objects of thought, they called far more truly objects of words, thus showing that from the earliest times they understood that no thought was possible except in a word, and that the objects of our knowledge became possible only after they had been named. Their language passed through an opposite process to that of Latin. Latin called every kind of knowledge or all known things gnomina, to know; but after a time, their gnomina become nomina, and were then supposed to be something different from the old and forgotten gnomina; they became nomina, i.e. mere names.

According to the Vaiseshikas, we have six Padarthas, i.e., six general meanings, categories or predicates, to which all words, i.e., all things can be referred. All known things must be either substances (9), qualities (24), or motions, the last meaning, however, more than mere local movement, so as to correspond in fact to our activity or even to our becoming. Knowledge (Buddhi) is here treated as one of the qualities of the soul, which itself is one of the substances, so that many things which with us belong to psychology and logic, are treated by the Vaiseshikas under this head.

The next two, the general and the particular, comprehend what is shared in common by many objects, and what is peculiar to one, and thus distinguishes it from all others.

Samavaya or intimate connection is a very useful name for a connection between things which cannot exist one without the other, such as cause and effect, parts and the whole and the like.

The seventh category, Abhava, or negation, was added, it would seem, at a later time, and can be applied to previous, to present or to subsequent non-existence, or even to absolute Abhava.

Madhavacharya in his Sarvadarsana-samgraha, the compendium of all the systems of philosophy, says, the Nyaya-sastra consists of five books, and each book contains two daily portions or Ahnikas. In the first Ahnika of the first book the venerable Gotama discusses the definitions of nine subjects, beginning with "proof" (Pramana), and in the second those of the remaining seven, beginning with discussion (Vada). In the first daily portion of the second book he examines doubt (8), discusses the four kinds of proof and refutes all objections that could be made against their being considered as instruments of right knowledge; and in the second he shows that "presumption" and other Pramanas are really included in the four kinds of "proof" already given. In the first daily portion of the third book he examines the souls, the body, the senses, and their objects; in the second, "under-standing" (Buddhi) and mind (Manas). In the first daily portion of the fourth book he examines activity (Pravritti), faults (Dosha) transmigration (Pretyabhava), fruit or reward (Phala), pain (Dukha), and final liberation (Apavarga); in the second he investigates the truth as to the causes of the "faults", and also the subject of "wholes" and "parts". In the first daily portion of the fifth book he discusses the various kinds of futility (Jati), and in the second the various kinds of objectionable procee-dings (Nigrahasthana).

After having held out in the first Sutra the promise of eternal salvation to all who study his philosophy properly, Gotama proceeds at once to a description of the steps by which the promised Nihsreyasa, or highest happiness, is to be attained, namely, by the successive annihilation of false knowledge, of faults, of activity, and, in consequence, of birth and suffering. When the last or suffering has been annihilated there follows *ipso facto* freedom, or blessedness (Apavarga), literally abstersion or purification. This process reminds us strongly of some of the links in the Patichcha Samuppada of the Buddhists.

I. Pramana

Gotama proceeds next to examine each of the sixteen topics. The first topic or Padartha is Pramana, which is of four kinds.

Perception or Pratyaksha: Perception (Pratyaksha) is explained as knowledge produced by actual contact between an organ of sense and its corresponding object, this object being supposed to be real.

Inference or Anumana: Inference (Anumana), preceded by perception, is described as of three kinds, purvavat, proceeding from what was before, i.e., an anticedent; Shesavat, prodeeding from what was after, i.e., a consequent; and Samanyato Drishta, proceeding from what is constantly seen together.

The meaning of the three kinds of inference differs considerably according to different commentators. It is generally explained that a Purvavat, preceded by or possessed of a prius, refers to the mutual relation between a sign and what is signified by it, so that the observation of the sign leads to the observation or rather inference of what is universally associated with it or marked by it. This unconditional association is afterwards treated under the name of Vyapti, literally pervasion of one thing by another.

Different from this very natural explanation of the three kinds of Anumana is another, according to which Sesha is not supposed to mean subsequent effect, allowing us to infer its invariable cause, but is to be taken in the sense of what is left.

The third, or Samanyato Drishta, inference, is illustrated by our inferring the existence of senses, which are by themelves imperceptible (*Indriyani atindriyani*), because we do perceive colour etc., and as no actions can take place without instruments we may infer the existence of senses as instruments for our action of seeing, etc. Samanyato Drishta thus becomes very like the seeing of a general concept. It is inference from the sensible to the supersensible.

Comparison or Upamana: Next follows Comparison (Upamana) or recognition of likeness, explained as an instrument for ascertaining what has to be ascertained by means of similarity with something well known before. For instance, having been told that a Gavaya is like a cow, and seeing an animal like a cow, but not a cow, a man may infer that it is a Gavaya.

Word or Sabda: Word (Sabda) is explained either as a precept of one worthy to be trusted, or as a right precept. It refers, either to visible or invisible objects. It is curious to see that among the people to be trusted (Apta) the commentator should mention not only Rishis and Aryas, but Mlechchas or barbarians also, provided they are well informed. Strictly speaking, the Veda would not come under Sabda, unless it can be proved to be Aptavachana, the word of one worthy to be trusted.

II. Prameya

The second Padartha or topic is Prameya, that is, all that can be established by the four Pramanas, or what we should call *omne scibile*. Twelve such objects are mentioned: (1) Self or soul, (2) body, (3) senses, (4) sense-objects, (5) understanding, (6) mind, (7) activity (will), (8) faults, (9) transmigration (10) rewards of deeds, (11) suffering, and (12) final beatitude. The first six of these are called causative, the other six caused.

III. Samasya

Samasya or doubt. Doubt, we are told, arises from our recognition of various attributes opposed to one another in one and the same object, as when we recognise in a distant object the qualities of a man and of a post. The definition given of doubt shows that the ancient logicians of India had carefully thought about the different causes of doubt, so that they were led to the admission of three of even five kinds of it.

IV. Prayojana, V. Drishtanta, VI. Siddhanta

But these disquisitions, as well as those referring to (IV) Prayojana, purpose or motive; (V) Drishtanta, example, familiar case; (VI) Siddhanta, tenets, contain nothing that is of peculiar interest to the historian of philosophy, except so far as they offer once more the clearest evidence of a long continued previous study of logic in the ancient schools or settlements of India.

VII. The Avayavas, or Members of a Syllogism

Much more important is the next subject, the so-called members, that is, the members of a syllogism. To us a syllogism and its structure are so familiar that we hardly feel surprised at meeting with it in the schools of logic in India.

VIII. Tarka

Tarka is explained as refutation, or reasoning from the fitness of the case, as when a person, though seeing smoke on a hill, does not see that there must be fire, and is thereupon made to see that if the hill were without fire, it would of necessity be without smoke.

IX. Nirnaya

The next topic is Nirnaya, ascertainment.

X-XVI. Vada, Jalpa, Vitanda, Hetvabhasa, Jati, Chhala, Nigrahasthana

Then follow the paragraphs connected with rhetoric rather than with logic, such as, Vada or argumentation, consisting of objections and answers, both disputants, however, caring for truth only; Jalpa, sophistical wrangling or attacking what has been established, by means of fraud; Jati, futility, arising from false analogies; Chhala, quibbling; and Nigrahasthana, unfitness for discussion. In the last five cases disputants are supposed to care for victory only, and not for truth. If this wrangling is devoid of any attempt at really establishing an opposite opinion, it is called, Vitanda, cavilling.

We next come to Hetvabhasas, or specious arguments, that is, paralogisms and sophisms. These are Savyabhichara, arguments that prove too much, Viruddha, that prove the reverse, Prakaranasama, that tell equally on both sides, Sadhyasama, that stand themselves in need of proof, and Kalatita, mistimed.

As to Chhala, fraud in using words in a sense different from what is generally understood, and, Jati, futility arising from change of class, it is difficult to understand why Jati, i.e., birth or genus, should mean a futile argument, unless it meant originally a *transitio in alterum genus*, as when, in answer to an argument that a man is unable to travel, because he has a fever, it should be answered that he is able to travel, because he is a soldier.

The last, Nigrahasthana, unfitness for discussion, is when a man by misunderstanding or not understanding, yet continuing to talk, renders himself liable to reproof.

This may seem a long list, though in several cases there are subdivisions which have here been left out, and yet at the end of the list, Gotama actually apologises and says that there are many more sorts of futility, which have been passesd over by him, but will have to be discussed hereafter.

JUDGEMENTS ON INDIAN LOGIC

European philosophers would no doubt be justified in saying what Ritter said in his History of Philosophy that the exposition of the Nyaya is tedious, loose, and unmethodical. It is certainly mixed up with subjects which have nothing to do with pure logic, but so was Greek logic in its beginning, in the school of Zeno, for instance. It may be also too minute for our taste, but it cannot be called loose at the same time. It is equally unfair to charge the Nyaya and all the other systems of Indian philosophy, with being unpractical and with entirely ignoring all the problems of ethics.

We must remember that philosophy in India had very different antecedents from what it has with us. We ourselves can hardly conceive a philosophy which in the end is not to be of practical usefulness, and which ignores all questions of morality. But we must learn to take philosophers as they are. Morality with the Brahmins depends either on prescriptive *sacra* (Dharma), or on what is called Samaya, the agreement of good people. But its strongest support is a firm belief in the solidarity of life here and hereafter, and a firm conviction that nothing can ever be lost. The popular mind of India seems never to have doubted the fact that every good or every evil thought or deed will grow and bear fruit, and that no one can ever escape from the consequences of his own acts and thoughts. Whether such a belief is right or wrong is not the question, but it produced at all events a deep sense of responsibility.

That highest freedom and beatitude, according to Indian views, depended on philosophy or knowledge; it could not be acquired by good works or good thoughts alone. This again may be right or wrong, but I can discover no looseness of reasoning in it, nor in Indian philosophy in general. We must not forget that, from a Hindu point of view, this life on earth is but an episode that may be very important in itself, but is a mere nothing compared with what lies behind and before, the eternal life of the soul. If they hold that a knowledge of the true relation between man and the world, and between man and the Author of the world is essential to true freedom and true happiness, are they so far wrong?

SPHOTA

Hindu philosophers have actually elaborated an idea which does not exits in any other philosophy, that of Sphota. Derived as it is from Sphut, Sphota must have meant originally what bursts forth. It has been translated by expression, notion, concept or idea, but none of these renderings can be considered as successful. It really means the sound of a word as a whole, and as conveying a meaning, apart from its component letters. The subject has been well treated by Madhava in his Sarva-darsana-samgraha. Here, when examining the Panini Darsana, he shows first of all that the Sabda or word which Panini professes to teach in his Sabdanusasana, or grammar, is really the same as Brahman. 'The eternal word,' he writes, 'which is called Sphota, and is without parts, is the true cause of the world,' is in fact Brahman, and he adds thereupon some lines from Bhartrihari's Brahmakanda:

'Brahman, without beginning or end, the indestructible essence of language,

Which developed in the form of things, and whence springs the creation of the world.'

What more could be said of the Neo-platonic Logos?

This shows, as we knew already from the Pratisakhyas, that the Hindus had elaborated the idea of letters, may even of vowels and consonants, long before they became acquainted with the written letters of a Semitic alphabet, and I only wonder that those who believe in an ancient indigenous alphabet, should never have appealed, though vainly, to the discussions of Sphota, in support of their opinion. Kaiyata explains 'Grammarians maintain that it is the word, as distinct from the letters, which expresses the meaning, since, it the letters expressed it, there would be no use in pronouncing the second and following ones (as the first would already have conveyed all that is wished). It is therefore something distinct from the single letters which conveys the meaning, and that is what we call the Sphota.'

This shows that the conventional character of the relation between sound and meaning was fully recognised in India, whether that sound was called Sabda or Sphota. Nor is it enough that the letters should be the same, they must also follow each other in the same order.

Sphota is in fact the word before it had been analysed into letters, the breaking forth of a whole and undivided utterance, such as it Go, 'cow', conveying a meaning which does not depend on any single letter nor on any combination of them. Though from our point of view the idea of such a Sphota may seem unnecessary, we cannot help admiring the ingenuity of the ancient philosophers of India in inventing such a term, and in seeing difficulties which never attracted the attention of European philosophers. For it is perfectly true that the letters, as such, have no reality and no power, and that every word is something different from its letters, something undivided and indivisible. In such a word as Vak, Vox, we have not a combination of three letters, v, a, k, which would be nothing, but we have an indivisible explosion, expressive of its meaning in its undivided form only, and this may be raised to the status of a word by means of a grammatical suffix which, as we should say, makes an organised whole of it. All this is true and recognised now by all students of the Science of Language, though never even suspected by the philosophers of other countries.

PRAMEYAS, OBJECTS OF KNOWLEDGE

Gotama, in his third book, is chiefly concerned with the Prameyas, the objects of knowledge established by the Pramanas; and the first question that meets us is whether the senses or Indriyas, the instruments of objective knowledge, should be treated as different from the Atman, the Self, or not.

INDRIYAS, SENSES

Gotama holds that they are different from the Atman; and in order to prove this, he argues, that if each sense could perceive by itself, each sense would perceive its own objects only, the ear sound, the eye colour, the skin warmth, etc.; and that therefore what preceives all these impressions together, at the same time and in the same object, must be something different from the several senses, namely, the Atman, or, according to other systems, the Manas or mind.

Sarira, Body: Next follows the questions whether the body is the same as the Atman, a question which would never occur to a Vedantist. But Gotama asks it and solves it in his own way. It cannot be, he says, because, when the body has once been destroyed by being burnt, the consequences of good and evil deeds would cease to pursue the Self through an endless series of births and rebirths. A number of similar objections and answers follow, all showing how much this question had occupied the thoughts of the Nyaya philosophers. Some of them suggest difficulties which betray a very low state of philosophical reasoning while other difficulties are such that even in our own time they have not ceased to perplex minute philosophers. We meet with the question why, with the dual organ of vision, there is no duality of perception; why, if memory is supposed to be a quality or mode of the Self, mere remembrance of an acid substance can make our mouth water. After these questions have been, if not solved, at least carefully considered, Gotama goes on to show that if the body be not Atman, neither can Manas, mind, be conceived as the Atman.

Manas, Mind The Self is the knower, while the mind or Manas is only the instrument (Karana) of knowledge by which attention is fixed on one thing at a time. The Self is eternal, not of this life only, without beginning and therefore, without end.

The rest of the third book concerned with the nature of Self (Atman), the mind (Manas), the difference between the two, and their relation to knowledge. Though there are many manifestations of Manas, its distingushing feature, we are told, is what we should call attention, or as Gotama explains it 'the preventing of knowledge arising altogether.' This is declared to be due to attention, and in many cases this would be the best rendering of Manas, Manas is therefore often called the doorkeeper, preventing sensation from rushing in promiscuously and all at once. If therefore we translate Manas by mind, we must always remember its technical meaning in Indian philosophy, and its being originally different from Buddhi, understanding.

The Buddhi of the Nyaya philosophers, is totally different from the Buddhi of the Samkhyas. Their Buddhi is eternal, while the Buddhi of Gotama is distinctly declared to be non-eternal. The Buddhi of the Samkhya is a cosmic principle independent of the Self, in the Nyaya philosophy it signifies the subjective activity of thought in the acquisition of knowledge, or in the lighting up and appropriating of the inert impressions received by the senses. This knowledge can come to an end and vanish by forgetfulness, while an eternal essence can never be destroyed.

Atman: Gotama declares quite clearly that real knowledge belongs to the Atman only, the Self or the soul. It cannot belong to the senses and their objects (Indriyartha), because knowledge abides even when the senses have been suppressed. Nor does knowledge belong to the Manas, which is but the instrument of knowledge, but it arises from the conjunction of Atman (Self) with Manas (attention), and on the other side of Manas with Indriyas (senses). Manas is the instrument, and the wielder of that instrument, like the wielder of an axe, must be someone different from it; this, according to the Nyaya, can only be the Self who in the end knows, who remembers who feels pain and pleasure, who desires and acts.

Memory: Memory, Smriti, has not received from Indian philosophers the attention which it deserves. If it is treated as a means of knowledge, it falls under Anubhava, which is either immediate or mediate, and then called Smriti. Every Anubhava is supposed to leave an impression or modification of the mind, which is capable of being revived. The various associations which awaken memory are enumerated in some detail.

KNOWLEDGE NOT ETERNAL

The important point, however, which Gotama wishes to establish is this, that knowledge, though belonging to the eternal Self, is not in itself eternal, but vanishes like any other act. Lastly, he states that the Manas is Anu, infinitely small, or, as we should say, an atom.

MORE PRAMEYAS

The fourth book which is devoted to the remaining six Prameyas, such as (7) Pravritti (activity), (8) Dosha (faults), (9) Pretyabhava (transmigration), (10) Phala (rewards), (11) Dukha (pain), and (12) Apavarga (final beatitude), is naturally of a more practical character, and less attractive to the student of the problems of being and thinking.

LIFE AFTER DEATH

One of the seven interesting subjects treated here is Pretyabhava, literally existence after having departed this life.

As the Self has been proved to be eternal, Gotama says it follows that it will exist after what is called death. Some of the objections made to this tenet are easily disposed of, but nothing is said to establish what is meant by transmigration, that is, being born again in another world as either a human or as some other animal being, or even as a plant.

EXISTENCE OF DEITY

Another important subject, is treated by Gotama, incidentally only, I mean the existence of a Deity. It comes in when a problem of the Buddhists is under discussion as nothing can be produced from nothing, nor from an annihilated something, the world also cannot have sprung from nothingness, but requires the admission of an Isvara, the Lord, as its real cause. And this admission of an Isvara, even though in the capacity of a governor rather than of a maker of the world, is confirmed by what was evidently considered by Gotama as a firmly established truth, namely, that every act of man invariably produces its result, though not by itself, but under the superint-endence of some one that is, of Isvara.

We then meet with a new argument, that if work done continued to work entirely by itself, the fact that some good or evil deeds of men do not seem to receive their reward would remain unaccounted for. This is certainly a curious way of proving the existence of God by the very argument which has generally been employed by those who want to prove His non-existence. Gotama's real object, however, is to refute the Buddhist theory of vacuity (Sunya), or of Nothing being the cause of the world, and after-wards to disprove the idea that effects can ever be fortuitous. He also differs from the Samkhya philosophers, who hold that all things, as developed out of Prakriti, are real only so long as they are noticed by the Purusha.

He holds, on the contrary, that some things are real and eternal, but others are not, because we actually see both their production and their destruction. If we were to doubt this, we should doubt what has been settled by the authority of all men, and there would be an end of all truth and untruth. This is a novel kind of argument for an Indian philosopher to use.

CAUSE AND EFFECT

If, however, we call the Nyaya philosophy theistic, we should always remember that such terms as theistic and atheistic are hardly applicable to Indian philosophy in the sense in which they are used by Christian theologians. With us atheistic implies the denial of a supreme and absolute Being; but we saw that even the so-called atheism of the Samkhya philosophy does not amount to that. It is simply the denial of an Isvara, as an active and personal creator and ruler of the world.'

In the Tarka-Samgraha, it is distinctly stated that 'the Atman or Self is twofold, the Jivatman (personal Self), and the Paramatman (the Highest Self).' It must not be supposed, however, that Isvara, the omniscient Lord, is Paramatman, which is one only, while the Jivatman is separate for each individual body, all-pervading and eternal. Though Paramatman is Isvara, Isvara is not Paramatman, but a phenomenal manifestation of Paramatman only. The argument which we met with before is fully stated in Gotama's Sutras. The actions of men, it is said, do not always produce an effect. Good actions do not always produce good results, nor bad actions bad results, as they ought, if every act continued to act (Karman). Hence there must be another power that modifies the continuous acting of acts, and that can be Isvara only. It is not denied thereby that human actions are required, and that no effects would take place without the working of human agents, only they are not the sole cause of what happens, but we require another power, an Isvara, to account for what would otherwise be irrational results of human actions.

EMANCIPATION

After examining the meaning of pain, and expressing his conviction that everything, even pleasure, is full of pain, Gotama at last approaches the last subject, emancipation (Apavarga). He begins as usual with objections, such as that it is impossible in this life to pay all our moral debts, that certain sacrificial duties are enjoined as incumbent on us to the end of our lives. If, therefore, good works continue, there will be rewards for them, in fact there will be paradise, though even this would really have to be looked upon as an obstacle to real emancipa-tion. Nothing remains but a complete extinction of all desires, and this can be effected by knowledge of the truth only.

Therefore knowledge of the truth or removal of all false notions, is the beginning and end of all philosophy, and of the Nyaya philosophy in particular. The first step towards this is the cessation of Ahamkara, here used in the sense of personal feelings, such as desire for a beautiful and aversion to a deformed object. Desire therefore has to be eradicated and aversion also. And this leads him on to what is the distinguishing doctrine both of the Nyaya and of the Vaiseshika philosophies, namely, the admission of Anus or atoms. If wholes are constantly divided and subdivided, we should in the end be landed in nihilism, but this is not to be. There cannot be annihilation because the Anus or the smallest parts are realities, and, according to their very nature, cannot be further reduced or compressed out of being. Ether is said to be intangible, neither resistant nor obstructing, that is, neither occupying space against others, nor preventing others from occupying space; and in the end an appeal is made that there must never be a regression in infinitum, as there would be in attempting to divide an atom.

KNOWLEDGE OF IDEAS, NOT OF THINGS

And now the opponent, again, it would seem, a Buddhist, makes a still bolder sweep by denying the existence of any external things. All we have is knowledge, he says, not things; nothing different from our knowledge, or indpendent of our knowledge, can exist for us. Gotama objects to this (Vidyamatra) doctrine, first of all because, if it were impossible to prove the existence of any external things, it would be equally impossible to prove their non-existence. And if an appeal were made to dreams, or visions produced by a mirage, or by jugglery, it should be remembered that dreams also, like remembrances, presuppose previous perception of things; and that even in mistaking we mistake something, so that false knowledge can always be removed by true knowledge.

After granting that, one more question arises, how that true knowledge, if once gained, is to be preserved, because we saw that knowledge is not eternal, but vanishes. And here the Nyaya suddenly calls the Yoga to its aid, and teaches that Samadhi or intense meditation will prove a safe preservative of knowledge, in spite of all disturbances from without, while the Nyaya philosophy retains its own peculiar usefulness as employed in the defence of truth against all comers, in which case even such arts as wrangling and cavilling may prove of service.

This may seem a very humble view to take with regard to a system of philosophy which at the very outset promised to its students final beatitude as the highest reward. But considering the activity of philosophical speculation, we can well understand that philosophers would secure for their system that high position which the Nyaya certainly held and still holds among the recognised systems of orthodox philosophy.

•••

8

The Vaiseshika

Nyaya and Vaiseshika have been often treated as sister philosophies, so we must give, for the sake of completeness, at least a general outline of Kanada's system. It does not contain much that is peculiar to it, and seems to pre-suppose much that we found already in the other systems. Even the theory of Anus or atoms, generally cited as its peculiar character, was evidently known to the Nyaya, though it is more fully developed by the Vaiseshikas. It begins with the usual promise of teaching something from which springs elevation or the *summum bonum*, and that something Kanada calls Dharma or merit. From a particular kind of merit springs, true knowledge of certain Padarthas, or categories, and from this once more the *summum bonum*. These categories embrace the whole realm of knowledge, and are: (1) substance, Dravya; (2) quality, Guna; (3) action, karman; (4) genus or community, Samanya, or what constitutes a genus; (5) species or particularity, Visesha, or what constitutes an individual; (6) inhesion or inseperatability, Samavaya; (7) according to some, privation or negation, Abhava.

These are to be considered by means of their mutual similarities and dissimilarities. Here we have, indeed, what comes much nearer to Aristotle's categories than Gotama's Padarthas. These categories or predicaments were believed to contain an enumeration of things capable of being named, of being known. If number of Aristotle's categories was controverted, no wonder that those of Kanada should have met with the same fate. It has always been a moot point whether Abhava, non-existence, deserves a place among them, while some philosophers were anxious to add two more, namely, Sakti, potentia, and Sadrisya, similitude.

SUBSTANCES

The substances, according to the Vaiseshikas, are: (1) earth, Prithivi; (2) water, Apah; (3) light, Tejas; (4) air, Vayu; (5) ether, Akasa; (6) time, Kala; (7) space, Die; (8) self, Atman; (9) mind, Manas. These substances cannot exist without qualities, as little as qualities can exist without substances. The four at the head of the list are either eternal or non-eternal, and exist either in the form of atoms (Anus) or as material bodies. The non-eternal substances again exist as either inorganic, organic, or as organs of sense. The impulse given to the atoms comes from God, and in that restricted sense the Vaiseshika has to be accepted as theistic. God is Atman in its highest form. In its lower form it is the individual soul. The former is one, and one only, the latter are innumerable.

QUALITIES

The principal qualities of these substances are: (1) colour, Rupa, in earth, water, and light; (2) taste, Rasa, in earth and water; (3) smell, Gandha, in earth; (4) touch. Sparsa, in earth, water, light, and air; (5) number, Samkhya, by which we perceive one or many; (6) extension or quantity, Parimana; (7) individua-lity or severalty, Prithakatva; (8) conjunction, Samyoga; (9) disjunction, Viyoga; (10) priority, Paratva; (11) posteriority, Aparatva; (12) thought, Buddhi; (13-14) pleasure and pain, Sukhaduhkha; (15-16) desire and aversion, Ichchha-dveshau; and (17) will, effort, Prayatna.

ACTIONS

The principal actions affecting the substances are: (1) throwing upwards, Utkshepana; (2) throwing downwards, Avakshepana (or Apa); (3) contracting, Akunchana; (4) expanding, Utsarana; (5) going, Gamana. These actions or movements are sometimes identified with or traced back to the Samskaras, a word which has been rendered by dispositions and instincts, as applied to either animate or inanimate bodies.

In the Sutras which follow, Kanada tries to point out certain features which the three categories of substance, quality, and action share in common, and others which are peculiar to two, or to one only. In the course of this discussion he has frequently to dwell on the effects which they produce, and he therefore proceeds in the next lesson to examine the meaning of cause and effect, and likewise of genus, species, and individuals. It may be that the name of Vaiseshika was given to Kanada's philosophy from the differences, or Viseshas, which he establishes between substances, qualities, and actions, or, it may be, from Visesha as a name of individual things, applicable therefore to atoms.

CAUSE

As to cause and effect, Kanada remarks that cause precedes the effect, but that, in order to be a true cause, it must be a constant antecedent, and the effect must be unconditionally subsequent to it. There is an important and often neglected difference between Kaarana and Karana. Kaarana, though it may mean cause, is properly the instrumental cause only, or simply the instrument. An axe, for instance, is the Karana, or instrument, in felling a tree, but it is not the Kaarana, or Cause. Causes, according to Kanada, are threefold, intimate, non-intimate, and instrumental. The threads, for instance, are the intimate cause of the cloth, the sewing of the threads the non-intimate, and the shuttle the instrumental cause.

QUALITIES EXAMINED

In the second book Kanada examines the qualities of earth, water, etc. He, like other philosophers, ascribed four qualities to earth, three to water, two to light, one to air (Akasa). These are the principal and characteristic qualities, but others are mentioned afterwards, making altogether fourteen for earth, such as colour, taste, smell, touch, number, extension, individuality, conjunction, disjunction, genus, species, gravity, fluidity, and permanence. Qualities ascribed to Isvara, or the Lord, are number, knowledge, desire, and volition. In the case of air, which is invisible, he uses touch as a proof of its existence, also the rustling of leaves; and he does this in order to show that air is not only one. Curiously enough Kanada, after explaining that there is no visible mark of air but that its existence has to be proved by inference and by revelation, takes the opportunity of proving, as it were, by the way, the existence of God by saying that 'work and word are the signs of the substantial existence of beings different from ourselves.' This, at least, is what the commentators read in this Sutra, and they include other beings different from ourselves, not only God, but inspired sages also. As far as God is concerned, it seems certain that Kanada thinks he is able to prove His existence, His omnipotence and omniscience by two facts, that 'His name exists, and that His works exist, perceptible to the senses.'

Kanada proceeds to prove the existence of Akasa, ether, by showing that it must exist in order to account for the existence of sound, which is a quality, and as such requires the substratum of an eternal and special substance, as shown before. A distinction is made afterwards between characteristic and adventitious qualities. If a garment, for instance, is perfumed by a flower, the smell is only an adventitious quality of the garment, while it is characteristic in the case of earth. Thus heat is characteristic of light, cold of water, etc.

TIME

Time, which was one of the eternal substances, is declared to manifest its existence by such marks as priority, posteriority, simultaneity, slowness, and quickness. The arguments in support of the substantiality of air and ether apply to Time also, which is one, while its division into past, present, and future, hibernal, vernal, and autumnal, is due to extrinsic circumstances, such as the sun's revolutions. Time itself is one, eternal, and infinite.

SPACE

Space, again, is proved by our perceiving that one thing is remote from or near to another. Its oneness is proved as in the case of Time; and its apparent diversity, such as east, south, west, and north, depends likewise on extrinsic circumstances only, such as the rising and setting of the sun. Like Time it is one, eternal, and infinite.

ATMAN

He now proceeds, to consider the eighth substance, Atman, the Self, the first in the list of his sixteen Padarthas. Like Gotama, Kanada also argues that the Atman must be different from the senses, because while the senses apprehend each its own object only, it follows that there must be something else to apprehend them all, the work which in other philosophies was ascribed to Manas, at least in the first instance. Besides, the organs of sense are but instruments, and as such unconscious, and they require an agent who employs them. If we see a number of chariots skilfully driven, we know there must be a charioteer, and we know also that chariots and horses are different from the charioteer. The same applies to the senses of the body and to the Self. In defending this argument against all possible objections, Kanada, following the example of Gotama, is drawn away into a discussion of what is a valid and what is an invalid argument, and more particularly into an examination of what is a Vyapti, or an invariable concomitance, fit to serve as a true foundation for a syllogism.

MANAS

He proceeds to a consideration of Manas, the ninth and last of the Dravyas or substances. This, too, is to him much the same that it was to Gotama, who treats it as the sixth of the Prameyas. In this place, as we saw, Manas might be translated by attention rather than by mind.

ANUS OR ATOMS

What is thought to be peculiar to Kanada, nay, the distinguishing feature of his philosophy is the theory of Anus or atoms. They take the place of the Tanmatras in the Samkhya philosophy. Though the idea of an atom is not unknown in the Nyaya philosophy it is nowhere so fully worked out as in the Vaiseshika. Kanada argued that there must be somewhere a smallest thing, that excludes further analysis. Without this admission, we should have a *regressus infinitum*, a most objectionable process in the eyes of all Indian philosophers. A mountain, he says, would not be larger than a mustard seed. These smallest and invisible particles are held by Kanada to be eternal in themselves, but non-eternal as aggregates. As aggregates again they may be organised, organs, and inorganic. Thus the human body is earth organised, the power of smelling is the earthly organ, stones are inorganic.

It is, no doubt, very tempting to ascribe a Greek origin to Kanada's theory of atoms. But suppose that the atomic theory had really been borrowed from a Greek source, would it not be strange that Kanada's atoms are supposed never to assume visible dimensions till there is a combination of three double atoms (Tryanauka), neither the simple nor the double atoms being supposed to be visible by themselves. I do not remember anything like this in Epicurean authors, and it seems to me to give quite an independent character to Kanada's view of the nature of an atom.

We are told that water, in its atomic state, is eternal, as an aggregate transient. Beings in the realm of Varuna (god of the sea) are organised, taste is the watery organ, rivers are water inorganic.

Light in its atomic state is eternal, as an aggregate transient. There are organic luminous bodies in the sun, sight of the visual ray is the luminous organ, burning fires are inorganic.

Air, again, is both atomic and an aggregate. Beings of the air, spirits etc., are organised air; touch in the skin is the aerial organ, wind is inorganic air. Here it would seem as if we had something not very unlike the doctrine of Empedocles. But the form which it takes in India is characteristically different from its Greek form.

Ether is always eternal and infinite. The sense of hearing is the ethereal organ: nay, it is supposed by some that ether is actually contained in the ear.

As to atoms, they are supposed to form first an aggregate of two, then an aggregate of three double atoms, then of four triply atoms, and so on. While single atoms are indestructible, composite atoms are by their very nature liable to decomposition, and, in that sense, to destruction. An atom, by itself invisible, is compared to the sixth part of a mote in a sunbeam.

SAMANYA

As to Samanya, community, or, as we should say genus, the fourth of Kanada's categories, it is supposed to be eternal, and a property common to several, and abiding in substance, in quality, and in action. It is distinguished by degrees, as high and low; the highest Samanya, or, the highest genus (Jati) is Satta, mere being, afterwards differentiated by Upadhis, or limitations, and developed into ever so many subordinate species. The Buddhist philosophers naturally deny the existence of such a category, and maintain that all our experience has to do with single objects only.

VISESHA

These single objects are what Kanada comprehends under his fifth category of Visesha, or that which constitutes the individuality or separateness of any object. This also is supposed to abide in eternal substances, so that it seems to have been conceived not as a mere abstraction, but as something real, that was there and could be discovered by means of analysis or abstraction.

SAMAVAYA

The last category, is one peculiar to Indian philosophy. Samavaya is translated by inhesion or inseparability. With Kanada also it is different from mere connection, Samyoga, such as obtains between horse and rider, or between milk and water mixed together. There is Samavaya between threads and cloth, between father and son, between two halves and a whole, between cause and effect, between substances and qualities, the two being interdependent and therefore inseparable.

Though this relationship is known in non-Indian philosophies, it has not received a name of its own, though such a term might have proved very useful in several controversies. The relation between thought and word, for instance, is not Ṣamyoga, but Samavaya, inseparableness.

ABHAVA

In addition to these six categories, some logicians required a negative category also, that of Abhava or absence. And this also they divided into different kinds, into (1) Pragabhava, former not-being, applying to the cloth before it was woven; (2) Dhvamsa, subsequent non-being, as when a jar, being smashed, exists no longer as a jar; and (3) Atyantabhava, absolute not-being, an impossibility, such as the son of a barren woman; (4) Anyonyabhava, reciprocal negation, or mutual difference, such as we see in the case of water and ice.

It may seem as if the Vaiseshika was rather a disjointed and imperfect system. Though it presupposes a knowledge of the Nyaya-system, it frequently goes over the same groung as the Nyaya. We should hardly imagine that the Vaiseshika-Sutras would argue against Upamana, or comparison, as a separate Pramana, in addition to Pratyaksha (sense) and Anumana (inference) unless in some other school it had been treated as an independent means of knowledge; and this school was, as we saw, the Nyaya. Kanada denies by no means that comparison is a channel through which knowledge may reach us, he only holds that it is not an independen channel, but must be taken as a subdivision of another and larger channel, Anumana or inference. He probably held the same opinion about Sabda, whether we take it in the sense of the Veda or of an utterance of a recognised authority.

THE SIX SYSTEMS

It must have been observed how these six systems of philosophy, though they differ from each other and criticise each other, share nevertheless so many things in common that we can only undersated them as products of one and the same soil, though cultivated by different hands. They all promise to teach the nature of the soul, and its relation to the God-head or to a Supreme Being. They all undertake to supply the means of knowing the nature of that Supreme Being, and through that knowledge to pave the way to supreme happiness. They all share the conviction that there is suffering in the world which is something irregular, has no right to exist, and should therefore be removed. Though there is a strong religious vein running through the six so-called orthodox systems, they belong to a phase of thought in which not only has the belief in the many Vedic gods long been superseded by a belief in a Supreme Deity, such as Prajapati, but this phase also has been left behind to make room for a faith in a Supreme Power, or in the Godhead which has no name but Brahman or Sat, 'I am what I am.'

The Hindus were fully aware that some of their systems of philosophy differed from each other on essential points, and that some stood higher than others. Madhusudana clearly looked upon the Vedanta as the best of all philosophies, and so did Samkara, provided he was allowed to interpret the Sutras of Badarayana according to the principles of his own unyielding

Monism. Vijnana-Bhikshu, a philosopher of considerable grasp, while fully recognising the difference between the six systems of philosophy, tried to discover a common truth behind them all, and to point out how they can be studied together, or rather in succession and how all of them are meant to lead honest students into the way of truth.

If it should be objected that we have already a logical treatment of these subjects in the Nyaya and Vaiseshika systems, rendering the Samkhya superfluous, and that it is hardly possible that both—the Samkhya as well as the Nyaya and Vaiseshika—could be means of right knowledge, considering that each represents the Self in a different form, the Nyaya and Vaiseshika with qualities, the Samkhya as without, thus clearly contradicting each other, we answer No, by no means! Neither is the Samkhya rendered superfluous by the Nyaya and Vaiseshika, nor do they contradict each other. They differ from each other so far only as Nyaya and Vaiseshika treat of the objects of empirical knowledge, but the Samkhya of the highest truth. The Nyaya and Vaiseshika, as they follow the common-sense view that it is the Self that feels joy and pain, aim at no more than at the first steps in knowledge, namely, at the recognition of the Atman as different from the body, because it is impossible to enter *per saltum* into the most abstruse wisdom. If therefore we read the following verse from the Bhagavad-gita:

'Those who are deceived by the constituent Gunas of Prakriti, cling to the workings of the Gunas (Sattva, Rajas, and Tamas). Let therefore those who know the whole truth take care not to distract men of moderate understanding who do not as yet know the whole truth;'—we see that here the following of the Nyaya and Vaiseshika systems, though they hold to the false belief that the Self can be an agent, are not treated as totally in error, but only as not knowing the whole truth, if compared with the Samkhyas, who know the whole truth. Even such knowledge as they possess, leads step by step by means of the lower impassiveness (Apara-vairagya) to liberation; while the lower knowledge of the Samkhyas only, as compared with the lower knowledge, is absolute knowledge, and leads by means of higher impassiveness (Paravairagya) straight to liberation.

But admitting that there is here no difference between Nyaya-Vaiseshika and the Samkhya systems, is there not a clear contradiction between the Samkhya on one side and the Brahma-Mimamsa (Vedanta) and the Yoga on the other? The former denies the existence of an eternal Isvara, the two others maintain it. Surely it cannot be said that here also the contradiction between these systems, the atheistic and theistic, can be removed by simply admitting, as before, two points of view, the metaphysical and the empirical, as if the theistic doctrine existed only for the sake of the worship of the multitude. Such a decision would here be impossible. The atheistic view that an Isvara is difficult to know and therefore non-existent, may well have been merely repeated by the Samkhyas, as a popular idea, and in order to put an end to the desire of men for acquiring a divine status and divine honours (by means of penance etc.), as in the case of the Naiyayikas when they say that the Self possesses qualities (which must be taken as merely a provisional remark). In the Veda or elsewhere Isvara, the anthropomorphic deity, is never explicitly denied, so that one could say that theism should be taken as the common popular view only.

•••

9

Summing Up

We have explored the recognised systems of Indian philosophy, so far as it seemed necessary to a general survey of the work done by the ancient thinkers of India. It seemed to me undersirable to enter here on examination of what has been called the later Vedanta which can be studied in such works as the Panchadasi or the Vedanta-Sara, and in many popular treatises both in prose and in verse. But-a general discussion is certainly in orders.

LATER VEDANTA

It would be unfair and unhistroical, to look upon this later development of the Vedanta as simply a deterioration of the old philosophy. Though it is certainly rather confused, if compared with the system as laid down pin the old Vedanta-Sutras, it represents to us what in the cource of time became of the Vedanta, when taught and discussed in the different schools of philosophy in medieval and modern India. What strikes us most in it is the mixture of Vedanta ideas with ideas borrowed chiefly, as it would seem, from Samkhya, but also from Yoga, and Nyaya sources. But here again it is difficult to decide whether such ideas were actually borrowed from these systems in their finished state, or whether they were originally common property which in later times only had become restricted to one or the other of the six systems of philosophy. In the Panchadasi, for instance, we meet with the idea of Prakriti, nature, which we are accustomed to consider as the peculiar property of the Samkhya-system. This Prakriti is said there to be the reflection, or as we should say, the shadow of Brahman, and to be possessed of the three Gunas or elements of goodness, passion and darkness or as they are sometimes explained, good as indifferent, and bad. This theory of the three Gunas however is altogether absent from the original Vedanta; at least, it is not to be met with in the purely Vedantic Upanished, occurring for the first time in the Svetasvatara Upanishad.

Again in the later Vedanta words Avidya and Maya are used synonymously, or if distinguished from one another they are supposed to arise respectively from the more or less pure character of their substance. The omniscient, but personal Isvara is there explained as a reflection of Maya, but as having subdued her, while the individual soul, Prana or Jiva, is represented as having been subdued by Avidya and to be multiform, owing to the variety of Avidya. The individual soul being endowed with a causal or subtle body, believes that body to be its own, and hence error and suffering in all their variety. As to the development of the world, we are told that it was by the command of Isvara that Prakriti, when dominated by darkness, produced the elements of ether, air, fire, water and earth, all meant to be enjoyed, that is, to be experienced by the individual souls.

In all this we can hardly be mistaken if we recognise the influence of Samkhya ideas, obscuring and vitiating the monism of the Vedanta pure and simple. In that philosophy there is no room for a second or for a prakriti, nor for the three Gunas, nor for anything real by the side of Brahman.

How that influence was exercised we cannot discover and it is possible that in ancient times already there existed this influence of one philosophical system upon the other for we see even in some of the Upanishads a certain mixture of what we should afterwards have to call the distinctive teaching of Vedanta, Samkhya, or Yoga-philosophy. We must remember that in India the idea of private property in any philosophic truth did hardly exist. The individual, was of little consequence, and could never exercise the same influence which such thinkers as Socrates or Plato exercised in Greece. If the descriptions of Indian life emanating from the Indians themselves, and from other nations they came in contact with, whether Greek conquerors or Chinese pilgrims, can be trusted, we may well understand that truth, or what was taken to be truth, was treated not as private, but as common property.

If there was an exchange of ideas among the Indian seekers after truth, it was far more in the nature of co-operation towards a common end, than in the assertion of any claims of originality or priority by individual teachers. That one man should write and publish his philosophical views in a book, and that another should read and criticise that book or carry on the work where it had been left, was never thought of in India in ancient times. If A referred to B often, as they say, from mere civility, Pujartham, B would refer to A, but no one would ever say, as so often happens with us, that he had anticipated the discovery of another, or that some one else had stolen his ideas. Truth was not an article that, according to Hindu ideas, could ever be stolen. All that could happen and did happen was that certain opinions which had been discussed, Shifted, and generally received in one Asrama, hermitage, Arama, garden, or Parishad, religious settlement, would in time be collected by its members and reduced to a more or less systematic form.

What that form was in early times we may see from the Brahmanas, and more particularly from the Upanishads, i.e., *Seances,* gatherings of pupils round their teachers, or later on from the Sutras. It cannot be doubted that these Sutras pre-suppose, by their systematic form, a long continued intellectual labour; nay, it seems to me difficult to account for their peculiar literary form except on the ground that they were meant to be learnt by heart and to be accompanied from the very beginning by a running commentary, without which they would have been perfectly unintelligible. I suggested once before that this very peculiar style of the Sutras would receive the best historical explanation, if it could be proved that they represent the first attempts at writing for literary purposes in India. Whatever the exact date may be of the introduction of a *sinis-trorsum* and *dextrorsum* alphabet for epigraphic purposes in India (and in spite of all efforts not a single inscription has as yet been discovered that can be referred with certainty to the period before Asoka, third century B.C.), every classical scholar knows that there always is a long interval between an epigraphic and a literary employment of the alphabet.

People forget that a period marked by written literary compositions requires a public, and a large public, which is able to read, for where there is no demand there is no supply. Nor must we forget that the old system of a mnemonic literature, the Parampara, was invested with a kind of sacred character, and would not have been easily surrendered. The old mnemonic system was upheld by a strict discipline which formed the principal part of the established system of education in India, as has been fully described in the Pratisakhyas. They explain to us by what process, whatever existed at that time of literature, chiefly sacred, was firmly imprinted on the memory of the young. These young pupils were in fact the books, the scribes were the Gurus, the tablet was the brain. We can hardly imagine such a state of literature, and the transition from it to a written literature must have marked a new start in the intellectual life of the people at large, or at least of the educated classes.

Anybody who has come in contact with the Pandits of India has been able to observe the wonderful feats that can be achieved by that mnemonic discipline even at present, though it is dying out before our eyes at the approach of printed books, nay, of printed editions of their own sacred texts; I need hardly say that even if Buhler's idea of the introduction of a Semitic alphabet into India by means of commercial travellers about 800 or 1000 B.C. were more than a hypothesis, it would not prove the existence of a written literature at that time. The adaptation of a Semitic alphabet to the phonetic system as elaborated in the Pratisakhyas may date from the third, possibly from the fourth century B.C., but the use of that alphabet for inscriptions begins in the middle of the third century only; and though we cannot deny the possibility of its having been used for literary purposes at the same time, such possibilities would form very dangerous landmarks in the chronology of Indian literature.

But whatever the origin of the peculiar Sutra-literature may have been—and I give my hypothesis as a hypothesis only-all—scholars will probably agree that these Sutras could not be the work of one individual philosopher, but that we have in them the last outcome of previous centuries of thought, and the final result of the labours of numerous thinkers whose names are forgotten and will never be recovered.

RELATIVE AGE OF PHILOSOPHIES AND SUTRAS

If we keep this in mind, we shall see that the question whether any of the texts of the six philosophies which we now possess should be considered as older than any other, is really a question impossible to answer. The tests for settling the relative ages of literary works, applicable to European literature, are not applicable to Indian literature. Thus, if one Greek author quotes another, we feel justified in taking the one who is quoted as the predecessor or contemporary of the one who quotes. But because Jaimini quotes Badarayana and Badarayana Jaimini, and because their systems show an acquaintance with the other five systems of philosophy, we have no right to arrange them in chronological succession. Kanada, who is acquainted with Kapila, is clearly criticised by Kapila, at least in our Kapila-Sutras.

Kapila, to whom the Samkhya-Sutras are ascribed, actually adopts one of Badarayana's Sutras, IV, 1, 1, and inserts it in his own work, IV, 3. He does the same for the Yoga-Sutras I, 5 and II, 46, which occur in II. 33, III, 34, and VI, 24 in the Samkhya-Sutras which we possess. Kanada was clearly acquainted with Gotama while Gotama attacks in turn certain doctrines of Kapila and Badarayana. It has been supposed, because Patanjali ignores all other systems, that therefore he was anterior to all of them. But all such conclusions, which would be perfectly legitimate in Greek and Latin literature, have no weight whatever in the literary history of India, because during its mnemonic period anything could be added and anything left out, before each system reached the form in which we possess it.

AGE OF KAPILA-SUTRAS

The Sutras of Kapila, which have come down to us, are so little the work of the founder of that system, that it would be far safer to treat them as the last arrangement of doctrines accumulated in one philosophical school during centuries of Parampara or tradition. It is easy to see that the Yoga-philosophy presupposes a Samkhya-philosophy, but while Patanjali, the reputed author of Yoga-Sutras, has been referred to the second century B.C., it is now generally admitted that our Samkhya-Sutras cannot ba earlier than the fourteenth century A.D. It is necessary to distinguish carefully between the six philosophies as so many channels of thought, and the Sutras which embody their teachings and have been handed down to us as the earliest documents within our reach.

Yoga, as a technical term, occurs earlier than the name of any other system of philosophy. It occurs in the Taittiriya and Katkha Upanishads, and is mentioned in as early an authority as the Asvalyana-Grihya-Sutras. In the Maitreya. Up. VI, 10 we meet even with Yogins. But it by no means follows that the Yoga, known in those early times, was the same as what we possess in Patanajali's Sutras of the Yoga-philosophy. We look in vain in the so-called classical Upanishads for the names of either Samkhya or Vedanta, but Samkhya occurs in the compound Samkhya-Yoga in the Svetasvatara Up. VI, 13 and in several of the minor Upanishads. It should be observed that Vedanta also occurs for the first time in the same Svetasvatara VI, 22, and afterwards in the smaller Upanishads. All such indications may become valuable hereafter for chronological purposes. In the Bhagavad-gita II, 39 we meet with the Samkhya as the name of a system of philosophy and likewise as a name of its adherents.

As to our Samkhya-Sutras their antiquity was first shaken by Dr. FitzEdward Hall. Vachaspati Misra, the author of the Samkhya-tattva-Kaumudi, who, according to Professor Garbe, can be safely referred to about 1150 A.D., quotes not a single

Sutra from our Samkhya-Sutras, but appeals to older authorities only, such as Panchasikha, Varshajanya, and the Rajavartika. Even Madhava about 1350 A.D., who evidently knew the Sutras of the other systems, never quotes from our Samkhya-Sutras; and why not, if they had been in existence in his time?

But we must not go too far. It by no means follows that everyone of the Sutras which we possess in the body of the Samkhya-Sutras, and the composition of which is assigned by Balasastrin to so late a period as the sixteenth century, is of that modern date. He declares that they were all composed by the well-known Vijnana-Bhikshu who, as was then the fashion, wrote also a commentary on them. It is quite possible that our Samkhya-Sutras may only be what we should call the latest recension of the old Sutras. We know that in India the oral tradition of certain texts, as, for instance, the Sutras of Panini, was interrupted for a time and then restored again, whether from scattered MSS., or from the recollection of less forgetfull or forgotten individuals. If that was the case, as we know, with so voluminous a work as the Mahabhashya; why should not certain portions of the Samkhya-Sutras have been preserved here and there, and have been added to or remodelled from time to time, till they meet us at last in their final form, at so late a date as the fourteenth or even the sixteenth century?

It was no doubt a great shock to those who stood up for the great antiquity of Indian philosophy, to have to confess that a work for which a most remote date had always been claimed, may not be older than the time of DesCartes, at least in that final literary form in which it has reached us. But if we consider the circumstances of the case, it is more than possible that our Sutras of the Samkhya-philosophy contain some of the most ancient as well as the most modern Sutras, the utterances of Kapila, Asuri, Panchasikha and Varsha-janya, as well as those of Isvara-Krishna and even of Vijnana-Bhikshu.

SAMKHYA-KARIKAS

But if we must accept so very modern a date for our Kapila-Sutras, we are fortunate in being able to assign a much earlier and much more settled date to another work which for centuries seems to have formed the recognised authority for the followers of the Samkhya in India, the so-called Samkhya-karikas or the sixty-nine or seventy *versus mcmoriales* of Isvara-Krishna (with three supplementary ones, equally ascribed to that author). That these Karikas are older than our Sutras could easily be proved by passages occurring among the Sutras, which are almost literally taken from the Karikas.

Alberuni, who wrote his account of India in the first half of the eleventh century, was well acquainted not only with Isvara-Krishna's work, but likewise, as has been shown, with Gaudapada's commentary on it. Nay, we can even make another step backward. For the Samkhya-karikas exist in a Chinese translation also, made by Chan-ti (lit. true-truth), possibly Paramartha, a Tripitaka law-teacher of the Chhan dynasty, A.D. 557 to 589 (not 583). Paramartha came to China in about 147 A.D. in the reign of the Emperor Wu-ti of the Lian dynasty which ruled in Southern China from 502 to 557 A.D. a and was followed by the Chhan dynasty. He lived till 582 A.D.; and there are no less than twenty-eight of his translations now in existence, that of the Suvarna-Saptati-Sastra being the twenty-seventh. The name given to it in Chinese, 'The Golden Seventy Discourse,' is supposed to refer to the number of verses in the Karika. Chan-ti was not considered a good Chinese scholar, and his translation of the Abhidharma-Kosha-sastra, for instance, had in consequence to be replaced by a new translation by Hiuen Tsang.

But though we are thus enabled to assign the Samkhya-karika to the sixth century A.D., it by no means follows that this work itself did not exist before that time. Native tradition, we are told, assigns his work to the first century B.C.

DATE OF GAUDAPADA

But even here new difficulties arise with regard to the age of Gaudapada, the author of the commentary on the Karikas. This commentary also, so we were informed by Beal, had been translated into Chinese before 582 A.D.; but how is that possible without upsetting the little we know of Gaudapada's date. Samkara is represented as the pupil of Govinda who was the pupil of Gaudapada. But Samkara's literary career began, as is generally supposed, about 788 A.D. How then could he have been the literary grandson of Gaudapma, and son or pupil of Govinda? As Mr. Beal could no longer be consulted I asked one of my Chinese pupils, the late Mr. Kasawara, to translate portions of the Chinese commentary for me; but the specimens he sent me did not suffice to settle the question whether it was really a translation of Gaudapada's commentary.

It is but right to state here that Telang in the Indian Antiquary, XIII, 95, places Samkara much earlier, in 590 A. D., and that Fleet, in the Indian Antiquary, Jan., 1887, assigns 630 to 655 as the latest date to King Vrishadeva of Nepal who is said to have received Samkara at his court, and actually to have given the name of Samkaradeva to his son in honour of the philosopher. In order to escape from all these uncertainties I wrote once more to Japan to another pupil of mine, Dr. Takakusu, and he, after carefully collating the Chinese translation with the Sanskrit commentary of Gaudapada, informed me that the Chinese translation of the commentary was not, and could not in any sense be called, a translation of Gaudapada's commentary. So much trouble may be caused by one unguarded expression! Anyhow this difficulty is now removed, and Samkara's date need not be disturbed. The author of the Karikas informs us at the end of his work that this philolsophy, proclaimed by the greatest sage, i.e., Kapila, had been communicated by him to Asuri, by Asuri to Panchasikha, and, as the Tattva-samasa adds, from Panchasikha to Patanjali, and had been widely taught until, by an uninterrupted series of teachers, it reached even Isvara-Krishna. He calls it the Shashti-tantra, the Sixty-doctrine.

A similar account is given by Paramartha in his comment on the first verse, Kipila (Kapila), he says, 'was a Rishi descended from the sky and was endowed with the four virtues, dutifulness (Dharma), wisdom (Prajna), separation from desires (Vairagya), and freedom (Moksha). He saw a Brahman of the name of O-shu-li (Asuri) who had been worshipping heaven or the Devas for a thousand years, and said to him: "O Asuri, art thou satisfied with the state of a Grihastha. or householder?" After a thousand years he came again, and Asuri admitted that he was satisfied with the state of a Grihastha. He then came a third time to Asuri, whereupon Asuri quitted the state of a householder and became a pupil of Kapila. These may be mere additions made by Paramartha, but they show, at all events, that to him also Kapila and Asuri were persons of a distant past.

TATTVA-SAMASA

But however far the Karikas of Isvara-Krishna may go back, they are what they are, a metrical work in the style of a later age, an age that gave rise to other Karikas like Bhartrihari's (about 650 A.D.) Karikas on grammar. Everybody has wondered, therefore, what could have become of the real Samkhya-Sutras, if they ever existed; or, if they did not, why there should never have been such Sutras for so important a system of philosophy as the Samkhya. There is clearly a great gap between the end of the Upanishad period and the literary period that was able to give rise to the metrical work of Isvara-Krishna. In what form could the Samkhya-philosophy have existed in that interval?

To judge from analogy we should certainly say, in the form of Sutras, such as were handed down for other branches of learning by oral tradition. The Karikas themselves presuppose such a tradition quite as much as the much later Sutras which we possess. They are both meant to recapitulate what existed, never to originate what we should call new and original thoughts. When we see the Karikas declare that they leave out on purpose the Akhyayikas, the illustrative stories contained in the fourth book of our Sutras, this cannot prove their posteriority to the Sutras as we have them; but it shows that at Isvara-Krishna's time there existed a body of Samkhya-philosophy which contained such stories as we find in our modem Sutras, but neither in the Karikas nor in the Tattva-samasa. Besides these stories other things also were omitted by Isvara-Krishna, comprehended under the name of Pravada, probably controversies, such as those on the necesaity of an Isvara.

Under these circumstances I venture to say that such a work in Sutras not only existed, but that we are in actual possession of it, namely, in the text of the much neglected Tattva-samasa. Because it contains a number of new technical terms, it has been put down at once as modern, as if what is new to us must be new chronologically also. We know far too little of the history of the Samkhya to justify so confident a conclusion. Colebrooke told us long ago that, if the scholiast of Kapila may be trusted, and why should he not? The Tattva-samasa was the proper text-book of the Samkhya-philosophy. It was a mere accident that he, Colebrooke, could not find a copy of it. 'Whether that Tattva-samasa of Kapila be extant,' he wrote, 'or whether the Sutras of Panchasikha be so, is not certain.' And again he wrote: 'It appears from the Preface of the Kapila-bhashya that a more compendious tract in the form of Sutras or aphorisms bears the title of Tattva-samasa, and is ascribed to the same author, i.e., to Kapila.'

I admit that the introductory portion of this tract sounds modern, and probably is so, but I find no other marks of a modem date in the body of the work. On the contrary, there are several indications in it of its being an earlier form of the Samkhya-philosophy than what we possess in the Karikas or in the Sutras. When it agrees with the Karikas sometimes almost verbatim, it is the metrical text that seems to me to presuppose the prose, not the metrical version. In the Sutras themselves we find no allusion as yet to the atheistic or non-theistic doctrines which distinguish the later texts of the Samkhya, and which are still absent from the Samkhya-karikas also.

The so-called Aisvaryas or superhuman powers, which are recognised in the Tattva-samasa, might seem to presuppose the recognition of an Isvara, though this is very doubtful; but the direct identification of Purusha with Brahman in the Tattva-samasa points certainly to an earlier and less pronounced Nirisvara or Lord-less character of the ancient Samkhya. It should also be mentioned that Vijnana-Bhikshu, no mean authority on such matters, and even supposed by some to have been himself the author of our modem Samkhya-Sutras, takes it for granted that the Tattva-samasa was certainly prior to the Kapila-Sutras which we possess. For why should he defend Kapila, and not the author of the Tattva-samasa, against the charge of Punarukti or giving us a mere useless repetition, and why should he have found no excuse for the existence of the Kapila-Sutras except that they are short and complete, while the Tattva-samasa is short and compact?

Not being able to find a MS. of the Tattva-samasa Cole-blooke decided to translate instead the Samkhya-karikas, and thus it came to pass that most scholars have been under the impression that in India also this metrical version was considered as the most authoritative and most popular manual of the Samkhya-philosophy. This is the way in which certain pre-possessions arise. We have learnt since from Ballantyne that at Benares, where he resided, these Karikas were hardly known at all except to those who had seen Professor Wilson's English edition of them, while the Tattva-samasa was well known to all the native assistants whom he employed. Nor can we doubt that in the part of India best known to Ballantyne it was really an important and popular work, if we consider the number of commentaries written on it, and the frequency of allusions to it which occur in other commentaries. The commentary published by Ballantyne is, if I understand him rightly, anonymous. It gives first what it calls the Samkhya-Sutrani, and then the Samkhya-Sutras-vrittih. Hall, quotes one commentary by Kshemananda, called Samkhya-kramadipika, but it is not quite clear to me whether this is the same as the one published by Ballantyne, nor have I had access to any other MSS.

We must not forget that in modem times the Samkhya-philosophy has ceased to be popular in several parts of India. Even in the sixteenth century Vijnana-Bhikshu, in his commentary on the Samkhya-Sutras, complains that it has been swallowed up by the sun of the time, and that but a small part of the moon of knowledge remained; while in the Bhagavata Purana 1, 3, 10, the Samkhya is spoken of as Kala-vipluta, destroyed by time. Professor Wilson told me that, during the whole of his intercourse with learned natives, he met with one Brahman only who professed to be acquainted with the writings of this philosophical school, and Professor Bhandarkar states that the very name of Samkhya-pravachana was unknown on his side of India. Hence we may well understand that Samkhya MSS are scarce in India, and entirely absent in certain localities.

It is possible also that the very smallness of the Tattva-samasa may have lowered it in the eyes of native scholars, and that in time it may have been eclipsed by its more voluminous commentaries. But if we accept it as what it professes to be, and what, up to the time of Vijnana-Bhikshu at least, it was considered to be in India, it seems to me just the book that was wanted to fill the gap to which I referred before. By itself it would fill a few pages only. In fact it is a mere enumeration of topics, and, as such, it would agree very well with the somewhat puzzling name of Samkhya, which means no more than enumeration. All other derivations of this title seem far-fetched as compared with this. According to Vijnana-Bhikshu in his commentary on the Sutras, both the Samkhya-Sutras and the Yoga-Sutras are really mere developments of the Tattva-samasa-Sutras. Both are called therefore Samkhya-pravachana, exposition of the Samkhya, the latter adding the peculiar arguments in support of the existence of an Isvara or Supreme Lord, and therefore called Sesvara, in opposition to the Samkhya, which is called An-isvara, or Lord-less.

And here it is important to remark also that the name of Shashti-tantra, the Doctrine of the Sixty, which is given by Isvara-Krishna, or at all events by the author of the 72nd of his Karikas, should occur and be accounted for in the Tattva-samasa, as containing the 17 (enumerated in 64 and 65), and the 33, previously exhibited in 64 and 63, together with the 10 Mulikarthas or fundamental facts which together would make up the sixty topics of the Shashti-tantra. At the end of the 25 great topics of the Tattva-samasa we find the straightforward declaration: 'It *tattva-samasakhya-samkhya-Sutras*. Here end the Samkhya-Sutras called Tattva-samasa.'

At first sight, no doubt, Samasa seems to mean a mere abstract; but Samasa may be used also in opposition to Brihat, and there is no other work in existence of which it could be called an abstract, certainly not either of the Karikas or of the modern Sutras, such as we possess them. The whole arrangement is different from the other and more recent treatments of Samkhya-philosophy. The three kinds of pain, for instance, which generally form the starting point of the whole system, are relegated to the very end as a separate topic. We meet with technical subjects and technical terms which are not to be found at all in other and, as it would seem, more modern Samkhya works. The smallness of the Tattva-samasa can hardly be used as an argument against its ever having been an important work, for we find similar short, yet old Sutra-works, for instance, the Sarvanukrama and other Anukramanis described in my History of Ancient Sanskrit Literatrue. However, in matters of this kind we must avoid being too positive either in denying or asserting the age and authenticity of Sanskrit texts. All I can say is that there is no mark of modern age in their language, though the commentary is, no doubt, of a later date. What weighs with me is the fact that Indian Pandits evidently considered the Tattva-samasa-Sutras as the original outlines of the Samkhya-philosophy, while the idea that they are a later spurious production rests, as far as I can see at present, on no real argument whatever.

ANTERIORITY OF VEDANTA OR SAMKHYA

It must be clear from all this how useless it would be, with the limited means at our disposal, to attempt to prove the anteriority either of the Vedanta or of the Samkhya, as systems of philosophy, and as distinguished from the Sutras in which we possess them. External or historical evidence we have none, and internal evidence, though it may supply a suggestion, can but seldom amount to positive proof. We can understand how, out of the seeds scattered about in the Upanishads, there could arise in time the systematic arrangement and final representation of systems such as have been handed down to us in the Sutras of the Vedanta, the Samkhya, and the other schools. It cannot be denied that in the Upanishad period Vedantic ideas were certainly more prevalent than those of the Samkhya.

I go even a step further and admit that the Samkhya-philosophy may have been a kind of toning down of the extreme Monism of the Advaita Vedanta. I think we can enter into the misgivings and fear of those who felt startled by the unflinching Monism of the Vedanta, at least as interpreted by the school which was represented rather than founded by Samkhya. Now, the two points which are most likely to have caused difficulty or given offence to ordinary consciences, would seem to have been the total denial of what is meant by the reality of the objective world, and the required surrender of all individuality on the part of the subject, that is, of our selves. These are the points which seem most startling even to ourselves, and it is quite possible that they may have given rise to another system free from these startling doctrines. They certainly formed the chief stumbling-block to Ramanuja and those who had come before him, such as Bodhayana and other Purvacharyas, and led them to propound their own more human interpretation of the Vedanta, though sacrificing the Isvara in order to save the reality of each Purusha.

These conflicting views of the world, of the soul, and of God, emerge already in the Upanishads; and in a few of them, the Svetasvatara, Maitray., and Katha Upanishads, for instance, there are utterances that come very near what we know as Samkhya rather than Vedanta doctrines. Vedanta ideas preponderate, however, so decidedly in the Upanishad literature, that we can well understand that in the oral tradition of the schools the Samkhya doctrines should have exercised Its limited influence only, whatever favour they may have found with those who were repelled by the extreme views of the monistic Vedanta. The followers of Kapila had an advantage over the Vedantists in admitting a Prakriti, or something objective, independent of Brahman or Purusha, though called into life and activity by the look of Purusha only, and disappearing when that look ceased.

They were also less opposed to the common consciousness of mankind in admitting the reality of individual souls. Dualism is always more popular than rigorous Monism, and the Samkhya was clearly dualistic when it postulated nature, not only as the result of Avidya or Maya, but as something real in the ordinary sense of that word, and when it allowed to the individual souls or jivas also an independent character. It should be remembered that the denial of an Isvara or personal Lord did not probably form part of the original Samkhya, as presented to us in the Tattva-samasa. It would seem therefore that on these very important points the Samkhya was more conciliatory and less defiant to the common sense of mankind than the Vedanta, and though this is far from proving that it was therefore posterior to the Vedanta in its severest form, it might well be accepted as an indication that these two streams of thought followed parallel courses, starting from a common fund of ancient Vedic thoughts, but diverging afterwards, the Vedanta unflinchingly following its straight course, the other, the Samkhya, avoiding certain whirlpools of thought which seemed dangerous to the ordinary swimmer.

To the people at large it would naturally seem as if the Vedanta taught the oneness of all individual souls or subjects in Brahman, and the illusory character of all that is objective, while the Samkhya allowed at all events the temporary reality of the objective world and the multiplicity of individual souls. Of course, we must leave it an open question for the present whether the extreme monistic view of the Veda was due to Samkara, or whether, like Ramanuja, he also could claim the authority of Purvacharyas in his interpretation of Badarayana's Sutras. If that were so, the difference between the two systems would certainly seem to be irreconcilable, while minor differences between them would in India at least admit of a friendly adjustment.

ATHEISM AND ORTHODOXY

Even on what seems to us so vital a point in every philosophy as theism or atheism, Indian philosophers seem to have been able to come to an understanding and a compromise. We must remember that in the eyes of the Brahmans the Samkhya is atheistic and yet orthodox. This seems to us impossible; but the fact is that orthodoxy has a very different meaning in India from what it has with us. What we mean by orthodoxy was with them not much more than a recognition of the supreme authority of the Veda. The Samkhya, whatever we may think of its Vedic character, never denies the authority of the Veda in so many words, though it may express a less decided submission to it. Whether in its origin the Samkhya was quite independent of the Veda, is difficult to say. Some scholars think that the recognition of the supreme authority of the Sruti was an afterthought with Kapila, a mere stroke of theological diplomacy. But if so, we should be forced to admit that the Samkhya philosophers wished, by means of this diplomacy, to be raised to the same position which others, such as the Vedantists, had occupied before them; and so far it might seem to indicate the posteriority of the Samkhya as a system of philosophy.

It is important here to remember that the Samkhya not only declared for the authority of the Veda, but had never openly rejected it, like Brihaspati or Buddha. It is quite another question whether it really carried out the spirit of the Veda, particularly of the Upanishads. That Samkara, the great defender of Vedantism, should deny the correctness of the interpretation of the Veda, adopted by Kapila, proves after all no more than that a difference of opinion existed between the two, but it would show at the same time that Kapila, as well as Samkara., had tried to represent his philosophy as supported by passages from the Veda. To judge from a passage in the beginning of the Samkhya-karikas it might seem indeed that Kapila placed his own philosophy above the Veda. But he really says no more there than that certain remedies for the removal of pain, enjoined by the Veda, are good, and that other remedies enjoined by philosophy are likewise good; but that of the two the latter are better, that is, more efficacious. This does not affect the authority of the Veda as a whole, as compared with philosophy, or human knowledge. We must not forget that after all it is Sruti or revelation itself which declares that all remedies are palliative only, and that real freedom (Moksha) from all suffering can be derived from philosophical knowledge only, and that this is incomparably higher than sacrifices or other meritorious acts (Samkhya-pravachana I, 5).

AUTHORITY OF THE VEDA

What authority Kapila assigns to the Veda may be gathered from what he says about the three possible sources of knowledge, perception, inference, and Aptavachana, that is the received, correct, or true word, or, it may be, the word of a trustworthy person. He explains Aptavachana in v. 5 by Aptasruti, which clearly means received revelation or revelation from a trustworthy source. However the commentators may differ, Sruti can here mean the Veda only, though, no doubt, the Veda as interpreted by Kapila. And that the Veda is not only considered as equal to sensuous perception and inference, but is placed by him on an even higher pedestal, is shown by the fact that Kapila (Sutras V, 51) declares it to be self-evident, Svatah-pramanam, while perception and inference are not, but are admitted to be liable to error and to require confirmation.

Though it is true, therefore, that with the true Samkhya philosopher the Veda does not possess that superhuman authority which is ascribed to it by Badarayana, I cannot bring myself to believe that this concession on the part of Kapila was a mere artifice to escape the fate which, for instance, befell Buddha. There are many passages where Kapila appeals quite naturally to Sruti or revelation.

In I, 36 he appeals to both Sruti and Nyaya, reasonmg, but in many places he appeals to Sruti alone. That revelation is to be looked upon as superior to experience or sensuous perception is stated by him in so many words in I, 147, where we read: 'There is no denial of what is established by Sruti.' Again, when the Nyaya philosophy tries to establish by reasoning that the organs of sense are formed of the elements, Kapila squashes the whole argument by a simple appeal to Sruti. 'They cannot be so formed,' he says, 'because Sruti says that they are formed of Ahamkara, self-consciousness.'

Other passages where the authority of Sruti is invoked as paramount by Kapila, or supposed to be so by the commentator, may be found in Samkhya-Sutras I, 36; 77; 83; 147; 154; II, 20, 22; III, 15; 80; IV, 22; etc.

PARALLEL DEVELOPMENT OF PHILOSOPHICAL SYSTEMS

The result of this desire to fix dates, where dates are impossible, has often proved most mischievous. Scholars of recognised authority have arrived at and given expression to convictions, not only widely different, but diametrically opposed to each other. The chief cause of this confusion has been that, by a very natural tendency, we always wish to arrange things *Nacheinander* or in causal connection, instead of being satisfied with taking things as *Nebeneinander,* parallel and formed under similar conditions, springing from a common source and flowing on side by side in the same direction.

A reference to the history of language may make my meaning clearer. None would say that Greek was older than Latin. Greek has some forms more primitive than Latin, but Latin also has some forms more primitive than Greek. It is true that we know literary productions in Greek at a much earlier time than literary productions in Latin, nor would any Sanskrit scholar deny that the Sutras of Badarayana are older than the Samkhya-Sutras, as we now possess the two. But for all that,

Greek, as a language, cannot be a day older than Latin. Both branched off, slowly it may be and almost imperceptibly at first, from the time when the Aryan separation took place. In their embryonic form they both go back to some indefinite date, far beyond the limits of any chronology. In India we may learn how, like language, religion, and mythology, philosophy also formed at first a kind of common property. We meet with philosophical ideas of a Vedantic character, though as yet in a very undecided form, as far back as the hymns of the Rig-veda; they meet us again in the Brahmanas and in some of the Upanishads, while the Samkhya ideas stand out less prominently, owing, it would seem, to the ascendency gained at that early period already by the Vedanta. Instead of supposing, however, that passages in support of Samkhya ideas occurring in certain of the older Upanishads were foisted in at a later time, it seems far more probable to me that they were survivals of an earlier period of as yet undifferentiated philosophical thought.

BUDDHISM SUBSEQUENT TO UPANISHADS

What remains of the chronological framework of Indian philosophy is in the end not much more than that both Vedanta and Samkhya ideas existed before the rise of historical Buddhism. The very name of Upanishad, for instance, is so peculiar that its occurrence in ancient Buddhist texts proves once for all the existence of some of these works before the rise of Buddhism.

The recognition of mendicant friars also, as a social institution, seems to me simply taken over from the Brahmans. The very name of Bhikkhu, applied to the members of the Buddhist fraternity, comes from the same source. It is true, no doubt, that the name of Bhikshu does not occur in the classical

Upanishads, but the right of begging, whether in the first or the third of the Asramas (Brahmacharin or Vanaprastha), is fully recognised, only that the third and fourth .Asramas are not so clearly distinguished in early times as they are in Manu and afterwards. In the Kaush. Up. II, 2 we read of a man who has begged through a village and got nothing (Bhikshitva); in the Chhand. Up. IV, 3, 5, a Brahmacharin is mentioned who has begged. The technical term for this begging is Bhikshacharya in the Brih. Ar. Up. III (V), 5, I, and exactly the same compound, Bhikkhacharya, occurs in the Dhammapada 392; Bhaikshacharya occurs also in the Mundaka I, 2, II, so that the fact that the substantive Bhikshu does not occur in the classical Upanishads can hardly be used as an argument to prove that the status of the mendicant friar was not known before the spreading of Buddhism. It is true that in its social meaning Asrama, the name of the three or four stages, does not occur in the classical Upanishads; but, as we find Asramin in the Maitray. Up. IV, 3, we can hardly doubt that the three or four stages (Brahmachari, Gahattho, Vanapattho, Bhikkhu) were known before the rise of Buddhism, and taken over by the Buddhists from the Vedic Brahmans. Socially, the only Asramas that remained among the Buddhists were two, that of the Grihins and that of the Bhikkhus.

That many of the technical terms of the Buddhists (Uposhadha etc.) could have come from the same source only, has long been known, so much so that it has been rightly said, Without Brahmanism no Buddhism.

The institution of the Vasso, for instance, the retreat during the rainy season, is clearly taken over from the Varshas, the rainy season, as kept by the Brahmans, and so is the quinquennial celebration of the Panchavarsha-parishad, and many other customs adopted by the Buddhists.

LALITA-VISTARA

I have explained before why at present I attribute less importance than I did formerly to the occurrence of a number of titles, including Samkhya, Yoga, Vaiseshika, and possibly Nyaya, in the Lalita-vistara. If the date assigned by Stanislas Julien and others to certain Chinese translations of this work could be re-established, the passage so often quoted from the twelfth chapter would be of considerable value to us in forming an idea of Indian literature as it existed at the time when the Lalita-vistara was originally composed. We find here the names not only of the Vedic glossary (Nighantu?) The Nigamas (part of Nirukta), Puranas, Itihasas, Vedas, grammar, Nirukta, Siksha, Chhandas, ritual (Kalpa), astronomy (Jyotisha), but, what would be most important for us: the names of three systems of philosophy also, Samkhya, Yoga, and Vaiseshika, while Hetuvidya can hardly be meant for anything but Nyaya. But until the dates of the various Chinese translations of the Life of Buddha have been re-examined, we must abstain from using them for assigning any dates to their Sanskrit originals.

ASVAGHOSHA'S BUDDHA-CHARITA

We may perhaps place more reliance on Asvaghosha's Buddha-charita, which, with great probability, has been ascribed to the first century A.D. He mentions Vyasa, the son of Sarasvati, as the compiler of the Veda, though not of the Vedanta-Sutras; he knows Valmiki, the author of the Ramayana, Atreya as a teacher of medicine, and Janaka, the well-known king, as a teacher of Yoga. By far the most important passage in it for our present purpose is the conversation between Arada and the future Buddha, here already called Bodhisattva in the twelfth book. This Arada is clearly a teacher of Samkhya-philosophy, it may be of Samkhya in an earlier state; and, though the name of Samkhya does not occur, the name of Kapila does (XII, 21), and even a disciple of his is mentioned. Here then we have in a poem, ascribed to the first century A.D., a clear reference to that philosophical system which is known to us under the name of Samkhya, and we have actually the name of Kapila, the reputed author of that system. The name of Kapilavastu also occurs, as the birthplace of Buddha and as the dwelling of the famous sage Kapila. No reference to the Vedanta has been met within Asvaghosha's Buddha-Charita, though the substitution of the Vedantic name of Brahman for the Samkhya name of Purusha deserves attention.

BUDDHIST SUTTAS

If we consult the Buddhist Suttas, which, whatever the date of their original composition may have been, were at all events reduced to writing in the first century B.C., and may be safely used therefore as historical evidence for that time, we find there also views ascribed to the Brahmans of Buddha's time which clearly breathe the spirit of the Samkhya-philosophy. But it would be very unsafe to say more, and to maintain that such passages prove in any way the existence of fully developed systems of philosophy, or of anything very different from what we find already in certain Upanishads. All we can say is that there are a number of terms in the Suttas which are the very terms used in the Vedanta, Samkhya and Yoga-philosophies, such as Atman, Sasvata, Nitya (Anitya), Akshobhya, Brahman, Isvara, Dharma, Parinama, and many more; but, so far as I know, there is not one of which we could say that it could have been taken from the Sutras only, and from nowhere else.

We should remember that in the Buddhist Canon we find constant mention of Titthiyas or Tirthakas and their heretical systems of philosophy. Six contemporaries of Buddha are mentioned, one of them, Nigantho Nataputta, being the well-known founder of Jainism, Purana Kassapa; Makkhali, Ajita, Pakudha and Sanjaya. Nor are the names of the reputed authors of the six systems of Brahmanic-philosophy absent from the Tripitaka. But we hear nothing of any literary compositions ascribed to Badarayana, Jaimini, Kapila, Patanjali, Gotama or Kanada. Some of these names occur in the Buddhist Sanskrit texts also, such as the Lankavatara where the names of Kanada, Kapila, Akshapada, and Brihaspati are met with, but again not a single specimen or extract from their compositions.

ASVALAYANA'S GRIHYA-SUTRAS

Another help for determining the existence of ancient Sutras and Bhashyas may be found in the Grihya-Sutras of Asvalayana and Samkhayana, works belonging to the age of Vedic literature, though it may be to the very end of what I call the Sutra-period. Here, as I pointed out in 1859 in my History of Ancient Sanskrit Literature, we find not only the Rig-veda with all its subdivisions, but such names as Sumantu, Jaimini, Vaisampayana, Paila, Sutras, Bhashyas, Bharata, Mahabharata, teachers of the law, Jananti, Bahavi, Gargya, Gautama, Sakalya, Babhravya, Mandavya, Mandukeya, Gargi Vachaknavi, Vadava Pratitheyi, Sulabha Maitreyi, Kahola Kaushitaka, Mahakaushitaka, Paimgya, Mahapaimgya, Suyajna Samkhayana, Aitareya, Mahaitareya, the Sakala (text), the Bashkala (text), Sujatavaktra, Audavahi, Mahaudvahi, Saujami, Saunaka, Asvalayana, etc. The Samkhayana Grihya-Sutras give the same list, though leaving out a few names and adding others. The most valuable part in both sets of Grihya-Sutras is their testifying at that early and probably pre-Buddhistic time, not only to the existence of Sutras, but of Bhashyas or commentaries also, without which, as I said before, neither the philosophical, nor the grammatical, nor any other Sutras would even have been intelligible, or even possible.

DID BUDDHA BORROW FROM KAPILA?

I may seem very sceptical in all this, but I cannot even now bring myself to believe that the author of Buddhism borrowed from the Samkhya or any other definite system of philosophy, as known to us in its final Sutras form, in the sense which we ourselves assign to borrowing. Buddha, it seems to me, had as much right to many of the so-called Samkhya or Vedanta ideas as Kapila or anybody else. Who would say, for instance, that his belief in Samsara or migration of souls was borrowed from Badarayana or Kapila? It belonged to everybody in India as much as a belief in Karman or the continuous working of deeds. In the great dearth of historical dates it may no doubt be excusable, if we lay hold of anything to save us from drowning while exploring the chronology of Indian literature. Our difficulties are very great, for even when the names of the principal systems of philosophy and the names of their reputed authors are mentioned, how do we know that they refer to anything written that we possess? Unless we meet with *verbatim* quotations, we can never know whether a certain book of a certain author is intended, or simply the general Parampara, that is, the tradition, as handed down in various Asramas, two things which should be carefully distinguished.

It is strange to see how often our hopes have been roused and disappointed. We were told that in Professor Hardy's most valuable edition of the Anguttara, a number of philosophical sects were mentioned which existed at the time of Buddha's appearance, such as (1) Ajivakas, (2) Niganthas, (3) Mundasavakas, (4) Jatilakas, (5) Paribbajakas, (6) Magandikas, (7) Tedandikas, (8) Aviruddhakas, (9) Gotamakas, and (10) Devadhammikas. But not one of these names helps us to a real chronological date. Ajivakas and Niganthas are the names of Jaina ascetics, the latter belonging to the Digambara sects, which could hardly have been established long before Buddha's appearance, while Mundasavakas, i.e., pupils of the shaveling, the Buddha, and Gotamakas would seem to be schools which owed their existence to Buddha himself.

The other names Jatilakas, ascetics, Paribbajakas, religious mendicants, Tedandikas, i.e., sanyasins carrying the three staves, would be applicable both to Brahmanic and Buddhist sects. Magandikas, if meant for Magadhikas, people of Magadha, would be Buddhists again. Aviruddhakas, a name not clear to me, may have been intended for ascetics no longer impeded by any desires, while Devadhammikas are clearly worshippers of the ancient national Devas, and therefore Brahmanic, and possibly Vedic. We get no historical dates from the names of any of these schools, if schools they were. All they teach is that at the time Brahmanic and Buddhist sects were existing side by side in large numbers, but by no means, as is commonly supposed, in constant conflict with each other. Of the six recognised systems of philosophy of their eponymous heroes or their written works, we do not hear a single word.

BANA'S HARSHACHARITA

Not even in later works, which have been referred to the sixth, seventh, and eighth centuries A.D., do we meet with actual quotations from our Sutras of the six Darsanas. Bana, in his Life of King Harsha, knows indeed of Aupanishadas, Kapilas, Kanadas; and if the Kapilas are the followers of the Samkhya, Kanadas the followers of the Vaiseshika school, the Aupanishadas can hardly be meant for anybody but the Vedantins. Varaha-Mihira, also in the sixth century A.D., mentions Kapila and Kanabhuj (Vaiseshika), but even this does not help us to the dates of any Sutras composed by them.

The Chinese translator of the Karikas, likewise in the sixth century, informs us that these Karikas contain the words of Kapila or of Panchasikha, the pupil of Asuri, who was the pupil of Kapila. We are told even that there were originally 60,000 Gathas, and all that Isvara-Krishna did was to select seventy of them for his seventy or seventy-two Karikas.

That Madhava (1350 A.D.), while mentioning the Sutras of the other systems, should not have mentioned those of the Samkhya, is no doubt, as I pointed out before, a strong argument in support of their non-existence in his time. But it is no proof, as little as we may conclude from the fact that Hiuen-tsang translated the Vaiseshika-nikaya-dasapadartha-sastra by Jnanachandra, and not the Vaiseshika-Sutras by Kanada, that therefore these Sutras did not exist in his time. We cannot be too careful in such matters, for the unreserved acceptance of a purely conjectural date is very apt to interfere with the discovery of a real date. Hiuen-tsang likewise mentions a number of Nyaya works, but not Gotama's Nyaya-Sutras. Does that prove that Gotama's Sutras were unknown in the seventh century? It may or may not. He relates that Gunamati defeated a famous Samkhya philosopher of the name of Madhava, but again he tells us no more. His own special study, as is well known, was the Yoga-philosophy. And here again, though he speaks of a number of Yoga works, he says not a word of the most important of them all, the Sutras of Patanjali. Yet I doubt whether we may conclude from this that these Sutras did not exist at his time.

VEDANTA SAYINGS

But teachers who follow the Vedanta such as Harihara, Hiranyagarbha, Vyasa and others, describe Purusha as one. Any why so? Because, as the Vedanta says,

1. Purush is all this, what has been and what is to be, he is lord of that immortality which springs up by (sacrificial) food, that is, he is beyond the immortality of the ordinary immortal gods.
2. That is Agni, that is Vayu, that is Surya, that is Chandramas, that is pure, that is Brahman, that is water and Prajapati.
3. That is true, that is immortal; it is liberation, it is the highest point, it is indestructible, it is the glory of the sun;
4. Higher than which there is nothing else, nothing smaller, and nothing greater, the One stands like a tree planted in the sky; by him and by the Purusha, all this is filled.
5. Having hands and feet everywhere, having mouth, head and eyes everywhere, hearing everywhere in this world, it stands covering everything;
6. Shining through the qualities (Guna) of all the senses, and yet free from all the senses, the master of all, the Lord, the great refuge of all;
7. He is all substances everywhere, the Self of all, the

source of all; that in which everything is absorbed, that the sages know as Brahman.

8. For there is but one Self of beings, settled in everybody, it is seen as one and as many, like the moon in the water.
9. For he alone, the great Self, dwells in all beings; whether moving or motionless, he by whom all this was spread out.
10. This Self of the world is one—by whom was it made manifold? Some speak of the Self as several, because of the existence of knowledge, and because knowledge is different in different people.
11. Wise people see the same (Atman) in the Brahman, in worms and insects, in the outcast, in the dog and the elephant, in beasts, cows, gadflies, and gnats.
12. 13. As one and the same string passes through gold, and pearls, jewels, corals, porcelain, and silver, thus is one and the same Self to be known as dwelling everywhere in cows, men, and in elephants, deer, etc.

We see in these extracts a mixture of Vedanta and Samkhya terms and ideas; and in verse 10 the two views of Brahman being one, and the Purusha being many, are given in the same breath.

EARLY RELATION BETWEEN VEDANTA AND SAMKHYA

The relation between Samkhya and Vedanta during the Upanishad-period is by no means clear. Most scholars seem to regard it as a kind of syncretism, but it may also represent to us a period of philosophic thought when these two views of the world were not yet finally differentiated, and were not felt to be altogether incompatible. Though there is in the

Upanishads which we possess a decided preponderance of a Vedantic interpretation of the world, the Samkhya philosophers are not altogether wrong when they maintain that their view also can be supported by Vedic authority. All these views were at first no more than guesses at truth, gropings in the dark; but the idea that if the one was right the other must be wrong, belongs decidedly to a later period, to that of systematised and controversial philosophy. There are certain technical terms, such as Purusha, Buddhi, Gunas, etc., which are looked upon as the peculiar property of the Samkhya, and others, such as Atman, Brahman, Avidya, Maya, etc., which remind us at once of the Vedanta-philosophy; but even these terms are used far more freely in the Brahmanas and Upanishads than in the Darsanas, nor are they always used in the same sense or in the same order by earlier and later authorities.

Thus we read in the Kathaka Up. III, 10, II:

'Beyond the senses are the objects (Artha), beyond the objects is the mind (Manas), beyond the mind is intellect (Buddhi), the Great Self (Mahan Atma) is beyond the intellect. Beyond the Great there is the Undeveloped (Avyakta), beyond the undeveloped there is the Purusha, beyond the Purusha there is nothing, that is the goal, the highest point.'

In the same Upanishad, VI, 7, 8, we read:

'Beyond the senses is the mind, beyond the mind the highest being (Sattvam Uttamam), higher than that being is the great Self (Mahan Atma), beyond this great (Self) is the highest, the Undeveloped.

'Beyond the Undeveloped is the Purusha, the all-pervading and imperceptible. Every creature that knows him is liberated, and obtains immortality.'

The successive development, as here described, is not in strict accordance with the systematic Samkhya, but still less does it represent to us Vedantic ideas. Even the two accounts, as given in the same Upanishad, vary slightly, showing to us how little of technical accuracy there was as yet during the Upanishad-period. We get:

	III, 10, 11	VI, 7, 8
1.	Indriyas	Indriyas
2.	Arthas	–
3.	Manas	Manas
4.	Buddhi	Sattvam Uttamam
5.	Mahan Atma	Mahan Atma
6.	Avyakta.	Avyakta
7.	Purusha	Purusha

The omission of the Arthas as objects would not signify because, as Indriyarthas, they are implied by the Indriyas or senses. But why should Buddhi, generally the first emanation of Prakriti in its undeveloped (Avyakta) state, be replaced by Sattvam Uttamam, the Highest Being? The word may be meant for Buddhi, for Buddhi is often called Mahat, the Great, but why it should be called Great is difficult to say. It is certainly not an equivalent of the Phoenician Mot, as Professor Wilson conjectured many yearg ago. Mahan Atma looks like a Vedantic term, but even then it would only occupy the place of Jivatma, the individualised Self, and how could this be said to emanate from the Avyakta?

Another passage which reminds us of Samkhya rather than of Vedanta-philosophy occurs in the Maitray. Up. II,S, where we read: 'He who has the name of Purusha, and is very small, intangible; invisible, dwells of his own will here in part, as a man who is fast asleep awakes of his own will. And this part, which is entirely intelligent, present in every single man, knowing the body, attested by conceiving (Manas), willing (Buddhi), and belief in subject and object (Ahamkara) is Prajapati, called Visva. By him, the intelligent, is the body made intelligent, and he is the driver thereof.'

This passage does not contain much of Samkhya thought, yet the words Purusha and possibly Buddhipurvam seem to allude to Kapila's ideas rather than to those of Badarayana. Other words also, such as Samkalpa, Adhyavasaya and Abhimana, in the sense of Ahamkara, point to the same source. The whole passage, however, is obscure, nor does the commentator help us much, unless he is right in recognising here the germs of the later Vedantic ideas of a Prajapati, called Visva or Vaisvanara (Vedanta-sara, 138), Taijasa and Prajna.

One more passage of the Maitray. Upanishad, III, 2, may here be mentioned, as reminding us of Samkhya doctrines. There we read: 'There is indeed that other different one, called the elemental Self (Bhutatma) who, overcome by the bright and dark fruits of action, enters on a good or evil birth, so that his course is upward or downward, and that overpowered by the pairs (the opposites) he roams about. And this is the explanation. The five Tanmatras (of sound, touch, light, taste, and smell) are called Bhuta (elements), and, the five Mahabhutas (gross elements) also are called Bhuta. Then the aggregate of all these is called Sarira, body, and he who dwells in that body is called Bhutatman (the elementary Atman). True, his immortal Atman (Self) remains untainted, like a drop of water on a lotus-leaf; but he, the Bhutatman, is in the power of the Gunas of Prakriti. Then, thus overpowered, he becomes bewildered, and because thus bewildered, he sees not the creator, i.e., the holy Lord, abiding within him. Carried along by the Gunas, darkened, unstable, fickle, crippled, full of devices; vacillating, he enters into Abhimana (conceit of subject and object), believing "I am he, this is mine," etc. He binds himself by himself, as a bird is bound by a net, and, overcome afterwards by the fruits of what he has done, he enters on a good or evil birth, downward or upward in his course, and, overcome by the pairs, he roams about.

Here we see again a mixture of Samkhya and Vedanta ideas, the Samkhya claiming such terms as Prakriti and Gunas, the Vedanta such terms as Atman and possibly Bhutatman. This Bhutatman, however, is by no means so clear as has sometimes been imagined. It is a term peculiar to the Maitray. Upanishad, and seems to have been borrowed from it when it occurs in some of the later Upanishads. If, like many other things in the Maitray. Upanishad, it is to be looked upon as belonging to the Samkhya-system, we must remember that Atman, though quoted sometimes as a synonym of Purusha., cannot be supposed to stand here for Purusha. A compound such as Bhuta-Purusha would be impossible. The Maitray, Up. III, I itself says that the Atman of Bhutatman is another, though likewise called Atman, and that he dwells in the body, Sarira, which is a compound of Tanmatras, Bhutas, and Mahabhutas. It would therefore correspond to the Vedantic Jivatman. But if this Bhutatman is said to spring from Prakriti, it could not possibly stand for the Purusha of the Samkhyas, because their Purusha does not spring from Prakriti, as little as Prakriti springs from him. Nor could any Atman be said to be purely objective. In fact, strictly speaking, this Bhutatman fits neither into the Vedanta, nor into the Samkhya-philosophy, and would rather seem to belong to a philosophy in which these two views of the world were not yet finally separated.

Another difficult and rather obscure expression in the Maitray. Upanishad is Niratman, an expression which would be impossible in the Vedanta-philosophy, and is certainly perplexing even in the Samkhya.

A similar mixture of philosophical terms meets us in the Svetasvatara Upanishad. In verse I, 10, for instance, we have Pradhana, which is Samkhya, and Maya, which is Vedanta, at least the later Vedanta, while in IV, 10 Maya is directly identified with Prakriti. Purusha occurs in III, 12, where it evidently stands for Brahman, IV, 1. But though in this Upanishad Samkhya ideas would seem to prevail, Vedanta ideas are not excluded. The very name of Samkhya and Yoga. occurs (VI, 13), but the name of Vedanta also is not absent, (VI, 22). In all this we may possibly get a glimpse of a state of Indian philosophy which was, as yet, neither pure Samkhya nor pure Vedanta, unless we look on these Upanishads as of a far more modern date, and on their philosophy as the result of a later syncretism.

THE TRUE MEANING OF THE SAMKHYA

In giving an account of the Samkhya, I have followed entirely the Tattva-samasa, without mixing it up with the Karikas or Sutras. I was quite aware that the Karikas or the Sutras might have supplied us with a clearer and better arranged account of that philosophy. But if I am right, that the Tattva-samasa is older than either, it seemed to me more important that we should know what the Samkhya really was in its original form. By comparing the Tattva-samasa with the Karikas and Sutras, we can easily see how this dry system was developed in later times. But though the Karikas and Sutras give us a more systematic account of the Samkhya, all that is essential can be found in the Samasa, if only we try to arrange the dry facts for ourselves. It must be confessed, no doubt, that neither in the Sutras, the Karikas, nor in the Tattva-samasa,do we find what we most value in every philosophy, an insight into the mind and heart of the founder of that philosophical system. If we were asked why such a system should ever have been imagined and elaborated, or what kind of comfort, whether intellectual or moral, it could have afforded to any human being, we should indeed have little to answer. All we can learn is that a man crushed by the burden of what is called the threefold misery, and seeing no hope of relief either by means of good actions or of sacrifices, which can promise no more than a temporary happiness on earth or in heaven, should seek advice from a philosopher, such as Kapila, believing that he could procure for him entire freedom from all his troubles.

At first sight no two philosophies would seem to be so different from each other, nay, to start from such opposite points of view as the Vedanta and the Samkhya. The Vedantist of the school of Samkara looks upon the whole world, including animate and inanimate nature, including the small gods and the still smaller men, as a phenomenal manifestation of an unknown power which he calls Brahman. There is nothing beside It, nothing that can be called real except this one invisible Brahman. Then came the question: But whence this phenomenal world or rather, as he starts with the idea of there being but one real being from eternity to eternity, How could that eternal Brahman ever give rise to the world, not only as its efficient, but also as its material cause, if indeed there is anything material in the objects known to the Vedantist. Under the circumstances thus given, but one answer is possible, that

Brahman is the world, and that the world, so far as it is Brahman, but so far only, is real. The phenomenal world, such as we see it and live in it, is changeful, ever passing away, and consequently never, in the Vedantic sense of that word, real. We never see it or know it, as it really is, until we have become Vedantists. It is impossible to think that this eternal Being, whatever name be given to it, could ever change or be changed. This view of the universe as a development of Brahman was possibly the original view taken by Badarayana, and it was clearly that of Ramanuja and his followers, who explain the world as an evolution (Parinama). But this was not Samkara's theory. He accepts the two facts that the world is changing and unreal, and yet that the real cause of it, that is, Brahman, is incapable of change.

VEDANTA, AVIDYA AND AVIVEKA

Hence nothing remains but to ascribe the changeful phenomenal character of the world to something else, and, according to the Vedanta, to ignorance, not, however, to our individual ignorance, but to some primeval ignorance directed towards Brahman as manifested and seen. This ignorance or Avidya, again, is not to be called real, it is nothing by the side of Brahman, nothing therefore that could ever have dominion over Brahman. All such views are excluded by the postulate that Brahman is free, is one and all; though here again, other Vedantists differ from Samkara, and represent Avidya as an actual power (Sakti) of Brahman, or as Maya, i.e., illusive power, which in fact performs, or is answerable for what we call creation. We should of course ask at once, Whence comes that Avidya or that Maya, and what is it? How can it be anything, if not again Brahman, the only thing that exists? The answer given by Samkara, which satisfied his mind, if not the minds of other Vedantists, was that we know as a fact that Avidya or Nescience is there, but we also know that it is not there, as soon as we see through it, in fact, as soon as we are able to annihilate it by Vidya or knowledge, such as is given to us by the Vedanta-philosophy.

The Vedantist holds that nothing that can be annihilated can claim true reality for itself. Therefore Avidya, though it is, must not be called something real. The great difficulty how Brahman could ever be affected by Avidya, which is a weakness or a defect, is avoided by looking upon Brahman, while affected by Avidya or seen through Avidya, as for the time under a cloud or forgetful of itself, but never really unreal. We ourselves also, that is the individual souls, can be in full reality nothing but Brahman, though for a while we are divided from it, because forgetful of Brahman through Avidya. While that state of Avidya lasts the true Brahman, neuter, may become to us Brahman, masculine, may become the creator and ruler of the world, and, as such, receive worship from his creatures. But as soon as the cloud of Avidya is lifted, this creator also recedes and is restored at once to his true state and dignity. He, the so-called Isvara, or Lord, or Creator, becomes what he is and always has been, the whole Brahman; and we ourselves also remember and thereby recover our true Brahmanhood, or Selfhood, not as if we had ever been divided from it, but only as having been blinded for a while by Avidya so as to forget ourselves, our true Self, that is Brahman.

If the Vedantist explains what we call Creation as the result of Avidya or Nescience, the Samkhya explains it by the temporary union between Purusha and Prakriti. This union is said to arise from a want of discrimination (Aviveka), and it is not in the highest sense a real union, because it vanishes again by discriminating knowledge (Viveka), nay, it is actually said to have the one object only of evoking at last in the Purusha a revulsion, and in the end a clear recognition of his complete independence, and his freedom from Prakriti. Thus the creation of the phenomenal world and our position in the phenomenal world are due to Nescience (Avidya) with the Vedantist, but to a want of discrimination (Aviveka) with the Samkhya philosopher, and this want of discrimination is actually called by the Vedantic term of Avidya in the Yoga-Sutras, II, 24.

Where then, we may well ask, is the difference between the two views of the universe? There is a difference in the mode of representation, no doubt, but in the end both Vedanta and Samkhya look upon what we call reality as the result of a temporary error, call it nescience, illusion, want of discrimination, or anything else. If, therefore, philosophers like Vijnana-Bhikshu recognised this original similarity in the tendencies both of the Vedanta and the Samkhya, it is hardly fair to blame them as having mixed and confounded the two. No doubt these two philosophies diverged in their later development, but they started with the same object in view, and they advanced for a time in the same direction. If the Vedantists desired to arrive at what is called Atmanatma-viveka, discrimination between Atman and Anatman, the Samkhyas looked forward to Prakriti-purusha viveka, discrimination between Purusha and Prakriti. Where then is the difference? If their later defenders forget their common interest and laid greater stress on the points of difference than on the points of similarity between them, it was but right that those who could see deeper, should bring to light whatever features there were left of the original family likeness between the two philosophies.

It is necessary, at all events that we should see all this clearly, just as Vijnana-Bhikshu and other philosophers saw it clearly, in order to perceive the unity that underlies the apparent diversity in the philosophy of India. Nor should we ever forget that our philosophical Sutras, whatever their age, whether of the fourteenth century A.D. or the fifth century B.C., are but the last outcome of the philosophical activity of a whole country, and that we are entirely ignorant of their historical antecedents. We should remember that the grammatical Sutras of Panini are contradicted again and again by grammatical forms which have fortunately been preserved to us in the earlier Brahmanas and Mantras of the Vedic period. We have no such remnants of an early period of philosophy anterior to the Sutras, with the exception of the as yet unsystematised Upanishads, and possibly of some of the more ancient parts of the Mahabharata; but in other respects we are left without any earlier facts, though not without a firm conviction that such perfect systems as we find in the Sutras cannot have sprung up in a day, still less from one brain, but that they must have passed through many changes for better or for worse, before they could assume that final and permanent form in which they are now presented to us in literature. The Sutras are, in fact, the final outcome of ages of inquiry and discussion.

It would seem then to follow from Vijnana-Bhikshu's remarks, that in India a philosopher might at one and the same time have been a follower of the Vedanta as well as of the Samkhya, if he could only see that, where the two follow different roads, they started nevertheless from the same point and were proceeding towards the same goal. If this is seen and accepted in a historical spirit, it can do no harm, though no doubt there is danger of the distinctive features of each system becoming blurred, if we dwell too much on what they share in common or on what they may have shared in common at an earlier period of their growth. In one respect Vijnana-Bhikshu, to mention him only, has certainly seen more rightly by not resorting at once to the idea that actual borrowing must have taken place, whenever Vedanta and Samkhya shared the same ideas. We should always remember that there must have been a period of unrestricted growth of philosophical thought in ancient India, and that during that period philosophical ideas, whether true or false, were common property and could be freely adopted by different schools of philosophy. It was in the Sutras that these schools became sterilised and petrified.

On one point Vijnana-Bhikshu may have gone too far, yielding to a temptation which does not exist for us. To him not only Vedanta and Samkhya, but all the six Darsanas or systems of philosophy were orthodox, they were all Smriti, though not Sruti. Hence his natural desire to show that they did not on any essential points contradict each other. After he had reconciled to his own satisfaction the conflicting tenets of Vedanta and Samkhya, and had certainly, at least to my mind, succeeded in discovering the common background of both of them, he attempted to do the same for the Nyaya and Vaiseshika. These two, as he says, as they represent the Self as endowed with qualities, might seem to be contradicted by the Vedanta and Samkhya which show that the Self, or the Purusha, cannot be endowed with qualities; but this is not so. Nyaya and Vaiseshika are intended, as he thinks, as a first step only towards the truth; and though they admit the self to be qualified by pain and joy, they teach that the Self is at all events different from the body. This is what marks the first advance toward a right understanding of the Self, not only as different from the body, but as unaffected by pain and joy, as neither suffering nor enjoying, as neither thinking nor acting in any way.

To the followers of the Nyaya-philosophy also, Brahman, the Absolute, is Anirvachaniya, undefinable or inexpressible. The full light, however, of the Samkhya-doctrine might dazzle the beginner, and hence, according to Vijnana-Bhikshu, the usefulness of the Nyaya and Vaiseshika, as slowly preparing him for the acceptance of the highest truth. There does not, however, seem to be any ancient evidence to support this view of Vijnana-Bhikshu's, that the Nyaya and Vaiseshika were intended as a preparation only, still less that they existed as systems before the doctrines of the Samkhya began to influence the thinkers of India. The Samkhya is indeed mentioned in the Mahabharata (XII, III, 98) as the highest truth, but the other systems are never represented as merely preparations for it. They present themselves as independent philosophies, quite as much as the other Darsanas: nor do I remember any passage where Gotama and Kanada themselves represent their teaching as a mere step leading to the higher knowledge of Vedanta or Samkhya, nor any utterance of Badarayana or Kapila to the effect that such preparation was required.

ORIGIN OF AVIDYA

The question which the Samkhya may seem to have left unanswered, but which is really unanswerable, is, how this Aviveka, this failure of Purusha to recognise himself as distinct from Prakriti, could ever have arisen, and how and by what stages the development of Prakriti may be supposed to have taken place which led in the end to the delusion of Purusha and made him look on the senses, on the Manas (central sense), on the Aham or ego, nay, on Buddhi or intellect, on everything, in fact, within his experience, as belonging to him, as his own.

What Kapila wishes to teach is that nothing is in reality his own or belongs to him except his Self, or, as he calls it, the Purusha. Here we can observe a real difference between Samkhya and Vedanta. And while in all these discussions Badarayana had only to appeal to the Veda in support of any one of his statements, Kapila, with all his regard for Aptavachana, had evidently meant to reason out his system by himself, though without any declared antagonism to the Vedas. Hence the Sutras of Kapila received the name of Manana-sastra, institute of reasoned truth.

THE SASTRA

If then it is asked how Kapila came to know anything about Prakriti which, as superintended by Purusha, is said to stand for the whole of creation, and how we ourselves can know anything about its various developments, beginning with Buddhi or intellect, and going on from Buddhi to Ahamkara, the making of the I or Ego, or subjectivity as inseparable from objectivity, and from Ahamkara to the Tanmatras or subtle substances, etc., we have to confess with the author of the Samkhya sastra that there was nothing but the Sastra itself to depend on in support of what may be felt to be very crude and startling assertions. Sastra sometimes stands for Veda, but it cannot well be taken in that sense here. It seems rather to point to the existence of a treatise, such as the Samkhya-karika or the original text of the Samkhya Sutras, or the whole body of Samkhya-philosophy, as handed down from time immemorial in various schools in India. At first sight, no doubt, it seems strange to us to derive Buddhi or Intellect from Prakriti, nature, or from Avyakta, the undeveloped. But we must remember that all these English renderings are very imperfect. Prakriti is very different from nature or though there is hardly a more convenient term to render it by. In the Samkhya-philosophy Prakriti is a postulated something that exists, and that produces everything without being itself produced. When it is called Avyakta, that means that it is, at first, chaotic, undeveloped, and invisible.

DEVELOPMENT OF PRAKRITI

In place of this one Prakriti we often read of eight Prakritis, those beginning with Buddhi or the Mahat being distinguished as produced as well as producing, while the first, the Avyakta, is producing only, but not produced. This need not mean more than that the seven modifications (Vikaras) and forms of Prakriti are all effects, and serve again as causes, while the Avyakta itself, the undeveloped Prakriti, has no antecedent cause, but serves as cause only for all the other forms of Prakriti.

RETROSPECT

After going through the long list of topics which form the elements of the Samkhya-philosophy, it may be well to try to give a more general view of Kapila's system.

Whether we begin with the beginning, the postulated Prakriti, or with the end, the phenomenal world as reflected by the Indriyas and the Manas, it is but natural that Kapila should have asked himself the question how what was postulated as the beginning, the undeveloped Prakriti, could account for all that was to follow, or how all that did follow could be traced back to this postulated Prakriti. Given the undeveloped Prakriti, he imagined that it was due to the disturbance of the equilibrium of its three constituents (Gunas) that it was first awakened to life and light or thought, to physical and intellectual activity. Some such impulse is required by all metaphysicians. This first step in the development of Prakriti, this first awakening of the inert substance, is conceived by

Kapila as Buddhi, the lighting up, and hence, so long as it is confined to Prakriti, described as Prakasa, or light, the chief condition of all perception.

After Prakriti has thus been lighted up and become Buddhi, or potential perception, another distinction was necessary in this luminous and perceiving mass, in this so-called Mahat or Buddhi, namely, the differentiation between perceiver and what is perceived, between subject and object. This was the work assigned, I believe, to Ahamkara, which I should prefer to translate by subjectivation rather than by Ego or Egoism.

This step from Buddhi to Ahamkara has been compared to DesCartes' *Cogito ergo sum*, but is it not rather *Sum, er go cogito*, as showing that being itself would be impossible unless it were first lighted up, and differentiated into subject and object; that *esse*, in fact, is *percipi*, or even *percipere*.

When the evolution of the Avyakta has gone so far, the question arises, how this process of perception could take place, how perception is possible subjectively, how it is possible objectively. If we begin with the objective side, the answer of Kapila is that there must be Tanmatras (This-only), potential perceptibilia, which are not the potentialities of everything in general, but of this and this only (Tan-matra). These five potentialities are sound, touch, odour, light, and taste. They are not yet what is actually heard, seen, etc., nor what actually hears and sees, but they contain the possibilities of both. As there is no hearing without sound, the Samkhyas seem to have argued, neither is there any sound without hearing. But there is in the Tanmatras the potentiality of both. Hence, according to the division produced by Ahamkara into subject and object, the five Tanmatras are realised as the five subjective powers of perception, the powers of hearing, touching, smelling, seeing, and tasting, and corresponding to them as the five objects of sense, the objects of sound, touch, odour, sight, and taste. In their final form the five potential Tanmatras stand before us in their material shape, subjectively as ear, skin, nose, eyes, and tongue, objectively as ether, air, light, water, and earth (the five Mahabhutas). These five supply all possible and real forms under which perception can and does take place.

It should be remembered, however, that in order to account for perception such as it really is, another, a sixth sense, is necessary, in addition to the five, which is called Manas, generally translated by mind, but really a kind of central organ of perception, acting as a door-keeper, meant to prevent the crowding in of perceptions, to arrange them into percepts, and, as we should say, into concepts also, being in fact the *conditio sine que non* of all well-ordered and rational thought. One might feel inclined to translate Manas by brain, if brain had not become so unscientific a term in our days. It might also be called the point of attention and apperception, but even this would hardly help us to a clear view of what Kapila really meant by Manas. Only we must guard against taking this Manas, or mind, for the true Self. Manas is as much a mere instrument of knowledge and a product of Prakriti as the five senses. They all are necessary for the work of perception, conception, and all the rest, as a kind of clockwork, quite different from the highest Self, whether it is called Atman or Purusha. The Purusha watches the clockwork, and is for a time misled into believing in his identity with the workings of Prakriti.

This is but a poor attempt, to make the Samkhya view of being and knowing intelligible, and I am far from maintaining that we have gained, as yet, a full insight into the problems which troubled Kapila, or into the solutions which he proposed.

What I feel is, that it is not enough simply to repeat the watch words of any ancient philosophy, which are easily accessible in the Sutras, but that we must at least make an attempt to bring those ancient problems near to us, to make them our own, and try to follow the ancient thinkers along the few footsteps which they left behind.

There is an illustration in the Samkhya-tattva-Kaumudi, which suggests a very different view of the process of knowing, and deserves to be taken into consideration: 'As the seniors of a village,' they say, 'collect taxes from the householders and hand them over to the governor of the district, who again remits them to the treasurer, and the treasurer to the king, thus do the outer senses, when they have perceived anything, hand it on to the inner sense, the Manas, the organ which determines what there is and then hands it over to Ahamkara, and the Ahamkara, after appropriating it, to the Buddhi, the supreme Lord.' Here Buddhi, though supreme, is decidedly different from the cosmic Buddhi that springs from the Avyakta and leads to Ahamkara; nor is it easy to see how these two Buddhis, or rather that one Buddhi in its two functions, could have been admitted by one and the same philosopher.

IS SAMKHYA IDEALISM?

There is another point on which it is difficult to come to a clear understanding. We are asked whether the Hindus fully realised the fact that we are conscious of our sensations only, and that all we call bodies, or the outside or objective world, is no more than the result of an irresistible inference of our mind, which may be called Avidya. We are conscious, no doubt, that we are not ourselves the cause of our sensations, that we do not make the sky, but that it is given us. But beyond that, our world is only an inductive world, it is, so to say, our creation;

we make the sky concave or blue, and all that remains, after deducting both the primary and secondary qualities, is Prakriti as looked at by Purusha, or, as we should say, *das Ding an sich,* which we can never know directly. It is within us, or under our sway, that this Prakriti has grown to all that it is, not excluding our own bodies, our senses, our Manas, our Tanmatras, our Ahamkara, our Buddhi. Was this the view taken by the Samkhyas? Did they see that the Sanchara, the development of the world, takes place within us, is our growth, though not our work, that the light which, as Buddhi emerges from Prakriti, is the light within us that has the power of perceiving by its light; that both the Aham, the Ego, and the Tvam, the Non-Ego, determine not only ourselves, but the whole world, and that what we call the real, the sensuously perceiving and perceived world, is no more than the development of thoughtless nature as reflected through the senses on our enchanted Self?

The riddle of the world which the Samkhya philosophy has to solve would then be no more than to account for the mistaken interest which the Self takes in that reflex, the consciousness which he assumes of it, the fundamental error by which, for a time at least, he actually identifies himself with those images. This identifying process would, from this point of view, really take the place of what we call creation. The closing of the mental eyelids would be the dropping of the curtain and the close of the drama of the world; and this final recognition of our cosmic misconception would lead the Self back from the stage of the world to himself, would undo all creation, and put an end to that suffering which is the result of bondage or finiteness.

It sometimes seems to me as if such views had been at the bottom of all Hindu philosophy, though forgotten again or obscured by a belief in that reality which determines our practical life (Vyavahara). By admitting this blending of cosmic and psychological views, much in the Samkhya-philosophy would cease to be obscure, the Buddhi of the world and the Buddhi of ourselves would indeed become one, and the belief in the reality of things, both objective and subjective, might truly be explained as due to Aviveka, the absence of discrimination between the Self and the imagery of nature. It would become intelligible why Prakriti should be supposed to play her part so long only as it was noticed by Purusha; it would explain why Prakriti, by itself, was taken as Achetana, objective, thoughtless, and the Purusha only as subjective, conscious and thinking; why in its solitude Purusha was conceived as not active, but Prakriti as always active; why Purusha should sometimes mean the eternal Self, and sometimes man such as he is or imagines himself to be, while interested in the world, believing in the world, and yet with a constant longing after a higher and truer state, freedom from the world, freedom from pain, freedom from all cosmic being, freedom as alone with himself.

Purusha and Prakriti

But if we may credit the founders of the Samkhya, whether Kapila or Asuri or Panchasikha, with such advanced views, if they really had made it quite clear to themselves that human beings cannot have anything but their own knowledge, we can understand why they should have represented the whole process of perception and combination, all joy and pain, and, in consequence, all willing also, as belonging, not to the Purusha or the Self, hut to a stranger, to the Manas, and indirectly to Prakriti, while the Purusha, when he seems to see, to combine, to rejoice, to suffer, and to will, does so by misapprehension only, like a spectator who is carried away by his sympathies for Hecuba, but who in the end dries his tears and stops his sighs, leaves the theatre of the world, and breathes the fresh air of a bright night. The Samkhya uses this very simile. The whole development of Prakriti, it is said, takes place only when Purusha is looking on the dancer, that is, on Prakriti, in all her disguises. If he does not look, she does not dance for him, and as soon as he turns his eyes entirely away from her, she altogether ceases to try to please him. She may please others who are still looking at her, and so far it may be said that she is never annihilated, because there will always be new Purushas to be enchanted and enchained for awhile, but at last to be set free by her.

STATE OF PURUSHA, WHEN FREE

Often has the question been asked, What then becomes of the Purusha, after the spell of Prakriti has been broken, and he has ceased to take any interest in the phantasmagoria of the world, thrown on him by the Manas and all the products of Prakriti that support the Manas. But this is a question which no philosophy can be expected to answer. All that can be said is that Purusha, freed from all Prakritic bonds, whether ignorance or knowledge, joy or sorrow, would remain himself, would be what he alone can be, unrestricted, not interfered with, free and independent, and hence, in the highest sense of the word, perfect and happy in himself. This ineffable state of bliss has naturally shared the fate of similar conceptions, such as the oneness with Brahman, the Nihsreyasa or *Non plus ultra,* and the Nirvana of the Buddhists. In the eyes of less advanced thinkers, this unfathomable bliss assumed naturally the character of paradisiacal happiness painted in the most brilliant and even sensuous colours, while to the truly enlightened it represented tranquillity (Santi), perfect rest, and self-satisfaction.

While I agree with Dr. Dahlmann that the Buddhist idea of Nirvana was the same, originally, as that of the higher bliss of the Vedanta and Samkhya philosophy, I cannot believe that it was borrowed by the Buddhists from either of those systems. Nirvana was one of the ideas that were in the air in India, and it was worked out by Buddha as well as by Kapila and Badarayana, but by each in his own fashion. The name itself, like many technical terms of Buddha's teaching, was no doubt Brahmanic. It occurs in the Vedanta, though it is absent in the Samkhya-Sutras. We see in the Buddhist Suttas how it was used by the Buddhists, at first, in the simple sense of freedom from passion, but was developed higher and higher, till in the end it became altogether negative. If it had been simply taken over by Buddha from some individual teacher of an established philosophy, it would betray its origin, while we see it spring up as naturally in Buddha's philosophy as in that of Badarayana and Kapila. They all took their materials from the same stratum of thought, and elaborated them into systems, probably about the same time. But in spite of Dr. Dahlmann's very learned and very able pleading, I must say once more that I cannot yet see any evidence for supposing that either Buddha borrowed direct from Kapila or that Kapila borrowed from Buddha.

Kapila does not enter into a minute analysis of his Nirvana, or, as he calls it, Kaivalya, aloneness. His object was to show how pain arose and how pain can be absolutely removed. If freedom from limitation and pain is happiness, that happiness can be secured by the Samkhya just as much as by the Vedanta and the Buddhist philosophy; but though the Vedantist admits happiness (Ananda) by the side of existence and perception (Sat-chit), as peculiar to the highest Brahman, he does not attempt to explain what kind of happiness he means; and some Vedanta philosophers have actually objected to Ananda or happiness as a positive predicate of the highest Brahman. Negatively, however, this happiness may surely be defined as freedom from pain, freedom from all limits or fetters, and therefore perfect bliss.

MEANING OF PAIN

It would seem extraordinary, and wholly unworthy of a great philosopher, if Kapila had had eyes for the ordinary sufferings only which are entailed on all the sons of men. He must have known that there is happiness also for them, and something between suffering and happiness, the even tenor of a man's life. Kapila meant something else by pain. He seems to have felt what Schelling felt, that sadness cleaves to all finite life, but that is very different from always being intent on getting rid of the sufferings inherent in life on earth. Kapila evidently meant by Duhkha or pain something more than physical or even mental suffering, namely, the consciousness of being conditioned, limited, or fettered, which is inseparable from this life. But whatever suffering he may have meant, the method suggested by him for its removal is certainly bold and decided. All this suffering, he tells us, is not, as we imagine, our suffering. Like the whole evolution of Prakriti, this suffering also belongs to Prakriti and not to ourselves, not to the Purushas.

PURUSHA

In order to explain the world, we have to admit not only Prakriti, rising in the form of Buddhi, Ahamkara, and Manas to the height or the depth of individual existence, perception, and action, but likewise another quite independent being, the Purusha, the real or the better and truer Self, and therefore very much the same as the Atman of the Vedanta. Both Purusha and Atman, it should be remembered, are absent in Buddha's teaching, and by their removal the idea of Nirvana has become almost meaningless. But on this point also we must wait for further light.

With Kapila the Purusha or Self always remains, after as well as before his release. It is true he is only the looker on of all that takes place through Prakriti, looking as it were into a glass in which all the doings of Prakriti are mirrored. For a time by some strange want of discernment, this Purusha, always one of many Purushas, forgets his true nature and identifies himself with this image of Prakriti. He imagines therefore that he himself sees and hears, that he himself suffers and rejoices, that he himself is an I, really possessing all that the world offers to him, and unwilling to give it up again, whether in life or in death. His very body, however, his organs of sense, nay, his mind and his individuality, are neither he, nor his; and if he can only learn the wisdom of Kapila, he is for ever above the body, above all sensation, above all suffering. Nay, Prakriti even, which has no soul, but acts only as impelled by her nature when looked at by Purusha, ceases her jugglery as soon as Purusha turns away.

PRAKRITI AN AUTOMATON?

It might possibly help us to understand the relation between Purusha and Prakriti better, if we saw in Prakriti an automaton, such as DesCartes described, performing all the functions which we consider our own and which are common to man and animals, as in fact a mere mechanism, and if we took the rational soul, the Purusha, as the *chose pensante,* superadded to the automaton. It was Professor Huxley who showed that, as a consequence of this assumption, all our mental conditions might be regarded as simply the symbols (Pratibimba) in consciousness of the changes which take place automatically in the organism. In the same way all the changes of Prakriti, from mere sensation to conceptual thought, might be taken as including pain and joy and consequent action, the working of Prakriti, independent of the looker on, although that looker on in his enchanted state imagines that he is himself doing what in reality Prakriti is doing for him. This is beautifully illustrated by the simile of the dancing-girl to which we referred before, but who is here represented not only as intent on pleasing and beguiling Purusha, but as trying herself to open his eyes and make him free from her charms and fetters. We thus get a new application of the simile mentioned before.

PRAKRITI'S UNSELFISHNESS

We read in the Karikas 59-62: 'As a dancer having exhibited herself on the stage ceases to dance, so does Nature (Prakriti) cease, when she has made herself manifest to Purusha.

60. In many ways Prakriti serves Purusha, who yet does nothing for her in return; she is noble-minded and cares only for the welfare of him who is so ungrateful to her.
61. There is nothing more modest, I think, than Prakriti, who does not expose herself again to the gaze of Purusha after she knows that she has been gazed at.
62. No Purusha is therefore really chained, nor does he become free, or wander; Prakriti alone, dependent as she is on different Purushas, wanders from birth to birth, is bound, and is freed.'

In fact it would seem that Prakriti, in enchanting or binding Purusha, has no object in view except that Purusha should in the end perceive his fetters, and by discrimination become free from them (Karika 59).

Here is indeed the Gordian knot of the whole Samkhya philosophy. We believe for a time in our own physical nature and in the nature by which we are surrounded, and so long as we do this, we suffer. We are exposed to all kinds of pain, till our eyes are opened and we learn that it is Prakriti that sees and acts, that kills and is killed; that suffers, while we imagine that we ourselves do and suffer all this. As soon as this insight has been gained, as soon as Purusha has distinguished between himself and what is not himself, liberation is achieved at once, and the dance of life is ended for ever, at least so far as the liberated Self is concerned. Until that final liberation has been accomplished and everything like body has been completely removed, transmigration continues, and the Purusha is supposed to be clothed in what is called the Linga-sarira, or subtle body. Whatever we may think of the truth of such a system we cannot help admiring its consistency throughout, and its boldness and heroism in cutting the Gordian knot.

THE ATHEISM OF KAPILA

We have still to say a few words about the charge of atheism brought against the Samkhyas. It seems certainly strange that at this early time and surrounded as he no doubt was by sacrifices and hymns addressed to the innumerable Vedic Devas, nothing should have been said by Kapila either for or against these beings. Most likely at his time and before his time, the different Devas of the popular religion had already been eclipsed in the minds of thoughtful people by one Deity, whether Prajapati, Visvakarman, or Brahman. Both Prajapati and Brahmans are mentioned in the Tattva-samasa-bhashya.

But even such a supreme Deva or Adhideva is never asserted or denied by Kapila. There is a place in his system for any number of subordinate Devas, but there is none for God, whether as the creator or as the ruler of all things. There is no direct denial of such a being, no outspoken atheism in that sense, but there is simply no place left for him in the system of the world, as elaborated by the old philosopher. He had, in fact, put nearly everything that belonged to God into Prakriti, only that this Prakriti is taken as purely objective, and as working without a conscious purpose, unless when looked at by Purusha, and then working, as we are told, for his benefit only.

This has sometimes been illustrated by what must have been a very old fable, that of a cripple who could not walk, meeting another cripple who could not see. As they could not live by themselves, they lived together, the lame one mounting on the shoulders of the blind one. Prakriti, we are told, was the blind, Purusha the lame traveller.

We must remember, however, that Prakriti, though blind, is always conceived as real, because the Samkhya philosophy looks upon everything that is, as proceeding out of something that is real (Satkaryavada). And here we see again the fundamental difference between the Samkhya and the other philosophies, as Vachaspati Misra has pointed out in his commentary on the Samkhya-karika. The Buddhist takes the real world as the result of nothing, the Vedantist takes the unreal world as proceeding from something real, Naiyayika and Vaiseshika derive what does not yet exist from what does exist, while the Samkhyas derive what is from what is.

If it be asked how the unconscious Prakriti began to work and attract the attention of Purusha, Kapila has an answer ready. The Gunas, he says, are first in a state of equipoise, but as soon as one of the three preponderates, there is tension, and Prakriti enters on the course of her unceasing labours, beginning with the emanation of Buddhi, and ending with the last of the twenty-four Tattvas.

There is this difference also between the atheism of Kapila and that of other atheistic systems of philosophy, that Kapila nowhere puts himself into a hostile attitude towards the Divine idea. He nowhere denies distinctly the existence even of the purely mythological gods, such as Indra, which is strange indeed; nor does he enter on any arguments to disprove the existence of one only God. He simply says—and in that respect he does not differ much from Kant—that there are no logical proofs to establish that existence, but neither does he offer any such proofs for denying it. We know that Kant, honest thinker as he was, rejected all the logical proofs of the existence of Deity as insufficient, and based the arguments for his belief in God on purely ethical grounds. Though we have no right to assume anything of the kind with regard to Kapila, when brought face to face with this great religious and moral problem, the existence of a supreme God, we ought to mark his impartiality and the entire absence, in the whole of his philosophy, of anything like animus against a belief in God. The Devas he could hardly have seriously believed in, we should say, and yet he spares them and allows them to exist, possibly with the reservation that people, in worshipping them, were unconsciously approaching the true Purusha. We should not forget that with many people atheism meant, and means, a denial of Devas rather than the denial of the one, only God, the First Cause of the world.

IMMORALITY OF THE SAMKHYA

It has also been said that Kapila's system is not only without a God, but likewise without any morality. But though it is quite true that, according to Kapila, Purusha in his perfect state is non-moral, neither merit nor demerit, virtue nor vice, existing any longer for him, he is certainly not allowed to be immoral. The Samkhya, like the Vedanta and other systems of Indian philosophy, implies strong moral sentiment in the belief in Karman (deed) and transmigration. Kapila also holds that deeds, when once done, can never cease, except at the time of Moksha, but produce effect after effect, both in this life and in the lives to come. This is one of the unalterable convictions in the Hindu mind. There is, besides the admission of virtue and vice, the dispraise of passion and the praise of dispassion. These are represented as forms of Buddhi, as Rupas or Bhavas, forms or states, inhering in Buddhi, and therefore following the Linga-sarira from birth to birth. Nay, it is distinctly added that going upward is due to virtue, going downward to vice, so that virtue, as a preliminary, is really indispensable to final liberation. It may be true that in this way morality is reduced to mere calculation of consequences, but even such a calculation, which is only another name for reasoning, would serve as a strong incentive to morality. Anyhow, there is no ground for saying that Kapila's system ignores ordinary morality, still less that it encourages vice.

SAMKHYA PARABLES

There is one more feature of the Samkhya that deserves to be mentioned, because it is not found in the other Indian philosophies, but may be supposed to have suggested to the Buddhists their method of teaching by parables. A whole chapter of the Sutras, the fourth, is assigned to a collection of stories, each of which is meant to illustrate some doctrine of Kapila's. Some are very much to the point, and they can be appealed to by one word, so as to recall the whole lesson which they were meant to teach. The first is meant to illustrate the complete change that comes over a man when he has been taught his true nature by means of the Samkhya: 'As in the case of the son of a king.' The story which follows is that a young prince who was born under an unlucky star, was taken out of his capital and brought up by a Sabara, a kind of wild man of the woods. When he grew up he naturally thought that he himself was a Sabara, and lived accordingly. But a minister, who had found out that the prince was alive, went to him secretly and told him that he was the son of the king, and not a Sabara. At once the prince gave up the idea that he was a savage, believed that he was a prince, and assumed a truly royal bearing. In the same manner a man who has been told his true character by his teacher, surrenders the idea that he is a material and mortal being, and recovers his true nature, saying, 'As a son of Brahman I am nothing but Brahman, and not a being different from him in this phenomenal world.'

The commentator adds an extract from the Garuda-Purana which must have been borrowed from a Samkhya source:

'As everything that is made of gold is known as gold, if even from one small piece of gold one has learnt to know what gold is, in the same way from knowing God the whole world becomes known.

'As a Brahman possessed by an evil spirit, imagines, that he is a Sudra, but, when the possession is over, knows that he is a Brahman, thus the soul, possessed by Maya, imagines that it is the body, but after Maya has come to an end, it knows its own true being again, and says, I am a Brahman.'

The seventh illustration is 'like a cut-off hand,' and is meant to teach that, as no one takes his hand again after it has once been cut off, no one should identify himself with anything objective, after having once surrendered the illusion of the objective. The sixteenth, to which I called attention many years ago as connected with old Aryan folklore, is meant to teach that even an accidental negligence may be fatal to our reaching the highest goal, as in the case of the 'frog-wife.'

The story is that of a king who, while hunting, had seen a beautiful girl in a forest. She became his wife on condition that he should never let her see water. He gave the promise, but once when the queen, tired after playing, asked him for some water, he forgot his promise, and brought her some, whereupon the daughter of the frog king became a frog (Bheki), and disappeared in the lake. Neither nets nor anything else was of any avail for bringing her back, the king had lost her for ever. Thus true knowledge also will disappear by one act of negligence, and will never return.

This system of teaching by parables was very popular with the Buddhists, and it is just possible that the first impulse may have come from the followers of Kapila, who are so often called Krypto-Buddhists or Prachchhanna-Bauddhas.

I have called attention already to the fact that these illustrative parables, though they do not occur in the Karikas and in the Tattva-samasa, must have existed all the time in the Parampara of the Brahmans, because they appear in the modern Sutras, that is, in the sixteenth century. Like the Sutras referring to these stories, other Sutras also may occur in our modern collection of Samkhya-Sutras, which existed for centuries, as handed down by tradition, but were omitted in the Karikas and even in the Tattva-samasa.

•••

Other Books on

PHILOSOPHY, RELIGION & CULTURE

1. The Vital Truths of Hinduism (New)
2. Philosophy India (New)
3. The Dhammapada (New)
4. The Last Days of Lord Buddha (New)
5. Complete Book of Hindu Gods And Goddesses (New)
6. Vatsyayana's Kamasutra Select and his Times
7. The Kamasutra of Mallinaga Vatsyayana
8. Judgment : No Aircrash No Death
9. Patriot: Netaji Subhas Chandra Bose
10. The Life of Lord Buddha
11. The Discourses of Lord Buddha
12. The Golden Book of Buddhism
13. The Golden Book of Hinduism
14. The Golden Book of Islam
15. The Golden Book of Rigveda
16. The Golden Book of Jainism
17. The Golden Book of Upanishads
18. Learn Rajayoga From Vivekananda
19. Colossus Vivekananda Select
20. Intellect India

21. Culture India

22. My Experiments With Truth

23. Mahatma Gandhi The Bhagavadgita

24. Shirdi Sai Baba

25. The Ramayana For Every Home

26. The Mahabharata For Every Home

27. Sai The Age of Cosmic Family

28. Sathya Sai and His Miraculous Powers

29. To Bloom Like A Lotus

30. The History of Sikh Gurus

31. Intelligence Beyond Thought

32. Indian Mythology

Lotus PRESS

Unit No. 220, Second Floor, 4735/22,
Prakash Deep Building,Ansari Road, Daryaganj,
New Delhi- 110002